Survival of the Sickest: Leadership, Co-Dependence, and the Spiritual Journey

Rev. Marc Lanoue, Ph. D.

DEDICATION

For all those who are held back from being who God wants them to be.

CONTENTS

ACKNOWLEDGMENTS

I need to thank a few people who have been instrumental in bringing this book to fruition. To Mrs. Debbie Resta and Mrs. Linda Gosman, I offer heartfelt thanks for their willingness to read through the entire manuscript and offer helpful advice to its improvement. I note Mrs. Mary Logue's contributions through our conversations and the several stories that she shared with me that I have adopted within the body of the writing. Her creativity in story-telling has provided modern parables of lasting value.

I would also like to thank my sister Elyse B. Lanoue for the cover that she created for the book. I am also indebted to my brother Bernard A. Lanoue, who provided the namesake for and story behind Bernard's Law, which is fundamental to my appreciation of leadership at large.

Those whose works I consulted are noted in the text and footnotes. I hope that I have duly acknowledged their contributions to this work. In no way do I wish to take credit for their intellectual property.

In acknowledging the contributions of others, I wish also to assert that I am fully and solely responsible for the content of this book. All errors are mine and mine alone.

Rev. Dr. Marc L. Lanoue, Ph. D.

Marc Lanoue

FOREWARD

Pope Emeritus Benedict XVI and Pope Francis have invited all of us to work toward a "New Evangelization," a term first used by Pope Benedict at the Ordinary General Assembly of Bishops in 2012. Many priests have wondered to me what is different about the New Evangelization versus what they have been doing for the past number of years in their ministries. They are puzzled, since they believe that their past accomplishments are seen as having no value. On another front, a man with whom I was speaking kept asking me why people needed to be "fed" spiritually, since he fed daily on the Eucharist at Mass and couldn't understand how people are leaving the Church in droves because they said that they weren't being spiritually fed.

Failing to see beyond ourselves and opening ourselves to other individuals in the examples above point to a closed point of view due to complacency, lack of insight, willingness to follow the crowd mentality—in a word, resistance, active and passive. Resistance is a strategy for avoiding change or growth in one's life, so that a person can remain where he or she is without change. It also reflects a manner of acting so as to avoid examining why a person does not want to look into the depths of one's being, that is, one's darkness.

Someone had attended a conference and was impressed by a young man who told the story of his life. He came from a family where the father was an alcoholic, and the mother spent her energies trying to keep the household of many children together with the father. God, religion, spirituality were never discussed, and pretty much anything was the rule of the day: alcohol, drugs, carousing, and dysfunction. The young man of note was a large person and a gifted athlete. People of import who could have had a positive impact on him chose to avoid addressing his addiction for their own selfish motives. Unresolved, his drug problem finally led him to an overdose and a near-death experience. According to his story, he was given a second chance by God, but was sucked into the life of an addict once again. He hit bottom again and asked God for yet another chance. God heard his impassioned plea, and he was miraculously healed of his addiction entirely this time. I believe in God profoundly and I believe this story of miraculous healing. I also believe that miracles are called such because they don't happen every day, in every circumstance. They are unique gifts of God that provide hope that God will intervene because of gravely difficult circumstances.

God's miraculous healing above should not obscure the fact that many times those in positions of authority or those in positions to help the young man did not do so. This book explores how and why people would use the gifted athlete from this story to advance their cause or wish for success, ignore him as a person, and pretend that everything will turn out "for the best" for him, his family, and society at large. In other words, they believed that wishful thinking was enough to change the athlete — so long as it doesn't involve them, while they got what they could out of him. Let's pray to God for our success and ignore our callousness in not providing the athlete with what he really needs — we'll just enable him with drugs, since we like to see him win for us on the field.

This book is about leadership, but should be understood in broad terms. Anyone who leads others: a father or mother leads a family; a CEO a company; a pastor a church; a coach a team; a manager a group of workers; a teacher students, all of these are leaders. Whatever darkness that person has not dealt with in his or her life will follow that person throughout life until it is recognized, brought to consciousness, acknowledged as one's own, appreciated as damaging others, assessed, restitution offered, and transformed by God. In a word, this is the nature of repentance or recovery or consciousness, and it is the underlying thrust of the New Evangelization. It is easy to implement new programs and offerings within a company or parish setting, but these can be Band-aids applied to deal with cancer. Superficial engagement in anything leads nowhere. True soul-searching delves into the heart of our darkness, so that Christ's Light can actually shed light on those areas that all of us avoid examining, except those few whose lives have taken them to the brink of devastation, even death, so that they had no choice but to do so. The long-term avoidance of such a gaze into darkness, a lack of depth, and general malaise in a superficial stupor has led us as a Church quite literally nowhere, but the suggestion that it involves only the Church is ridiculous, as we will examine in the pages that follow.

I did a great deal of copy editing when I worked in industry, which means simultaneously recognizing the rules of English grammar, acceptable stylistic variances of an author or authors, inconsistencies, and aspects that are, simply put, wrong—this is form. The form of a work is distinct from its content, which requires an understanding about finer points within a field of study, for instance, biology, philosophy, or theology, depending on the subject under review. But when it comes to religious experience, we tend to gloss over the fact that people's home lives (form) can impact their views (content) and can leave them and everyone whom they touch damaged from the encounter. Real life involves both form and content.

This book is about the implications of leadership: how it blocks the people being led from examining their darkness and how leaders avoid their own need for repentance and the consequences of such actions, both on individuals and on communities. I believe in miracles, but I recognize their exceptional quality. This book is about how ignoring the actions of real human beings is undermining people's salvation, spirituality, and quality of life. Wishful or positive thinking may be nice, but they lead us to nowhere of any enduring value. The spiritual journey, coupled with a trip into one's darkness, with revelation of our shared suffering with Christ, leads to the Kingdom. Some present kings and queens will have to give up their scepters, so that God's Kingdom can reign supreme. This is why there is resistance. This is why there is pain, psychic and otherwise, in society; constant deadlock in the halls of government; no depth in our hearts; and no shared compassion for our fellow human beings. The fruits of the Kingdom are something that leaders can banter around, as though they know what they are talking about. I leave them to it, as I invite readers to consider the difficult inner work of plodding through their darkness. The journey's fruit is suited only to personal taste. Don't take any else's word for it.

Fr. Marc Lanoue.

INTRODUCTION

In my first book, *"Remove the Stone": Using Your Sins to Redirect Your Spiritual Energy*, I developed the idea that spirituality is an investigation into the spirits or motivations or energies or forces or voices within, that determine a person's actions. All of these energies figure into the picture for someone attempting to recognize one's own true voice amidst the cacophony of other voices that are competing for attention within a person. One of these voices is God's and another is the true self's or soul's; they are always present. But the other voices may drown them out, so that these unique two cannot be recognized. By careful attention to the "characteristics" within a given circumstance, one can recognize their sources and treat each appropriately. It is my position that misdirected energies compel us to support circumstances, practices, and systems that do not have God as their source, so they lead to sin, whose ultimate end is death. All energies are not sinful, such as the energy that leads us to breathe without thinking about it, but if one is listening to one's ego as though it were one's only voice, then damage to others, and even to oneself, tends to occur. If we are working toward the wrong goal, then our efforts will be stunted, more or less, not only toward growing in awareness of the Kingdom and working for its establishment, but misdirected energies can also commandeer our objectives and make us believe that they reflect the Kingdom, when, in fact, our goals are merely idols. The Kingdom brings life, not stupor, numbness, or death. If the values of the Kingdom are not being developed, then values supporting idols are.

My intent with this second book is different from psychology, which attempts to help a person to unpack emotions and other concerns in one's mind and heart. This project is a reflection on the discovery of the true self or soul, which is not usually within the purview of psychology apart from Carl Jung (1875-1961) and those who adopt his insights in their work and lives. This second book takes up the subject of leadership, as a discussion in itself, but also as a topic related to the New Evangelization. However, it also appreciates how leadership types can silence one's inner voice in place of someone else's voice. We will have reason to examine this throughout this work because of its implications.

Many organizations like the military and, in some instances, the Church, operate using a top-down and closed system. Classifying systems uses terms like 'open' and 'closed.'

> In closed systems, information that cannot be processed within the existing paradigm will not be allowed in or recognized. By definition, it simply does not exist. Open systems take new information, they espouse flexibility as one of the characteristics of their system, and they are open to new information as a way to initiate change.[1]

As I noted in *"Remove the Stone"*, the military establishment knew about sexual assaults at the various military academies and elsewhere, but did nothing about them for some time. The "chain of command" kept victims' complaints quiet, as it also isolated the victims.[2] The sex-abuse crisis in the Catholic Church—until relatively recently—was handled by Church officials in a similar manner. In a closed system, no outside force can influence decision-making or the development of policy. This situation has undoubtedly worked as "negative evangelization" for the

---

[1] Anne Wilson Shaeff and Diane Fassel, *The Addictive Organization: Why We Overwork, Cover Up, Pick Up the Pieces, Please the Boss and Perpetuate Sick Organizations* (San Francisco: Harper Collins, 1988), 60.

[2] See Rev. Marc Lanoue, *"Remove the Stone": Using Your Sins to Redirect Your Spiritual Energy* (Saarbrücken, Germany: Blessed Hope Publishing, 2014), 115.

Church, driving people away.[3]

We will begin our investigation by identifying some scriptural texts that reflect appropriate leadership values from Jesus, as well as those that do not. We will further see how certain circumstances and cultural expectations stand in the way of realizing the values espoused by Jesus even while he walked the earth. It is my position that the inadequacies of any leader, particularly within a closed system, will impact the health of the system in which the leader functions, especially if that leader does not deal well with resistance. We will not be dealing exclusively with Church-based scenarios, since most systems from all areas of life have a leader or leaders associated with them. Models developed by Dr. Donna Markham, OP, Ph. D. will help us to classify various leadership styles to recognize what to expect from them. I do not suggest that these are the only models for making such an assessment; however, I found them helpful in categorizing leadership situations that I have experienced in my life and also for recognizing what is possible and not possible under the leadership of certain individuals.[4]

Using the same approach as in *"Remove the Stone"*, though more broadly reflected, I shall evaluate examples that reflect Markham's models and attempt to appreciate how resources can be misdirected. I believe that these examples can offer valuable information for developing parish systems that will be true to Catholic heritage and identity and also true to the need for growth and development that leads to a community of believers who are working toward Kingdom values and who will experience Kingdom blessings. We will draw from several sources to illustrate these points, especially Pope Francis' Apostolic

---

[3] See Sherry A. Waddell, *Forming Intentional Disciples: The Path to Knowing and Following Jesus* (Huntington, IN: Our Sunday Visitor, 2012), 28, 160-161, 245-247.

[4] Pope Francis has identified several types of "ills" besetting Church leadership, which have made the news frequently. For the Pope's list to the curia on 22 December 2014, see (as of this writing [28 January 2015]): http://www.religionnews.com/2014/12/22/doctor-pope-francis-list-ails-church/

Exhortation *Evangelii gaudium*.[5] We shall also reference *The Addictive Organization* by Anne Wilson Schaef and Diane Fassel and their revolutionary insights about addictive organizations. Anne Wilson Shaef also provides us with important insights into how to approach the phenomenon of co-dependence, especially in her work *Codependence: Misunderstood-Mistreated*, which has such long-standing implications, it would be difficult to overstate its influence on all aspects of society, especially the closed systems of the Church and military.[6]

Viktor Frankl and several others offer their findings about how people react when they are under duress; this is important for recognizing the implications of superficial vs. deep-seated commitment to something, especially as it relates to interactions with others. We will also be examining several consequences of leadership from the business world, since leaders affect business as well as every other area of life, so, to exclude them, would be omitting this vital component from our examination. Fr. Thomas Keating, a Trappist monk, offers insights about how new prayer forms are necessary for bringing people to a deeper place in their experience of God, themselves, and each other. He is reliant upon his confreres, especially Fr. Thomas Merton.

Fr. Thomas Merton, a Trappist monk and prolific writer on the spiritual life and other areas, offers his understanding of the isolation that is possible when an institutional *persona* is imposed to replace one's unique personal identity. Merton's characterization is a timeless reminder that, despite Vatican II, institutional understandings, which far outlast those who implement and enforce them, are long-lasting caricatures of ideals that gain ground, whether this is healthy or not. All of these writers recognize the need for a new way of operating or doing business. We shall examine some of these recommendations and how

---

[5] All references to statements made by Pope Francis come from *Evangelii gaudium*, unless otherwise indicated. For the complete text, see, as of this writing (15 February 2015): http://w2.vatican.va/content/francesco/en/apost_exhortations/documents/papa-francesco_esortazione-ap_20131124_evangelii-gaudium.html
[6] Anne Wilson Schaef, *Co-dependence: Misunderstood-Mistreated* (San Francisco: HarperSanFrancisco, 1986).

they might play out.

As we begin our study, we draw from the fourth chapter of Mark's Gospel, the parable of the seeds (Mark 4:1-20), describes how seeds, used as a metaphor for the Word of God, are sown within various environments and the yield of fruit that each sowing brings. This parable serves as a starting point for appreciating that a person's environment and his or her interaction with it impact how people receive the Word and deliver fruit from it.

> Mark 4:1 On another occasion he began to teach by the sea. A very large crowd gathered around him so that he got into a boat on the sea and sat down. And the whole crowd was beside the sea on land. 2 And he taught them at length in parables, and in the course of his instruction he said to them, 3 "Hear this! A sower went out to sow. 4 And as he sowed, some seed fell on the path, and the birds came and ate it up. 5 Other seed fell on rocky ground where it had little soil. It sprang up at once because the soil was not deep. 6 And when the sun rose, it was scorched and it withered for lack of roots. 7 Some seed fell among thorns, and the thorns grew up and choked it and it produced no grain. 8 And some seed fell on rich soil and produced fruit. It came up and grew and yielded thirty, sixty, and a hundredfold." 9 He added, "Whoever has ears to hear ought to hear." 10 And when he was alone, those present along with the Twelve questioned him about the parables. 11 He answered them, "The mystery of the kingdom of God has been granted to you. But to those outside everything comes in parables, 12 so that 'they may look and see but not perceive, and hear and listen but not understand, in order that they may not be converted and be forgiven.'" 13 Jesus said to them, "Do you not understand this parable? Then how will you understand any of the parables? 14 The sower sows the word. 15 These are the ones on the path where the word is sown. As soon as they hear, Satan comes at once and takes away the word sown in them. 16 And these are the ones sown on rocky ground who, when they hear the word, receive it at once with joy. 17 But they have no root; they last only for a

time. Then when tribulation or persecution comes because of the word, they quickly fall away. <u>18</u> Those sown among thorns are another sort. They are the people who hear the word, <u>19</u> but worldly anxiety, the lure of riches, and the craving for other things intrude and choke the word, and it bears no fruit. <u>20</u> But those sown on rich soil are the ones who hear the word and accept it and bear fruit thirty and sixty and a hundredfold."

Jesus' words about how to interpret this passage (vv. 14-20) should not be understood as an exhaustive discourse on the spreading of the Word or the yield of fruit. Instead, it is our hope to take a modern approach to examining ways that can help and hinder the spread of the Word of God, particularly at this point in the history of the Church, as we apply it to Church and other leaders and the impact that these leaders have on the groups entrusted to their care.

1 LEADERSHIP ACCORDING TO JESUS

Introduction

A religious brother involved extensively in negotiation ministry at the individual and community levels once suggested that no discussion about leadership could begin without first addressing the issues raised in the passage involving Jesus' interaction with the sons of Zebedee. I agree with his assessment. Jesus' sense of leadership should, after all, be at the heart of any consideration that involves religious institutions claiming a connection with Christ. Before we examine the models of leadership as described by Dr. Markham, we shall consider the leadership concerns voiced by the sons of Zebedee to Jesus on his way to Jerusalem in Mark 10:32-45.

The Journey to Jerusalem and Request for Position

> Mark 10:32 [The disciples] were … going up to Jerusalem, and Jesus went ahead of them. … Taking the Twelve aside again, he began to tell them what was going to happen to him. 33 "Behold, we are going up to Jerusalem, and the Son of Man will be handed over to the chief priests and the scribes, and they will condemn him to death and hand him over to the Gentiles 34 who will mock him, spit upon him, scourge him, and put him to death, but after three days he will rise." 35 Then James and John, the sons of Zebedee, came to him and said to him, "Teacher, we want you to do for us whatever we ask of you." 36

He replied, "What do you wish [me] to do for you?" 37 They answered him, "Grant that in your glory we may sit one at your right and the other at your left." 38 Jesus said to them, "You do not know what you are asking. Can you drink the cup that I drink or be baptized with the baptism with which I am baptized?" 39 They said to him, "We can." Jesus said to them, "The cup that I drink, you will drink, and with the baptism with which I am baptized, you will be baptized; 40 but to sit at my right or at my left is not mine to give but is for those for whom it has been prepared." 41 When the ten heard this, they became indignant at James and John. 42 Jesus summoned them and said to them, "You know that those who are recognized as rulers over the Gentiles lord it over them, and their great ones make their authority over them felt. 43 But it shall not be so among you. Rather, whoever wishes to be great among you will be your servant; 44 whoever wishes to be first among you will be the slave of all. 45 For the Son of Man did not come to be served but to serve and to give his life as a ransom for many."

This exchange illustrates two understandings of leadership, one from the sons of Zebedee and one from Jesus.

The disciples have just heard about how Jesus will be mistreated by Jewish and Gentile officials, who will ultimately put him to death (vv. 33-34), and before that about the difficulty that the wealthy have with gaining eternal life (10:17-27). In light of these statements, the sons of Zebedee present themselves to Jesus and question him about who will take over for him when he is gone (v. 37). However, they do this in a manipulative fashion. They place their demand at the start of their questioning in order to hem Jesus in: "Teacher, we want you to do for us whatever we ask of you" (v. 35). This is something akin to saying, "What are you doing tonight?" without revealing what the intent of the question is about. Jesus seeks further information from them. They indicate that they want to bask in the glory that Jesus will receive when he assumes power. Though what power they believe he will be assuming is ambiguous, it seems likely that it will have to do with Messianic and, therefore, political power. They also want to be his principal attendants.

Jesus, however, recognizes that they do not appreciate what it is that they are asking and goes on to ask if they are able to be baptized with the baptism that he will experience, which means a process of purification that will involve suffering (see vv. 33-34).[7] They state that they can accept this baptism (v. 39a), but Jesus separates the special roles that they are seeking from the suffering that must take place, recognizing that the criteria for filling these roles have already been determined (by God) and involve more than simple discipleship.

The other ten disciples become indignant at the sons of Zebedee because of their attempt to assume superior positions for themselves (v. 41). In reaction to this, Jesus summarizes the way in which others assert their authority: "You know that those who are recognized as rulers over the Gentiles lord it over them, and their great ones make their authority over them felt" (v. 42). Bullying, arrests and even killing by occupying forces serve to emphasize who is in charge. (See Luke 3:14.) However, Jesus has a different understanding of and approach to authority: "But it shall not be so among you. Rather, whoever wishes to be great among you will be your servant; whoever wishes to be first among you will be the slave of all" (vv. 43-44). The sons of Zebedee were looking to bask in the glory achieved by Jesus when he assumed authority as Messiah. Jesus, instead, points the disciples to service. Assisting others permits others the ability to recognize authority themselves. They don't have to have someone's authority forced upon them to recognize it. Instead, they have the ability themselves to appreciate its presence in the service provided to them. It is possible that people may not recognize this authority; but force is not what Jesus wants the disciples to use to get people to recognize their authority. Service is the means to that end. He uses his

---

[7] Adela Yarbro Collins (*Mark: A Commentary* [Hermeneia; Minneapolis: Fortress, 2007] 496-497) notes that Jer 25:15-29 and Isa 51:17 (LXX) describe drinking a cup of divine wrath, which she views as the closest Old Testament image to Jesus' statement here. See also Josephus, *Ant.* 18.5.2 §§116-17; Joseph A. Fitzmyer, SJ, *The Gospel According to Luke X-XXIV: Introduction, Translation, and Notes* (AB 28, 28A; New York: Random House, 1985) 2. 996. Note also Col 1:24: "Now I rejoice in my sufferings for your sake, and in my flesh I am filling up what is lacking in the afflictions of Christ on behalf of his body, which is the church."

own life as an example to reflect what he has in mind: "For the Son of Man did not come to be served but to serve and to give his life as a ransom for many" (v. 45). His deeds will point to his authority and authorization by God, even to the point of shedding his blood to ransom many. One's willingness to be the slave of all is the hallmark of the true disciple of Jesus.

This account, then, offers insights into assumptions regarding leadership, which operate contrary to Jesus' words, such as:

1. We are in competition with others, so we must put ourselves, including our family members, forward to get ahead.
2. Manipulation will get you what you want—putting someone on the spot; getting a person off guard achieves the desired effect.
3. Glowing in someone else's glory to share authority with them obfuscates your own lack of personal authority.
4. Having authority will make you better or happier.
5. Boldness is preferable to sitting on the sidelines or exhibiting humility.
6. Boasting of readiness for pre-requisites that you know nothing about can make you look qualified.
7. Lording one's authority over others is the name of the game— everyone does this.
8. Those in authority do not require purification; they are the purifiers.
9. One must force one's authority on others for them to appreciate it.

For the follower of Jesus, however, leadership has different values:

1. There is a plan established by God that we fit into, which does not require the use of force.
2. People do not need to be compelled to appreciate authority.
3. Service is the way that you win people's hearts.
4. Non-acceptance by others, even rejection, and possibly suffering, is possible for true leaders.
5. You may have to pay the price for others' lack of appreciation.
6. Leadership leaves some loose ends and doesn't necessarily bring everyone along.

The values of the sons of Zebedee reflect ego-based concerns, which means one's position is taken by force from others with whom one is in competition. Violence and competition are two qualities reflective of ego-based values. Such authority is not recognized as coming from within, as is the case with Jesus. The people who hear Jesus are discerning enough to recognize him as someone with something unique about him—an internal quality—versus those who believe themselves special—through external achievements or authorization. (See Mark 1:22.) This makes people with inner authority dangerous to those who do not have it, which is the underlying reason Jesus was turned over to the Romans for execution (Mark 14:53-64). This inner sense of authority versus an external installation into it makes all the difference in determining what constitutes Christ-based leadership in contrast with leadership based on something else.

Who Determines What "Successful" Leadership Is?

This part of our exploration will examine various leadership styles that will help to appreciate how energies are focused towards various ends. They may lead to "success" in worldly terms, but the question must always be asked whether this success is reflective of the expectations of worldly leadership models (ego-driven, fear-based, forced upon others) or those of Jesus (the power of service to arouse the recognition of others).

Family Systems

We know from the study of family systems that certain dynamics within a family can manifest themselves in various behaviors and actions among its members, as the example below illustrates.[8]

> A woman came for reconciliation confessing acts of promiscuity, drinking, and other matters. She was 42 and had a parent who was an alcoholic.

An alcoholic parent, as is true with any alcoholic or addict, can drain the energies of a family into supporting that addiction, especially in maintaining the secret that everything is fine within the family unit.

---

[8] Schaef, *Co-dependence: Misunderstood-Mistreated*, 15-19.

Everyone in the household, more or less, will pay the price for the addiction, since parental (or other) nurturing will be stymied by the energies directed to support the addiction. The 42 year-old woman's emotional development reflected someone in her twenties. My part was to appreciate where she was coming from, so that I, in turn, could speak with her in the most compassionate and helpful way that I could. Her parents lacked the emotional depth to deal with their lives, because the addiction served to offset dealing with their emotions. The ability to deal with one's emotions is learned within one's family. If there are no teachers, then these "lessons" will not be taught and therefore not learned. Acting out behaviors, as related above, are how people deal with the lessons that they never received or emotional depth that they are incapable of handling. Either way, this woman's emotional situation was arrested and she would continue to inflict damage on herself and others until this matter was addressed in her life. No matter where she goes or what she does to escape this reality, her lack of emotional depth will go with her, rendering her incapable of dealing with emotions at a deep level. Leadership begins in the home, where we learn how to deal with the events that face us. In this case, the unwillingness to deal with those events in an emotionally mature way is what is passed on to the subsequent generation.

Parish & Business Systems

When it comes to parish or business systems, similar dynamics predominate. If we use the example of a parish, a Pastor or Administrator or Lay Associate running a parish will have a leadership style peculiar to that person; however, if the person has pathological issues that have not been addressed through formation or development in life, then, as in the case above, these matters will stymie the development of the parish or other organization. Some leaders with more serious pathologies will engage in replication, where they will rework an organization's structures to accommodate the pathological problem. For instance, if a leader is an addict, then the leader will have key employees ensure isolation for the leader to hide the secret of the addiction. The family system that supported the addiction will be reproduced or "replicated" within the organization to ensure that the addiction remains hidden, and the addict will continue receiving the "fix" of choice.

In our discussion below, we will use the models presented by Dr. Markham. Markham uses the term "spiritlinking" to reflect the process of bringing the spirits or energies of people together to achieve a common goal through mutual relationships. I shall note others' ideas where appropriate that I have found helpful in elucidating aspects of leadership styles. We begin with an understanding of what healthy leadership entails.

Healthy Leadership

Markham's definition of healthy leadership emphasizes relationships among members of a group, where the value of each of its members is maintained, as the group also works toward a goal of ensuring that the intent of the group is developed for future generations. This assumes healthy participants in the group, who are not co-opted by addictive or other pathologies.

> Leadership is about building relationships, about unifying a community of colleagues, about believing in the value and worth of each person, about serving and teaching and, when the time comes, about entrusting the next generation with what has been learned.... Just as excellent leaders are able to work through resistances that serve to fracture corporate unity in the service of the organizational mission, poor leaders can, themselves, become blocks to the possibility of a solid future because they failed to represent the truth.... What is essential is the recognition of these symptoms and expeditious treatment.[9]

Leaders need not be perfect, but they must be good communicators or be honest enough with themselves that they are not and enlist the help of those who are, which means that they are open to feedback—truth and honest exchange. They need to build relationships, not undermine them. Their peculiarities in exercising their leadership need not be wholly

---

[9] Donna J. Markham, *Spiritlinking Leadership: Working through Resistance to Organizational Change* (New York: Paulist, 1999), 114.

eradicated for a system to function in a healthy manner. Eccentricities are not necessarily unhealthy modes of behavior, whereas, dysfunctional ones are.

Healthy Community

Healthy communities have clear-cut values, goals, and vision, but they need to respect people first and foremost. A true community is a haven for souls, not a social club for superficial exchanges. A healthy community revisits values, goals, and vision periodically over time to see if they still reflect the community's future, and they have processes in place to address problems and make directional changes should the need arise. Change can bring growth, which may be accompanied by some anxiety or suffering for the community's membership. But planning can help to minimize the anxiety and its impact. Growth is sought, not avoided, in a healthy community, but appreciation of how much growth must also be taken into account.

Unhealthy communities attempt to avoid anxiety or suffering at all costs; they fear growth, where growth does not necessarily mean expansion, but, instead, facing "hard things" in the community's growth. The more the suffering or change of the community is a shared one, the better its members can bear the brunt of anything that comes their way. When, however, scapegoats are sought, shared suffering is undermined. Rewards for only a few will also lead in this direction, as the credit for the work everyone has accomplished is given to a select few, rather than the group as a whole. A good leader is critical to establishing that shared suffering and vision. Anyone afraid to grow with the community must be encouraged by the leader and healthy members of the community. The more people take ownership of the community, the more painful it will be to coordinate change, but it will be a shared experience, which has the power to unite people together and make bonds ever stronger. Common suffering, not common rewards, bring people together in substantial ways, as anyone who has experienced trauma as a group, such as soldiers or the police, can attest. The following example illustrates such a shared experience.

A husband and wife were taking their grandson to pick up their daughter after her final cancer treatment. When they went into the room of people receiving treatment, they were immediately struck that they were the only ones in the room who were not in hospital gowns. When their daughter came out, the nurse at the front desk announced over the loud speaker, to everyone present, that today she had received her final cancer treatment. Everyone in the room turned to look at her and applauded with genuine smiles on their faces. After a brief pause, the nurse returned to the microphone and mentioned to the group that the woman's parents had recently celebrated fifty years of marriage. Again, there was applause and huge smiles celebrating this life event. Everyone in the room shared an appreciation for life, which made them a community; they had all endured some level of treatment for cancer. The couple was envious of the community that the people receiving cancer treatments shared together.

In an interview on NBC News, the interviewer asks Joan Lunden, being treated for cancer at the time, how cancer had changed her. "It just gives you this much, much greater appreciation for life. And it's a shame that you have to go through something that almost takes away life to appreciate it more, but it certainly does do it to you."[10]

Dysfunctional Leadership

Definitions can offer a framework in which one can appreciate certain aspects of leadership, but seeing how they become realized in actual organizational settings offers a different dimensionality. The examples below will help to provide a framework that systematizes the important points of a given leadership type within a specific setting. However, we will set this up by a few case studies that will begin our discussion.

Bernard's Law

My brother Bernard was telling me about the program *Survivor*, which he had recently watched for a year. The premise of the show is that a number of people, men and women, are placed on a remote island, where

---

[10] *NBC News*, 1 October 2014.

they are divided into teams. They must obtain food by their own efforts from the natural resources available on the tropical island. They go through challenges developed by the producers of the program in order to win privileges for their team, such as: ready-made food or tools to make procurement of food or other living on the island easier. The challenges also determine who has what it takes to win further challenges. The losing team has to eliminate one of its members through the vote of its team members. My brother noticed that those who have little to nothing to offer to the team are eliminated most quickly. The gifted, who have what it takes to complete the challenges and stock up privileges, are picked off one by one, as other team members make alliances with one another to stay together for a given purpose or timeframe. The one who wins "the game" of *Survivor* is the person who is the most cunning and manipulative, not the best or brightest person. It's the person with the most savvy, who uses the resources at hand—human or other—primarily to his or her own advantage, no matter what the moral or ethical cost may be. I call this "Bernard's Law," and it will serve as a metaphor for appreciating what kind of a person is "winning" in organizations and society at large, and why change and conversion are so necessary, but constantly thwarted or undermined. By Bernard's Law, I mean those who are a threat to the *Survivor* "winners" by virtue of their inner strengths. Such people have to be eliminated from the competition and the group, so that those who are benefitting from the system as it stands may continue to do so.

As an example of this, we can see that Pope Francis has inherited certain dilemmas from his predecessors. In the media, Pope Francis' actions have been characterized as "shaking things up" in the Vatican. He seems to be more than a new leader establishing a new regime; he seems to be changing the rules of "the game" at the highest levels of the Vatican. *Time Magazine* reports that some had been concerned about "the Italian problem," whereby families for generations have been guaranteed positions for life. By this schema, family loyalty replaces quality of service as the prime motivation behind retaining employees. (See the Sons of Zebedee above.) Advancing the Gospel received lip service as temporal concerns got in the way of sharing the Gospel and building the Kingdom. Pope Francis has reformed the curia and established a new group of Cardinal-advisors whose primary objective is evangelization, where a different set of values, namely those espoused by Jesus, become the norm of operations, rather than guaranteeing one's family's future through keeping a job. We will have reason to return to these points later as our study continues.

An Autocratic Abbot

As part of a college project, I visited several monasteries. I had visited one monastery and then another of the same religious order in another location, though each was financially independent. In speaking with the abbot of the second monastery, I told him that I had visited the other monastery and I mentioned how I had found the monastery patro-centric, meaning, everything revolved around the abbot, the so-called (spiritual) father-figure there. The abbot at the second monastery said, "You mean he is autocratic." I learned later during my visit that the second abbot had been tasked by his superiors to investigate the leadership of the earlier abbot. There were questions as to whether he was crushing rivals to his authority and so undermining any future leadership in his monastery. This proved true later on, when the monastery needed to elect another abbot, but there was no one in the monastery who could handle the mantle of leadership. All the monks who had any promise never had their potential fostered, so they withered on the tree under the previous abbot. There was no growth of leaders to take the monastery into the future. Thus, the financial stability that the abbot had worked to assure was actually impeded by the crushing of rivals.

The abbot described above prepared a great financial future for his monastery; that is not in question. However, the human toll was also enormous and notorious. Not dealing with one's problems may work for a time and may work to ensure a future for an institution, like a monastery, but the human toll is enormous and cannot be underestimated. A wealthy monastery with no spiritual leadership is one without a future; it is spiritually bankrupt. This type of leadership is a negative example, which we will attempt to classify using Markham's models below.

Models of Leadership

Dr. Markham notes that there are "blocks to the possibility of a solid future," and they come in the form of the leaders who are leading the group. The scenarios presented in the subsequent chapters reflect some situations from four types of leaders that Markham identifies. I have used these to guide our discussion. After all, Jesus himself related that many things can get in the way of the seed, that is, the Word of God, taking root in someone's life (see Mark 4 above). I would suggest that by examining the issue of leadership within an organization, we are appreciating the manner in which a person inhibits the Word from taking root or stands in the way of growth. The leader's unwillingness to deal with his or her inadequacies will impact how a community deals with growth in profound ways.

Conclusion

We are all formed in different ways, given our home life, physical (dis)abilities, and other resources. But we seldom remain confined to a family system forever. Instead, we venture out to experience new groups, people, and circumstances. But what we have been taught in our families goes with us, whether we acknowledge it or not. These experiences may have trivial or profound ramifications for how we interact with the outside world, especially if we are in charge. We take a great deal for granted and assume that things will continue in a positive direction. This may not always be the case, so it is important to acknowledge this and recognize that everyone is different, but also that sometimes "eccentricity" may be a euphemism for pathological dysfunction. Eccentricity is something that we can live with. Dysfunction is a sick way of doing things and will infect us with a diseased perspective, sapping the life within us, oftentimes without us knowing or recognizing it. The manners of leadership described below exemplify cases of sick individuals leading groups. Our purpose in reporting them is to illustrate how Markham's models reflect real-life circumstances and scenarios that affect real people. All names have been changed. Study details may reflect composite or altered experiences to respect the privacy of individuals.

We close this first chapter with a quote from the Gospel of Mark about Jesus' appreciation of leadership. The people were looking for direction to help them to live their lives. Even when Jesus recognized the need for a break, he put his needs aside to teach the people.

Mark 6:31 [Jesus] said to [the disciples], "Come away by yourselves to a deserted place and rest a while." People were coming and going in great numbers, and they had no opportunity even to eat. 32 So they went off in the boat by themselves to a deserted place. 33 People saw them leaving and many came to know about it. They hastened there on foot from all the towns and arrived at the place before them. 34 When he disembarked and saw the vast crowd, his heart was moved with pity for them, for they were like sheep without a shepherd; and he began to teach them many things.

Marc Lanoue

2 THE NARCISSIST AS LEADER

Introduction

Personality types are developed over time. Most people are familiar with what it means to be an introvert or an extravert, but no classification can encompass everyone. Such labels are attempts to appreciate certain qualities versus others. Some people use the signs of the Zodiac as an indicator. eHarmony and other such web-sites attempt to connect types of people in order to match them, "maximizing" compatibility. Whatever a person uses to classify, there's a reason for using certain criteria, whether recognized or not. No one can be defined by any label, no matter how precise such labels may be. That being said, we now turn to examine certain characteristics in leaders that can cause communities to fail in realizing or even having goals and vision. Every leadership type is not just as helpful to the community as any other. A dysfunctional leader can lead a team or individual to a championship or to excel, but this can be with great psychic and spiritual pain experienced by the participants. It's one thing to push a team hard; it's another to give pain relievers to athletes to cover up a serious injury, so that the player can continue in the game. The next four chapters address leaders with varying levels of dysfunction to recognize how much damage they inflict in the name of "success."

You Can Deny Your Cross

> [Jesus] summoned the crowd with his disciples and said to them, "Whoever wishes to come after me must deny himself, take up his cross, and follow me. (Mark 8:34; Luke 9:23).

When Jesus invites us to deny ourselves, his invitation is for us not to pursue the goals of the ego to the exclusion of anything and anyone else, which, in sum, may be described as being concerned with what I do; what I have (meaning even a spouse, children, material possessions, house), and what people think of me. The Gospel passage used for Ash Wednesday warns against actions done to impress others.

> <u>Matt. 6:1</u> "[But] take care not to perform righteous deeds in order that people may see them; otherwise, you will have no recompense from your heavenly Father. <u>2</u> When you give alms, do not blow a trumpet before you, as the hypocrites do in the synagogues and in the streets to win the praise of others. Amen, I say to you, they have received their reward. <u>3</u> But when you give alms, do not let your left hand know what your right is doing, <u>4</u> so that your almsgiving may be secret. <u>And your Father who sees in secret will repay you.</u> <u>5</u> "When you pray, do not be like the hypocrites, who love to stand and pray in the synagogues and on street corners so that others may see them. Amen, I say to you, they have received their reward. <u>6</u> But when you pray, go to your inner room, close the door, and pray to your Father in secret. <u>And your Father who sees in secret will repay you.</u>.... <u>16</u> "When you fast, do not look gloomy like the hypocrites. They neglect their appearance, so that they may appear to others to be fasting. Amen, I say to you, they have received their reward. <u>17</u> But when you fast, anoint your head and wash your face, <u>18</u> so that you may not appear to others to be fasting, except to your Father who is hidden. <u>And your Father who sees what is hidden will repay you.</u> (Matthew 6:1-6, 16-18).

The understanding is that God will reward in secret. Those who perform their works for others to see are being rewarded by others' praise and the building up of their reputation. Such people are thus falling into the trap of stroking their egos, which leads us to our discussion of the first type of leader—the narcissist.

A narcissist is someone who totally identifies with the ego; there is no acknowledgement of or connection with a true self or soul, so a narcissist's undertakings are to enhance one's value or esteem in the eyes of the world, ensuring that everyone can see how the narcissist is "successful." Success is understood as enhancing one's wealth, life, progeny, and reputation, to use the values of some of the Old Testament (see Job 1:1-3 and 42:10-16) or power, prestige, titles, and education in modern terms. In other words, things like the building of buildings and other tangible accomplishments are how the narcissist will evaluate whether he or she is successful. Money and wealth—whether the person has control over it or amasses it—will also reflect such success. Interior values are minimized; material things are maximized within this type of value system. It never occurs to the narcissist to go interiorly for checks and balances. Since the ego is fear-based, that is, constantly concerned with losing what it has accomplished or achieved, it will always evaluate people on the basis of their ability or intent to undermine or enhance what the ego has. This would not be so bad, except that any wrong step from someone against the narcissist will be met with backlash, given the insecurity that exists. Markham offers the following insight:

> Often seen as "saviors" in struggling organizations, [narcissists] assume unwavering control. The organizational enthusiasm is short-lived, however, as persons soon intuitively sense that something is lacking. Grandiosity and suspiciousness in the narcissistic leader begin to give rise to impulsive decision-making and random disregard of organizational processes. Believing that they alone possess the truth and that others simply exist to mirror their need to receive continued adulation, they engage in subtle tactics of devaluation of any employees who do not serve this purpose.[11]

When people do not value themselves in a real, God-centered way, they will devalue others. The narcissist has no appreciation of others, because

---

[11] Markham, *Spiritlinking*, 117.

it's all about the ego, so there would never be any interior reflection to recognize that the narcissist does not interiorly value him or herself.

The Narcissist: Image Isn't Everything, It's the Only Thing!

Narcissists find their identity in their egos. Catering to the ego will guide the way the person does everything in life. For the narcissistic leader, the source of "truth" is the maintenance of one's image, since status and remaining the "best" are of particular concern. If this is not the goal of the situation at hand, then the situation will be redirected so that it does not upset the current image—it can only maintain or enhance the image—or it will be rendered innocuous, through carefully controlled processes to undermine anything that does not benefit the ego.

> The grounds of the wealthy parish were sizeable and impeccable. But many people complained when a bulletin notice appeared threatening to take away the St. Vincent de Paul collection box for clothing for the poor, since it sometimes overflowed. The parishioners wanted to convey the image of being generous in sharing their goods with others. The Pastor wanted a beautiful campus. Images were at odds.

Narcissists lack the ability to deal with otherness, since their focus is entirely on their own ego, its support and aggrandizement. There is no interior depth, so any programs that they sponsor will also be without depth—you can't give what you don't have. The constant expansion of the ego, through building projects and construction and plans for physical growth, divert energy away from any interior, secret growth—the kind that God causes and desires.

> Narcissism is a failure not of conscience but of empathy, which is the capacity to perceive emotions in others and so react to them appropriately. The poor narcissist cannot see past his own nose, emotionally speaking, and as with the Pillsbury Doughboy, any input from the outside will spring back as if nothing had happened.[12]

---

[12] Martha Stout, Ph. D., *The Sociopath Next Door* (New York: MJF

Narcissists cannot take feedback, because they are the source of truth. They also have no place for others' shortcomings. Competition to maintain one's position and power is also constantly operative.

> A parish hired a Youth Minister. He was doing phenomenal work; he was charismatic and was drawing many kids into the program. The religious sister who oversaw another program witnessed his success, so undermined his work. He quit. The parish hired another Youth Minister who had no organizational skills—there was no threat there. The number of kids dwindled to less than a quarter of their numbers under the former Youth Minister. The other Youth Minister was hired by a neighboring community to run its Boys and Girls Club program. It is bursting at the seams and doing great work.

Creativity

Creativity is the word we use to convey how people share themselves with others through projects of various types. Within a parish setting, especially within a large parish, creative people will be those who manifest the Spirit in the proliferation of gifts that St. Paul talks about in First Corinthians (1 Cor 12:4-11). We call these charisms or gifts from God used to advance the Kingdom. (We will explore this topic further in chapter 10.)

If creativity is undermined or non-existent, then an organization's future is doomed, as was seen above in the case of the abbot. Others' potential—another word for "spirit"—is never tapped. There is no way to manifest the Spirit, so enterprises that may have begun under the power and guidance of the Holy Spirit at one time, turn into human enterprises, which have no power to give life or bring healing.

> The Pastor told the new priest that his predecessor had been inadequate to meet the needs of the Bible Study group, since he had only rudimentary training in Scripture. The new priest with advanced degrees in Scripture contacted the Bible Study's

Books, 2005), 127-28.

coordinator on multiple occasions. She finally said that she had no way for him to contribute to her group.

Narcissists tend to enable others with similar insecurities to keep a hold on their own control. Empowerment is lacking. The inability to be creative can be frustrating, as it can also sap one's life-force, unless a person recognizes other outlets to manifest creativity. Leaving a sick or dying group or organization may be the only way to preserve one's soul.

Finances

Lack of disclosure is a red flag. If someone has something to hide, then transparency is a problem, though not all lack of disclosure is problematic. However, the signs may not be cut and dry. Finances, as an example, can point to a deeper problem; they are not necessarily the root cause, though they may misdirect attention from other issues.

> An employee was moving to a new area in the company, but he had never dealt with finances. He recognized that he would need training in this area and so asked his boss for training repeatedly over the three years that he was there. The training never came. The boss kept a tight rein on all inquiries into the company books.

> A parishioner noted that there were twenty-six requests for monetary assistance in the parish bulletin, and the parish's payroll amounted to a million dollars each year. There were two collections per Mass each weekend. She wondered where the money was going and what all of the staff was doing that called for such large salaries. Questions were never answered.

Community

Real community involves a shared experience of suffering, which we call compassion. The appreciation of Jesus' Passion is not solely an objective reality; it is also something that takes on deeper meaning over time, as we recognize our own sufferings in life, as well as those of others. However, sharing these realities is necessary for people to get to know each other. Self-disclosure is the willingness to share oneself with others—sufferings and triumphs, but it assumes people willing to receive the self-disclosure on the other side, in a word: intimacy.[13] It also involves solitude, the ability to be comfortable with oneself and the ability to hold one's sufferings. If this does not start with oneself, then one cannot appreciate another's pain or difficulties—compassion and empathy. Networks that are superficial and closed to outsiders can become havens for both narcissists and ego-weak personalities, the type most open to stroking the ego-maniacal narcissist.

The image that is maintained to the outside world must be controlled, which means that the truth is never made clear.

Positive Points for the Narcissist

Given the examples above and the predominance of narcissism in American society, we should not think that narcissists are all bad—quite the contrary. Narcissists have many positive qualities. First and foremost, they have vision, so they can ensure that an organization stays on target when competing requests for attention come up. Since narcissists cannot live in the present moment, their future-thinking perspective can drive an organization. Narcissists can thus help others to focus their energies on a goal. However, the prime goal for the narcissist is the person's own ego. Through some careful wording and not a little manipulation and bullying, a narcissist can compel a person to follow a program to ensure

---

[13] Schaef and Fassel (*The Addictive Organization*, 143-144) write: "By intimacy we are not referring to sexual intimacy or even what might be seen as emotional intimacy. What we mean by intimacy is the willingness to know oneself and to let oneself be known by others. William Ouchi [*The M-Form Society: How American Teamwork Can Recapture the Competitive Edge* (Reading, MA: Addison-Wesley, 1984)] describes intimacy as a common thread binding people together in caring closeness and support in social relations. He observes that intimacy is very rare in American life and that we resist the notion that closeness can be achieved in a workplace. We have segmented our lives in such a way that personal feelings have no place at work. Interestingly, the inability to form and maintain intimacy is a prime characteristic of an addict. We do not feel that it is by accident that our corporations have been structured to reflect this lack of intimacy."

that the ego of the narcissist leader will get what it needs to be stroked and inflated. If the goal of others and the goal of the narcissist can work together, then there will be "success." Projects, especially physical projects like buildings, are ego-extensions of the narcissist, so their realization will be a reflection of the leader's ability to deliver. Since there is nothing substantial interiorly for a narcissist, it emphasizes why such projects must succeed—narcissists' identities are wedded to such projects.

> The parish had a financial connection with a third-world parish and school. A team of highly skilled workers: engineers, educators, and medical personnel from the parish would visit once a year for about two weeks, though some went for longer periods. They discovered that their funds to pay the teachers were being misdirected elsewhere. Additionally, they found that natural disasters regularly destroyed the projects that they had worked so hard to establish there. They devised ways to ensure that the funds from the parish went to the teachers in a consistent and guaranteed way. They also developed ingenious ways of diminishing the effects of natural disasters on the projects that the parish was working on, so that they would be stable and permanent, even during difficult times.

A narcissistic leader will ensure that his or her projects—ego-extensions—will be preserved and successful, which is the payoff. In this case, both the narcissist and the people benefit from the improved fail-safes for the projects. The problem develops when there is no payoff, that is, there is nothing "to show" for the work accomplished.

Negative Points about the Narcissist

The points from Markham above more than suggest that there are always negative points in dealing with narcissists, whether they are admitted or not.

> Some religious Sisters came to solicit funds for the poor from the wealthy parishioners. After Mass, the Associate Pastor greeted them and left the church, expecting that they would join the

Pastor and others for dinner. They didn't come. The next day, the Sister told the Associate that they were never invited to dinner; they were lucky to receive a cup of water. When the Bishop assigned a Sister from a different community to speak at all the Masses about a diocesan initiative, the Pastor had her stay overnight at the rectory; join him and others for dinner; and have breakfast the next day.

The image a parish wishes to present and financial considerations not to their benefit often makes outreach incidental, not fundamental, to the future of the parish from the perspective of the narcissistic leader. But outreach on the part of a true leader can turn a congregation in the right direction.

The new Pastor of the parish had worked in the missions for twenties years prior to his assignment at the growing church. The Vestry asked for a capital campaign to expand the church building in light of the phenomenal growth. The Pastor made it clear to everyone concerned that the capital campaign would have two equal parts: one for the church and the other for the missions. If they did not collect their goal for the missions, there would be no expansion of the church. Both components of the campaign exceeded their goals by hundreds of thousands of dollars, and the church is growing, both here and abroad.

No End in Sight

With a narcissist at the helm, everything will appear to everyone concerned to be running along smoothly, even beautifully. Catch phrases using superlatives will abound: "Our Lady of the Best School produces brilliant children through its superior teaching methods." However, if someone stops to look under the hood, there won't be much found. The resources—human, spiritual, physical, financial—will have all been diverted toward advancing the ego of the narcissistic leader. Within a parish situation, depending on the strength and longevity of the Pastor, the parish will appear "successful," but in whose terms, the narcissist's or those seeking spiritual nourishment? By substituting the term "parishioners" for "employees" below, Markham offers an interesting assessment of such a situation.

> By the time the source of the problem has been accurately targeted, employees have often been so manipulated and intimidated that they lack the stamina to take any action directed toward confronting the leader..... Narcissists lack the capacity for honest self-examination and are too rigidly defended to hear feedback. ... Narcissists do not fundamentally change.[14]

One parishioner in such a parish wrote: "I am eager for formation and shepherding," but it wasn't happening, nor was it ever going to happen. Another parishioner said: "The Pastor's a CEO, not a shepherd." Some Associate Pastors had attempted to provide spiritual nourishment, but over time such initiatives were co-opted to serve "the program" or left to die a slow death, since they did not serve the *modus operandi*.

Pope Francis writes:

> Spiritual worldliness, which hides behind the appearance of piety and even love for the Church, consists in seeking not the Lord's glory but human glory and personal well-being. It is what the Lord reprimanded the Pharisees for: "How can you believe, who receive glory from one another and do not seek the glory that comes from the only God?" (Jn 5:44). It is a subtle way of seeking one's "own interests, not those of Jesus Christ" (Phil 2:21). It takes on many forms, depending on the kinds of persons and groups into which it seeps. Since it is based on carefully cultivated appearances, it is not always linked to outward sin; from without, everything appears as it should be (§93).

Appearance, however, is not reality, that is, God's Reality. It saps life and is a debilitating system. The life that comes from the Gospel is always available, but the narcissistic leader will re-channel efforts leading to it toward his or her own agenda.

> A child with autism had been through the religious education training to receive her First Communion. On the day of the

---

[14] Markham, *Spiritlinking*, 120.

practice, the Director of Religious Education asked her parents if the child would "act out" during the service. They said that they didn't know. The family feared their child's exclusion, and the impact it would have on her. A different reaction occurred at another First Communion two years earlier at the same church when another child, with no disability, had pulled the fire alarm as First Communion was being distributed to the children and their parents to the piercing sound of the fire alarm.

The Gospel can always be accommodated to egotistical ends.

Where Does This Come From?

In a closed system, there are huge holes in checks and balances, so opportunities for avoidance of doing the right thing abound. Pastors, once canonically installed, cannot be removed, unless they engage in willful wrong-doing of a financial or moral nature. If there is no correction of bad behaviors, then the person will continue with them. Some people become adept at looking for the holes in the system, as Bernard's Law suggests, and it starts before they get to the seminary, but stays with them, as Markham points out above. Narcissists do not change. A case in point:

> A charitable organization in support of priestly vocations provided seminarians with a picnic dinner, closing out their day of prayer together. The seminarians were working with them to clean up after the event. One seminarian, already ordained a deacon, surreptitiously backed out of the room and left, so that he did not have to help with the clean up. A year later, this same deacon was on a trip. Whenever he was scheduled to serve Mass, he was conspicuously absent, whereas, when he served as deacon, he was present in finery. He returned to his diocese for a short time from an assignment overseas to say a special Mass for a select group, which took rehearsals of four hours to prepare.

Pope Francis can offer us insight:

> In some people we see an ostentatious preoccupation for the

liturgy, for doctrine and for the Church's prestige, but without any concern that the Gospel have a real impact on God's faithful people and the concrete needs of the present time. In this way, the life of the Church turns into a museum piece or something which is the property of a select few (§95).

Image and ego inflation become the prime motivations for narcissists, and we can see that Pope Francis is well aware. And when Prelates with or without knowledge encourage these individuals to continue in their endeavors, these "leaders" end up undermining the Gospel that they say they are supporting.

Summary

All people have egos, but they have to be strengthened through conflict. When there is too much conflict or trauma, a person has insufficient ego strength, which we will address below. When a person has too little conflict or avoids receiving feedback, then that person's ego will become too inflated, and the negative qualities of the ego will surface, though perhaps after it is too late. When inadequacies are not addressed, their concealment becomes the way of life for the person, even if they bring others down as a result. The narcissistic leader has little to no sense of interiority, so there will never be anything done that has depth. He or she will always see others as rivals. Jesus' identification of various ways that the Word of God can have its place in one's life overshadowed by other concerns is real. The narcissistic leader will never change, so the question becomes what does one do with this? We cannot answer this question before addressing the other types of leaders that Markham describes. We end this chapter, however, with a parable taken from Fr. Anthony De Mello's *Taking Flight*, which encapsulates how a community's compassionate concern is co-opted by social superficiality.

On a rocky seacoast where shipwrecks were frequent there was once a ramshackle little lifesaving station. It was no more than a hut and there was only one boat, but the few people who manned the station were a devoted lot who kept constant watch over the sea and, with little regard for themselves and their safety, went fearlessly out in a storm if they had any evidence that there had been a shipwreck somewhere. Many lives were thus saved and the station became famous.

As the fame of the station grew, so did the desire of people in the neighborhoods to become associated with its excellent work. They generously offered of their time and money, so new members were enrolled, new boats bought, and new crews trained. The hut, too, was replaced by a comfortable building which could adequately handle the needs of those who had been saved from the sea and, of course, since shipwrecks do not occur every day, it became a popular gathering place—a sort of local club.

As time passed the members became so engaged in socializing that they had little interest in lifesaving, though they duly sported the lifesaving motto on the badges they wore. As a matter of fact, when some people were actually rescued from the sea, it was always such a nuisance because they were dirty and sick and soiled the carpeting and the furniture.

Soon the social activities of the club became so numerous and the lifesaving activities so few that there was a showdown at a club meeting, with some members insisting that they return to their original purpose and activity. A vote was taken and these troublemakers, who provide to be a small minority, were invited to leave the club and start another.

Which is precisely what they did—a little further down the coast, with such selflessness and daring that, after a while, their heroism made them famous. Whereupon their membership was enlarged, their hut was reconstructed—and their idealism smothered.

If you happen to visit that area today, you will find a number of exclusive clubs dotting the shoreline. Each one of them is justifiably proud of its origin and its tradition. Shipwrecks still occur in those parts, but nobody seems to care much.[15]

---

[15] Anthony De Mello, *Taking Flight: A Book of Story Meditations* (New York: Image Books/Doubleday, 1990), 84-85.

3 THE AS-IF LEADER

Introduction

Our foray into the arena of leadership is meant to help us to appreciate the implications of leaders not dealing with their emotional or other inadequacies. This unwillingness to deal with these personal issues will hinder the growth of an organization or system, so that it will not realize its purpose, goal, mission, or potential. We saw above how the problem of the narcissist is one of empathy, but also of seeing one's identity in ego-extensions, rather than interior states of being, which we call the true self. Emotional awareness can lead one to a greater appreciation of depth of one's self as well as others, and even God, since "the Spirit scrutinizes everything, even the depths of God" (1 Cor 2:10). A lack of emotional awareness and its impact will be the common thread among these leadership types, which leads to the next classification from Dr. Markham, namely, the As-if Leader.

The As-if Leader

If you read the Gospel of Mark from the beginning, early on you encounter the following statement: "The people were astonished at [Jesus'] teaching, for he taught them as one having authority and not as the scribes" (Mark 1:22). The people say this after Jesus teaches in the synagogue (v. 21). His teaching in the synagogue is followed by the healing of someone possessed by a demon (vv. 23-27), which causes his fame to spread (v. 28). I would suggest that Jesus' teachings come from a deeper place, namely, alignment with his true self. Becoming aligned with one's true self, rather than one's ego, can eventually lead to the Kingdom.[16] We will have reason to explore this further below. The scribes, on the other hand, observe the Law, which does not have the same sort of impact. The old adage: "You can lead a horse to water, but you can't make him drink," is apt in this circumstance. The purpose of the Law is to dispose someone to God's will and thus love one's neighbor as he or she does oneself (Lev 19:18). However, this need not be the result if one is preoccupied with observance of the Law (an external observance) rather than having the Law written on one's heart (interior transformation). (See Jer 31:33. Cf. Mark 7:1-23.) From Mark 1:22, we can appreciate that the people discern a difference between Jesus' authority (and its deeper source) and that of the scribes.

Institutions, groups, and organizations provide us with ready-made value systems in which we are able to find our true selves, so long as we make the teachings or values of the institution a part of ourselves or reject them or both as we recognize who we are in relation to them. This is what we call individuation, that is, becoming who we are not in isolation from everyone else, but in light of everyone else around us. However, many factors can stand in the way of this occurring. We need the group during adolescent years and young adulthood especially—in these cases the peer group—to act as a go-between for the development of identity. If, however, someone is unable to manifest an identity without appeal to the group, then I call such a person "gregotistical," which means that the person does not have sufficient ego strength on his or her own, so adopts the group-ego—shorthand for a group's value system—as one's own in

---

[16] Thomas Merton (*Conjectures of a Guilty Bystander* [New York: Image/Doubleday, 1968], 36) writes: "We believe, not because we want to *know*, but because we want to *be*. And supernatural faith responds to the mystery of that natural faith which is the core and center of our personal being, the will to be ourselves that is the heart of our natural identity. The higher faith is the will not only to be ourselves, but to find ourselves truly in Christ by obedience to His Father." Emphasis his.

effect to tell the person who he or she is.[17] This understanding informs our appreciation of what Markham refers to as her second category of leadership, the "As-if" leader.

> As–if leaders [are people who] have learned how to interact and how to behave in [a leadership] role, but the substance of personal identity and inner authority is lacking. Because they have a well-developed talent for mimicry, they find themselves from time to time in positions of leadership. Superficially playing the role of what they believe is that of a leader, they're in a state of continued apprehension that the deceit will be discovered. Furthermore, as–if leaders' deep-seated feelings about being inauthentic and inadequate make it difficult for them to make any significant goal-directed decisions. Procrastination becomes the hallmark of their style and the organizations they lead become transfixed in paralysis. It goes without saying that these leaders' posturings have grave consequences for organizations seeking to engage in transformative change.[18]

An As-if leader will appeal to rules, policies, and roles to avoid taking personal responsibility for actions, since such a person is unaware of an interior identity. As-if leaders have permitted someone else, the group-ego, to speak for them. A case in point:

> A Pastor and Associate Pastor were assigned to hear confessions after Mass. The Pastor said the Mass, so the Associate went to his confessional before Mass ended and assumed that the Pastor would go to his confessional after Mass. After hearing

---

[17] Merton (*Conjectures of a Guilty Bystander*, 66-67) writes: "Mass society is indeed made up of individuals who, left to themselves, know they are zero, and who, added together in a multitude of zeroes, seem to themselves to acquire reality and power. But this is the negative individualism of the man who thinks he establishes himself as real by comparing himself with everything that is "not-I." (When you count up enough things that are not-I, you end up by discovering that even I is not-I.) But, meanwhile, what is to blame is not individualism but collectivism."

[18] Markham, *Spiritlinking*, 120-21.

confessions for an hour and a half, the Associate came out wondering where all the people had come from, since confessions normally lasted one hour. The Pastor had forgotten to stay for confessions. When the Associate asked him about this, the Pastor responded: "The Pastor provides priests for the confessions; he doesn't hear them"—stated in the third person. Rather than admitting his oversight and moving on, he related that he had something more important to do—the weekly letter for the bulletin, which he had waited until the last minute to do.

We can see how procrastination, as Markham describes, is found in this case. The role becomes the dominant force, not the person in the role. The group-ego becomes something that no one questions. A person can be "safe" in discussions with others as an As-if leader by appealing to the group-ego all the time. This keeps discussions running in circles, which obfuscates the As-if leader's inability to lead.

Another example illustrates how over identification with one's role can play out in personal interactions.

An Associate Pastor had been assigned to a new parish, so he introduced himself to a priest who offered weekend help there regularly. He not only ignored the new priest, but would never say his name. This went on for some time, so the new priest asked the Pastor about it and found that this priest had always been "quirky" like this. The priest was encouraged to ignore it, which he did. The "quirky" priest held another position within the diocese, and one day the Associate Pastor had occasion to call him to inquire about a matter, leaving a message. The "quirky" priest responded within a short time with great cordiality and depth of knowledge and insight, and spent as much time as was needed on the phone to address the problem. This same treatment occurred on several more occasions.

Institutional understandings or group-egos, which I use interchangeably, can provide us with clear-cut roles to determine our actions, but these roles should not obscure each person's need for growth as an individual person. "Keep the law and the law will keep you." This is an apt description, but what about growth as an individual? Everyone is called to address emotional immaturity no matter what state of life one is in. If someone needs professional help to overcome abuse or some other trauma in one's life, it is everyone's responsibility to do this. Many, however, will not, and the impact can be devastating.

Over-identifying with One's Role

The television program *60 Minutes* aired a segment on 3 March 2013 that described a Marine, Clay Hunt, who had returned to civilian life after several years in the military. He subsequently committed suicide. In the footage, he states: "We deserve a lot better coming home as veterans." Clay wondered why people were at the mall, whereas he had been in war. There was a huge disconnect for him. He could not transition from one institution—the military and its clear-cut value system—to American society, where containers or value systems are so fluid. He did not understand that he was also virtually disposable as far as his fellow citizens were concerned. He did not feel appreciated, which means that the external affirmation from the institution had not been replaced with an internal sense of self or one's true value before God.[19]

Recently a priest was ordained, who suffered from depression. This was known to his formators; however, he was given the go-ahead for ordination. Within months of ordination as a priest, he committed suicide. The communal life that he knew at the seminary fell away as he entered the real-life demands of his parish, and his depression closed in on him. This story represents a disconnect when institutional living—

---

[19] Excerpt from Lanoue, "Remove the Stone", 111. *The Baltimore Sun* published an article by Gregg Jaffe of *the Washington Post*, which described a program for addressing the alarming rate of suicides, which is on the rise, within the Navy SEALs, Army Rangers, and Green Berets. The suggestion at the command level is to hire people to ensure that the special-forces soldiers are in top physical shape. An anonymous person is quoted as saying: "You get guys who are healthy physically, and they have less [sic] problems." It's unfortunate that the commanders in the military are blind to the implications of someone who claims to have "moral flexibility," but "America, right or wrong," doesn't seem to ring true anymore. See *the Baltimore Sun*, 18 May 2014, p. 11.

which supports one's role—is over emphasized to the detriment of the individual's inner sense of identity.

In another instance, three newly ordained priests left the priesthood shortly after going to their new assignments, because their parish situations were so dramatically different from anything for which they had been prepared. They thought that they could not continue.

From my own perspective, I noted my concern in an article published in *Homiletics and Pastoral Review* that, as a seminarian studying for the priesthood in the Roman Catholic Church, given the sex-abuse crisis and its aftermath, that a discussion of celibacy never occurred there.[20] Seminarians at other seminaries have voiced similar concerns to me. But celibacy, that is, not having a spouse and being sexually continent, is only the obvious, practical aspect of this discipline. Being comfortable with oneself and being comfortable with the Church go hand in hand. The As-if leader has not adapted himself to the life-giving character of a relationship with Christ, which the Church is meant to foster and protect. He has aligned himself, as a child would, with following Church teachings with no personal transformation in view. Such leaders do not know who they are, and there will be serious implications for those who do not address this important matter in their lives. Removing the discipline of celibacy may be a response to the problem, but it is not the answer.

The As-if leader is good enough to be a scribe, i.e., identifying the rules, but without the interior sense of the purpose that observing the rules means. Such a leader cannot speak with the authority of Christ, because he has not experienced Christ himself, let alone worked to discern his own depths and darkness. We should expect that people will discern a difference between an As-if leader and someone with genuine leadership qualities; however, we must recall that Bernard's Law will be in effect, and As-if leaders will do everything that they can to avoid facing their inadequacies, which means that those whose lives expose them will be

---

[20] See, as of this writing (5 February 2015):
http://www.hprweb.com/2013/07/the-corporate-associate-effectively-addressing-the-affective-needs-of-the-newly-ordained/

viewed as rivals and, therefore, expendable. We should expect that betrayal and character assassination will be used to undermine people who witness from their interior authority, as the example of both Jesus and John the Baptist demonstrate. We will examine betrayal more in a later chapter.

Role vs. Humanity

If a person overemphasizes his or her role, then the connection to one's humanity suffers. There has to be a proper balance between the *persona* of a role and one's true self. Many television programs involving police and other occupations dramatically portray how a person can be sucked into one's role so much so that one's home life suffers, even to the point of a break-up. Everyone needs to make a living, but everyone also needs to protect one's true self. Marriages, families, and other relationships can be destroyed in light of such neglect of proper boundaries. The same is true within the priesthood and religious life.

The As-if leader is, in many ways, comparable to the narcissistic leader; however, there is a significant difference. The As-if leader has no ego strength nor does he or she have vision. Such a leader has given over any sense of identity to the group-ego. Ronald Heifetz and Marty Linsky of the Harvard Business School note: "Losing yourself in your role is a sign that you depend on the institution or community for meeting too many of your personal needs, which is dangerous."[21] Such a leader's accomplishments are motivated by and are the result of institutional authority for accomplishing anything or to a peer group that is as dysfunctional as he or she is, since the group-ego is always more insecure and problematic than any individual's ego: there are no checks on it and it has all of the problems that an ego does. Gregotistical people do not question the group-ego, which makes appeal to it all the better for them, and all the worse for the people whom they are leading. This scenario is a prime example:

---

[21] Ronald A. Heifetz and Marty Linsky, *Leadership on the Line: Staying Alive Through the Dangers of Leading* (Boston: Harvard Business Review Press, 2002), 190.

The Associate Pastor mistakenly attributed the title of "Doctor" [meaning holding a doctorate] to a chaplain in a hospital, and the Pastor corrected him, "If he's a doctor, it's one of those fake degrees." Another participant in the conversation pointed out that some monks with little connection to current Church affairs questioned how a deceased prelate could have received a doctorate in Canon Law (JCD) within a year of receiving a doctorate in Theology (STD). The Pastor said, "They don't hand those types of degrees out like that anymore," which means that they once did.

Every other group's credentials and rites must be inferior to those of the As-if leader's group. There is never any question about the integrity of the group-ego, despite examples to the contrary.

Creativity

No new ideas exist for the As-if leader. He or she is constantly searching for something—anything—to provide him with insights, since he has no interior well to draw from.

There were three Penance Services in one day, two during the day for the school children and one in the evening for about fifty children in religious education. One priest was scheduled to lead the first two, whereas, another priest was scheduled for the third. After the first two services, the second priest approached the first to do the one in the evening as well, since the first "hadn't had time to prepare a sermon." More than twenty years in the priesthood had left him bereft of ideas.

Leadership stems from one's connection to depth of some kind, as does one's creativity. If there is no connection to depth, then all tasks related to him will be difficult, troublesome, even baffling as to how one ought to proceed.

Community

Communal events can lead to community, but just calling something "community," with no grounding, does not make community or build community spirit, as this example illustrates.

> The seminarian and priests of the house gathered for Evening Prayer, since the Vocations Office recommended it as part of developing the prayer life of seminarians. When the seminarian left, so did the common prayer.

Community is about sharing oneself with others, especially through the sharing of intimacy, as mentioned above. Everyone needs intimacy. Prayer can foster such an exchange with God, which is its purpose, but its practice can never take the place of it with human beings.

No Vision

As-if leaders will have trouble getting people to follow them, because they lack vision and credibility in anything substantive. The narcissistic leader believes too much in himself or herself (=ego), whereas, As-if leaders don't believe in themselves at all, and this is conveyed subtly and overtly in everything that they say and do. They erroneously believe that people will follow them simply because they are in charge (=role), though facts suggest otherwise. For example:

> There was a need for more volunteers to help with Sister's ministries. People were burned out and saw their "ministry" week after week as a burden. Notices for months in the parish bulletin and contacts from new parish registrants led to two or three volunteers stepping forward, though dozens were needed. Direct invitations went nowhere. In spite of efforts to prove otherwise, the facts revealed that people were not stepping forward; there was no community or leadership to be found to prompt them to participate.

Pope Francis weighs in on this point: "A proposal of goals without an adequate communal search for the means of achieving them will inevitably prove illusory" (§33). Having a lot of activities operating at one's parish may seem as though it is a vibrant place (image). However, if the same faces keep surfacing and are getting burned out, then there is nothing substantive feeding the people at their core; it's all superficial.

People recognize depth. Superficiality seems to be a more difficult discernment process.

Employee Relations

As-if leaders are unable to express their needs and so attach themselves to others who will enable them, which means that they will provide for the As-if leader's needs without requiring them to express them. This takes its toll, both on the number of people who do not commit to anything, as well as to the overall well-being of those who are performing the needy leader's bidding. For those who are employees, decisions of any worth are hard to come by.

> Most significantly, these leaders have a strong need to be liked by others. In fact, their insatiable need to be appreciated by employees makes it extremely difficult for them to make hard decisions that could result in negative responses....[22]

The inability to handle employee issues is by far the most significant issue affecting the As-if leader, so it would be true in a company as in a parish. In a parochial setting, a Pastor must ensure that a parish is served well by its staff, both lay and clerical, and that both are effective.

> Auditors from corporate headquarters told managers that members of their committees needed to sign forms acknowledging their need to recuse themselves in cases where conflicts of interest existed. A recently hired staff member handed out papers in haste for signatures as committee members assumed their seats and became settled in for a meeting, though without explaining anything. The nature of the forms was not conveyed until the next meeting, where some cried foul about what had taken place. The CEO dismissed these concerns, until others told him that he had himself violated ethics by forcing people to sign documents without explaining their contents.

Though everyone avoids accountability at one time or another, avoiding one's mistakes all the time is an indication of a lack of ego strength. The

---

[22] Markham, *Spiritlinking*, 120.

As-if leader will find individuals who will enable his or her bad behaviors, so that he or she will never grow. We will address this point further below in our discussion related to the Unrecovered Addict and those who support such a leader.

Growth and the New Evangelization

Pleasant experiences make life enjoyable. Difficult experiences help us to grow. If all difficulties are removed from the equation, then there will be no life, because there is no growth. Transformation cannot occur, unless growth is possible.

> These poor leaders exhibit a need to be liked that outweighs their need to accomplish the transformative task.... If left in the position for very long, these leaders will attract dependent, needy workers whose subjective discomfort is as great or greater than that of the leader.... Should an organization leave in place an as–if leader, it passively colludes in resistance. It has effectively made it impossible for necessary change to proceed.[23]

The New Evangelization is the topic of conversation and focus for most dioceses and parishes these days, because Pope Francis, as did his predecessor, Pope Benedict XVI, recognizes that unless something is done to stem the current tide of people leaving the Church in droves, then the Catholic Church will be significantly impacted. Pope Francis recognizes that "business as usual" will not work anymore in shoring up the huge holes that exist, which means that energy is being exerted in areas that will not lead to growth. The New Evangelization involves transformative change in order to be realized.

An As-if leader will not be able to effect any substantive change any more than a narcissistic leader. Their preoccupations, though different, lead to the same result: Since they have not dealt with their own inadequacies, they will not have the leadership skills to help others to deal with theirs and so venture out further to gain depth. It is true that we cannot substitute for anyone on his or her journey, but we can create an

---

[23] Markham, *Spiritlinking*, 121.

environment that fosters growth rather than hampers it. Both the narcissistic leader and the As-if leader are stifled emotionally and will stifle others, the one so as not to be shown up, and the other because he would never do anything other than what the group-ego tells him. Both the narcissist and the As-if leader keep people entrusted to their care dependent for exploitational purposes. The freedom found in Christ is a foreign message for both of these leaders.

Summary

Balance is the key: institution and individual; they go hand-in-hand. The institution wants adherents to act without question, the way children are expected to act. However, closed systems are rife with loopholes allowing bad behaviors to mushroom into detrimental circumstances. Healthy attention to one's individual transformation is vital, but this is what adults do, not children. Institutions cannot be transformed; only people can. Reformation for institutions means that the group-ego has shifted emphases, not much else.

The As-if leader is one who has little ego strength of his or her own and has permitted the values of the institution to substitute for his or her identity. The Gospel of Christ invites us to die to self—the ego-strong self. People who have not grown in ego strength cannot die to a dominant ego self life, because they never lived one. They don't know who they are or what they want, because the ego is also the locus of making real choices, not just following initiatives from someone else. Interior authority stems from people willing to grow or suffer or accept what comes their way and deal with it—they don't run from difficult circumstances, but instead grow because of them. Growth comes through openness to that which is (Reality), rather than control of circumstances (ego-based manipulation). As-if leaders do not know themselves, their needs, or proper boundaries, and run from all difficulties and suffering, especially confrontation. There is no hope for transformation with As-if leaders. We need to recognize that if the institution is corrupt or is advocating unethical behavior, only someone with ego-strength can combat this. In a later chapter we will explore the implications of not pursuing one's inner self and embracing—usually blindly—what the institution advances as Gospel, and some of the grave consequences of such a poorly developed sense of self.

I close with an anecdote from an actual situation, which, I believe, encapsulates the legacy of the As-if leader.

> An organization had received a stately home and substantial property through a bequest in a will. They wanted the items in the home sold, since the organization had no use for them. An appraiser from a notable auction house came to evaluate the home and its contents. After going through the home, the appraiser came back with this conclusion: "A lot of money has been spent here, but there's nothing of any value."

Marc Lanoue

4 THE TALKING HEAD

Introduction

As we continue examining types of leadership, we now move to the Talking Head. The Talking Head is someone who does not consider emotion in decision-making, so everything will reflect a "black-and-white" approach. The Church, as it has become increasingly centralized, as Pope Francis admits, has seen this occurring in dioceses, which means that the institutional Church can oftentimes become more important than the people that it was meant to serve. Markham describes such a leader in the following way.

> Talking–head leaders are alexithymic; that is, they function from a fundamental base of denying emotion.... Classic organizational resistances of legalism and rigidity characterize groups led by talking heads.... left unaddressed, this type of dysfunctionality in the leader will block transformation.... Not only are they unable to enter into the process of spirit linking, but they also risk destroying whatever community networking may be developing through informal leadership channels.[24]

Community is a natural offspring of people coming together. It is the

---

[24] Markham, *Spiritlinking*, 122. See
http://en.wikipedia.org/wiki/Alexithymia for further information on alexithymia.

ability to have a common set of values and hold each other to higher standards, as it also relates at a deeper level in compassion. If there is no accountability within a community, then there can be no growth. Conversely, because compassion takes us beyond ourselves to recognize innate connection with others, the direction the Talking Head employs denies connection. Community suffers at the hands of the Talking Head. Pope Francis' action of setting up a panel of eight Cardinals to help him to address Church issues is an attempt to form a community of trusted advisors to see the Church on its path.

> At worst, the Cardinals are laying out a new set of best practices for far-flung dioceses to follow [related to sex-abuse cases]. At best, they are admitting that the Vatican had focused too much attention on the legal challenges of the sex-abuse crisis rather than on the behavioral problems at its core.[25]

Policies cannot change hearts, as we saw above with regard to celibacy. A community can provide an environment, but only the individual person can do what is necessary in his or her life to effect real change. By overemphasizing legal aspects related to sex abuse, dioceses have not directed resources toward combating the problem, which is a mature understanding of celibacy. Where the institution is more important than the people who comprise it, there is a general loss of the sense of vision for the institution apart from its maintenance from a purely functional-financial basis. This puts administrators of such institutions into a protectionist mode.

Closure of Parishes

Shortly after I was ordained a transitional deacon—meaning that I would be ordained a priest the following year—I returned to my family's home in Massachusetts and preached at all of the Masses at the various churches that had been joined together under a single Pastor. I was surprised that on this particular Sunday the priest was reading a letter from the Diocesan Bishop: that all but one parish in each of the towns in the county would be closed effective the following January 1st. Several

---

[25] *Time Magazine*, 23 December 2013, p. 60.

parishes objected, particularly those that were ethnically Polish, and they began occupying their church buildings. They sought Vatican intervention in their cases, as had parishioners in the Archdiocese of Boston, when Cardinal Sean O'Malley had announced closures there many years earlier.

> Although the Vatican has rarely sided with Catholics objecting to parish closings. … [In effect,] Church officials in Rome found that Bishop Timothy A. McDonnell [of the Diocese of Springfield, MA] acted appropriately in deciding to close or merge the parishes in Chicopee and Adams, but not in seeking to convert the buildings from religious to secular use.[26]

Those in the community of Adams, which is near my family home, saw their church reopened as a shrine, where they now have a weekly Sunday Mass, after they successfully appealed Bishop McDonnell's decision to close their church. The news from the Bishop about its closure came out of nowhere for them. Their parish's financial outlook was the strongest in the community, with a newly renovated church, a strong parochial identity, a parish school, and resources in the bank, with hard-working people supporting the parish through volunteerism, thanks to the leadership of their long-standing pastor, who retired at 82. They felt that their community was being threatened, to the point that they occupied their church for more than a year.

In the Bishop's defense, we have to recognize that the county was and continues to be financially depressed. He had to act in some way; that is not in question. Had he, however, considered the concerns of the people

---

[26]http://www.boston.com/news/local/massachusetts/articles/2011/02/18/d iocese_moves_to_remove_sacred_status_of_7_closed_churches/A step toward selling churches. It's interesting to note that the weekly publication of the Archdiocese of Baltimore, *The Catholic Review* (22 May 2014, p. 11) quotes Cardinal Raymond Burke, the prefect of the Vatican's Supreme Court at the time as saying: "When we [bishops] don't follow the requirements of [Canon] law, then people rightly claim that they've been aggrieved."

and seen the grounds of the church, he may have decided differently. Nonetheless, it is sad that so much animosity developed over this issue, and that the Vatican had to be brought in to decide the matter. A family member lives in Scituate, MA, which is in the Archdiocese of Boston. The parish in that town has been occupied for many years in protest. They were not satisfied by officials' explanations for why certain parishes were chosen over others to be closed.

Decisions have to be made in light of many different factors; but members of a community both individually and collectively want to know what's going on and they want to appreciate justice in the deliberations and actions. They also do not want to be slighted by their leadership, as though they are cogs in a wheel. The people of a parish need to be recognized as having emotional connections to a parish community, not just a building, which their occupation represents. Much more is lost when a parish is closed than a building. This is the aspect that is glossed over by a Talking Head leader, which I have heard many times.

A priest once told me that a bishop will be either a bishop for priests or a bishop for the people. But I believe that there is a third category, the Talking Head stance, where the institutional Church, not to be confused with either priests or people, is emphasized. The interest revolves around the patrimony or property of the local church. Neither priests nor people matter: the institution is what matters and the money that flows from parishes. Pope Francis is acutely aware of such a circumstance:

> This spiritual worldliness...can also lead to a business mentality, caught up with management, statistics, plans and evaluations whose principal beneficiary is not God's people but the Church as an institution (§96).

It's easier to lead by decree, which devalues people, than to lead them through discussion, which might get messy and require dealing with people where they are, instead of imposing one's will. This is foreign territory to the Talking Head leader.

Creativity

If the institution cannot benefit from the creativity of its priests or others, then creativity will be stifled.

> Several Associate Pastors inquired about attending courses in Pastoral Counseling, given the large number of their parishioners approaching them for marriage counseling. They were discouraged from attending any courses, as were other priests, since the diocese maintained that taking such courses would interfere with their duties in their parishes. Some, however, were tapped for studies in Canon Law, so that they could work in the Tribunal Office in the Chancery. The program generally required five summers to complete and on-line courses during the regular academic year.

> Unpaid volunteer cantors had been leading singing for more than ten years at the parish. The Pastor did not appreciate their contributions to the parish's worship, so he sent an e-mail to all of them out of the blue letting them know that their services would no longer be required. He had hired cantors for leading the congregation at Mass, and they would assume these responsibilities. This Pastor assumed a bigger leadership role in the diocese.

We will discuss creativity and its connection with realizing fulfillment in a later chapter, as well as its connection with isolation, but the seedbed for viewing the negative impact of such a stance seems clear. The institution will always benefit, whereas the individual will not when it comes to the Talking Head leader.

Summary

The individual member of an institution matters and if he or she does not, the institution has compromised the Gospel message in order to privilege another message: that the institution and its preservation are of more importance. When one's humanity is suppressed, as, for instance, by denying emotion and privileging "the bottom line," everyone loses. The institution may be maintained, but it is morally bankrupt and has ceased its human connection, as we saw above in the episode involving the abbot of the monastery. If a Talking Head leader is tied to such a bankrupt institution, then the error perpetuates itself.

We close this section with a parable from Anthony De Mello's *Taking Flight*, which describes the problem of an overly developed institutional focus.

> After many years of labor an inventor discovered the art of making fire. He took his tools to the snow-clad northwest regions and initiated a tribe into the art—and the advantages—of making fire. The people became so absorbed in this novelty that it did not occur to them to thank the inventor, who one day quietly slipped away. Being one of those rare human beings endowed with greatness, he had no desire to be remembered or revered; all he sought was the satisfaction of knowing that someone had benefited from his discovery.

> The next tribe he went to was just as eager to learn as the first. But the local priests, jealous of the stranger's hold on the people, had him assassinated. To allay any suspicion of the crime, they had a portrait of the Great Inventor enthroned upon the main altar of the temple, and a liturgy designed so that his name would be revered and his memory kept alive. The greatest care was taken that not a single rubric of the liturgy was altered or omitted. The tools for making fire were enshrined within a casket and were said to bring healing to all who laid their hands on them with faith.

> The High Priest himself undertook the task of compiling the *Life of the Inventor*. This became the Holy Book in which the Inventor's loving-kindness was offered as an example for all to emulate, his glorious deeds were eulogized, his superhuman nature made an article of faith. The priests saw to it that the Book was handed down to future generations, while they authoritatively interpreted the meaning of his words and the significance of his holy life and death. And they ruthlessly

punished with death or excommunication anyone who deviated form their doctrine. Caught up as they were in these religious tasks, the people completely forgot the art of making fire.

There was no fire.[27]

---

[27] De Mello, *Taking Flight*, 14-5.

Marc Lanoue

5 THE UNRECOVERING ADDICT

Introduction

The fourth and final type of leader for our discussion is the Unrecovering Addict, but it will involve a discussion of several other leadership/personality types as well, given its close association with the condition known as co-dependence. The Unrecovering Addict is someone who is addicted to a substance or process, and though the person may have stopped taking the addictive substance or otherwise withdrawn from the addictive process, the person has not addressed the underlying emotional issue that caused the difficulty to begin with. Addressing one's emotional problems that undergird addiction involves being in a recovery program, such as: Alcoholics Anonymous or something similar, which we render simply as "recovery."

Addiction Is Running The Show

If there is an addictive leader at the helm of an organization or system, then that individual, depending on the level of influence, will steer his or her concerns toward "scoring a fix," be it drugs, alcohol, food, or another payoff. Schaef and Fassel are clear about the outcome: "Ethical deterioration is the inevitable outcome of immersion in the addictive system.... [By] refusing to let in information that would alter the addictive paradigm, ... you are spiritually bankrupt."[28] This statement is particularly important for our study, given that we have been discussing Church leadership. People are looking not for more religion, but for more guidance in understanding their spiritual lives and gleaning fruit from them. If a Pastor is spiritually bankrupt, which will be a direct by-product of an addiction, no matter how things *seem* to be to the onlooker, the system will be bereft of spiritual nourishment.

> We believe the addictive system invites us to compromise our personal morality by inviting us to engage in [addictive] processes.... Besides establishing a social norm in which it is acceptable to cheat, steal, and lie, the very use of addictions separates us from our spiritual awareness. To the extent that religious systems are caught in the same processes as the addict, they themselves support our remaining in the addictive system. Indeed, whenever we confuse religion with spirituality, we are opting for the structure, control, and rules of an addictive system. This reliance on religion may remove us from the inner search only we can do from the depths of our own being.[29]

"The depths of our inner being" is a description of one's true self. If a person is alienated from this core, then that person will never realize who he or she is. Only someone in "contact" with one's true self will be able to cut through measures that will be brought to bear to alienate anyone questioning such a system. Schaef and Fassel continue:

> Invalidation is the process the addicted system uses to define into nonexistence those ideas and experiences that the system cannot know, understand, or most importantly, control. Invalidation is one of the main hallmarks of a closed system. It is knowledge that divergent ideas exist but will not let them into the frame of reference of the system, and it refuses even to recognize the existence of processes that are threatening to it.[30]

---

[28] Schaef and Fassel, *The Addictive Organization*, 67.

[29] Schaef and Fassel, *The Addictive Organization*, 67.

[30] Schaef and Fassel, *The Addictive Organization*, 71.

Invalidation ensures that the system remains in place just the way it is. This was the first mode of defense for dioceses in light of accusations of sexual abuse, as it has been for other organizations doing the same.[31]

Keeping Dysfunctional Systems in Place

Enabling behaviors are those that support addictive or codependent behaviors in another person, group, or system. Parents who provide their son or daughter with money to obtain drugs are enabling their child, not helping that child to get the real help he or she needs to get off drugs and deal with the issues that led to addiction. Parishes may have a policy to marry any couple who presents themselves, though the couple may be living together, pretending that a blessing over them will turn their union into a Sacrament. We hear talk about our justice system, and yet, we have all heard of cases where the accused are being freed from prison after their cases are re-examined and fraudulent proceedings and evidence are exposed.

Assumptions on the part of the individual or group or system is not only that these systems are acting uprightly, as much as it is that they should not be questioned. It is assumed that they have sufficient checks and balances in place to address any problems that develop, and that the people who are functionaries within these systems want the system to function with integrity, as they do themselves. But what happens when this is not the case or when the participants are actually manipulating the circumstances to ensure that no one discovers that the system in place is meant to undermine, undercut, and otherwise destroy? Bernard's Law is once again in play. One need only recall the situation with the Veterans Administration, where a full-scale investigation at the highest levels of government has been initiated to address administrators who mandated two lists for keeping track of wait times: the actual one and the one that was reported to the Government. This dishonesty has resulted in the deaths of many veterans due to denied or delayed care.[32]

---

[31] We will explore this further below when we discuss the case of Ray Rice of the Baltimore Ravens and his altercation with his then girlfriend.

[32] See, as of this writing (7 February 2015):

Pope Francis has something to say about systems trampling on the Gospel.

> We must recognize that if part of our baptized people lack a sense of belonging to the Church, this is also due to certain structures and the occasionally unwelcoming atmosphere of some of our parishes and communities, or to a bureaucratic way of dealing with problems, be they simple or complex, in the lives of our people. In many places an administrative approach prevails over a pastoral approach, as does a concentration on administering the sacraments apart from other forms of evangelization (§63).

Though Pope Francis is here speaking about institutional bureaucracy that may stand in the way of people's connection with the Church, I would suggest that the institution's dysfunction may also be systemic, so as to be a deterrent to people. They can sense the type of authority that is present and they can appreciate the sickness, though they probably have no way of articulating it. This does not mean that there is not something malevolent that is operative, even where the Church is involved.

---

http://www.cbsnews.com/feature/va-hospitals-scandal/. See also the case of the defective air bags from the Takata Company, (as of this writing 16 January 2015):http://www.consumerreports.org/cro/news/2014/10/everything-you-need-to-know-about-the-takata-air-bag-recall/index.htm: "According to a Nov. 7 *New York Times* report, Takata was aware of dangerous defects with its air bags years before the company filed paperwork with federal regulators. Based on interviews with two unnamed Takata employees, the Times [sic] stated that Takata began secretly testing for air bag defects in 2004—four years before the company claims it started testing for flaws. The Takata sources also told the Times [sic] that, after three months of testing in 2004, Takata's internal research was halted and research materials were destroyed."

Good Qualities (Covering) Over Good Leadership

Schaef and Fassel are on target in stating that addictions come in many shapes and sizes, and they are at various levels of intensity and seriousness. So I would suggest that addictions can be obfuscated by seemingly good leadership qualities. However, the problem is that they often go to extremes in producing boundaries, the very thing that addicts cannot recognize in themselves, but which they demand from others. Control in extreme terms is the area that I have encountered most often in my ministry, since control can be used to ensure that a system functions in the way that the leader may obtain the biggest payoff that he or she desires, no matter who is hurt in the process. The problem is that supernatural or grace-filled or God-given growth cannot be controlled. When there is no Presence of God's Grace in a given environment, where one would think that it would be found, namely, a parish or parochial group, then it's time to leave and find another group or parish. Co-dependents, however, the prime targets of other co-dependents, particularly addicts and narcissists, are experts at keeping things hidden. Since co-dependents don't trust their inner voices over the institutional voice, they will always be the prime victims of these predators.

> Human beings have struggled to find comfort in illusions of dependency.... They momentarily trick the victim into feeling comforted in the midst of massive change. At the same time, they increasingly and insidiously deprive the person of the very thing needed to promote healing: strong, mutual relationships.... Dependency [takes] the place of partnership. Community is missing in every aspect of life.[33]

Is anyone learning from others' mistakes? Or is everything presumed to be "the grace of God," when actually it is nothing more than a cover-up for sin? No transformation is possible, which means that the conduits for the Spirit have been blocked. Even Jesus had trouble performing healings where people had no faith in him in certain areas, as the Gospel reports (Mark 6:1-6). Trust is the necessary building block for creating a life-giving community, but if the leader is spiritually bankrupt and

---

[33] Markham, *Spiritlinking*, 116.

undermining people at every level, then trust is taking a hard hit. Dishonesty to preserve the closed system as an acceptable practice undermines everyone and everything attached to it.

Pope Francis has himself expressed his "wonder" at how religious—men and women who are members of religious communities—and priests can maintain their commitment within their respective communities, yet harbor deep-seated hatreds and other problems, which block transformation.

> It always pains me greatly to discover how some Christian communities, and even consecrated persons, can tolerate different forms of enmity, division, calumny, defamation, vendetta, jealousy and the desire to impose certain ideas at all costs, even to persecutions which appear as veritable witch hunts. Whom are we going to evangelize if this is the way we act? (§100).

Such persons are not acting from a deeper place, namely, the Stage of Authenticity, which we will treat in a later chapter.

The "Dry Drunk"

A "dry drunk" is someone who has addressed the physical aspects of his or her addiction, so the person has ceased drinking alcohol or taking drugs or is dieting (from a food addiction that has resulted in morbid obesity). These are good things but problematic when such people thwart true recovery by not addressing the underlying emotional difficulties that prompted them to take up the addiction in the first place. An episode from a confessional experience serves to illustrate this point.

> A man stated that he had not been to confession or to church in ten years. He was in his forties. He had been married and divorced twice. He said that he had never really loved his wives, but married them anyway. His kids didn't want to have anything to do with him. Further inquiry revealed that he had been a drug addict in his late teens, "but he was all done with that." I asked him if he knew what a dry drunk was. He said that he had never been into drinking, so I described what I meant. I told him that a

person who is not in recovery will do damage to everyone around him or her. I counseled him further about the difference between forgiveness and his long-term need to address his problem. He began to cry and thanked me for my counsel and the penance I offered, which involved recognizing his God-given value.

Everyone likes to see on-going difficult processes in one's life come to an end, be it the end of the school year, years in a job awaiting retirement, or watching children leave home to set up housekeeping on their own. There is a sigh of relief in coming to the end of something that has been painful, like cancer treatments, or for which we have worked, but we have to ask ourselves the question: What was the point of this sacrifice or growth or experience over time? In a general sense, depth comes through committing to something over time and holding one's suffering so as to grow from the experience. Avoidance of doing this can lead to addiction or to emotional superficiality, but there will also be damage.

A man came for counseling. He had left his wife, because she had been debilitated by a major medical issue. The woman whom he left her for later developed a worse condition. The man was sorry that he had left his wife, but it wasn't clear if this was because he left her or because the condition of the girlfriend was more difficult to contend with. All involved were in their seventies. He sought help because he was terminal. Both of his parents had been alcoholics.

The addiction of choice becomes the substitute for sitting with one's sufferings or difficulties. A person develops a relief mechanism—the addiction of choice to indulge in—to offset the need to stay with the absence of relief or end of pain or whatever else. In my experience, *a parent's or both parents' suffering from alcoholism is the number one problem by far that people ignore in their lives, which leads to serious emotional consequences for their children in the future.* All people need to sit with the difficulties of their lives, though no one can tolerate one hundred percent truth all the time, as this example illustrates:

A woman in her seventies lost her husband during the night at the hospital where he had been for more than a week. The next morning she went to the golf course, where she played nine holes of golf—as she had done countless times before. Her neighbor came to her home and began to berate her for playing golf after the death of her husband. She told her neighbor: "I will be mourning my husband for the rest of my life. If I can do something so as to distract myself from the loss, then I am going to do it."

Distractions can be helpful and healthy, but addicts use distractions to avoid experiencing their pain at all costs. If we don't sit with and deal with the underlying emotional issues that led to the addiction in the first place, then no change in the individual is going to take place, because no depth can occur, no matter how much the physical aspects of the addiction are addressed. For the addict, unrecovered or active, the addictive behaviors will continue, which means that the person will continue to privilege the fix over relationships and growth, and do damage to him or herself and others through lying, cheating, avoidance, or a host of other dishonest behaviors. In an institution, these behaviors will undermine what has been built, more or less, depending on the level of influence that the unrecovered addict has within the organization or system, be it a family or company or church.

I have personally never seen an active addict in charge. However, I have seen the damage that they have inflicted through the people with whom they have had relationships. Adult children of alcoholics (ACOA's) and others affected by addicts are known as co-dependents. These are people who do not have an identity of their own interiorly understood; they have no connection with their true self. Oftentimes, they live vicariously through the person with the addiction; however, they also exist apart from an association with an addict, as we shall see below. One might use the term "enabler" interchangeably with co-dependent, and this would be correct in certain circumstances. However, the two terms are distinct. Nonetheless, we need to appreciate the nature of the damage that addiction can do within an organization, and how addicts infect everyone and everything around them. Our discussion now turns to co-dependency, since co-dependency can feed into creating addicts as it can also enable them.

Co-dependency

Anne Wilson Schaef in her book, *Co-Dependence: Misunderstood-Mistreated*, takes the reader through some of the literature that describes a co-dependent as a term, in effect, corresponding to an enabler, that is, someone who colludes with an addict to feed his or her addiction. This means that the co-dependent in this circumstance is defined through the addict, not on his or her own.[34]

As-if leaders, as seen above, who are more than likely co-dependents, cannot give what they don't have as an example for others to model: a mature sense of self, adult emotional depth, integrity, substantial lived experience and suffering, vision, or wisdom beyond "playing the game." Those who ally themselves with them will not grow in any substantial way, which means they, too, will become co-opted into a life that supports these structures, in a word, co-dependence. Life will be frustrated, insecure, and constantly in flux, not because life has change embedded within it, but because everything is shifted around so often *to avoid* spiritual or emotional grounding and growth: I call it the "bait and switch." People are baited with innovation, playing on their hopes for change, but such hopes are undermined when any real change starts to take place. In a company setting, this is why people, when they see that things "aren't quite right" find other employment options. Such a company has little hope of any meaningful growth or progress. A parish "moving" in this direction is superficial and has no depth. There are many activities going on, constant expansion, but no one is being fed at a deep spiritual level. Morale is low, but confusion is high to ensure that no one figures it out.

Dishonesty and dysfunction will be the standard models for dealing with the normal ebbs and flows of life within a co-dependent environment.

---

[34] Schaef, *Co-dependence*, 9-10.

There will be no one there to help people to move from an ego-based life to a life based in the true self. Without a guide, people will mistakenly believe that what they are experiencing is what God wants for them. Without a leader who recognizes the superficiality and arrested development inherent to this situation, there is little hope of growth for them. A co-dependent leader is incapable of bringing anyone to spiritual or emotional growth, since it is beyond the co-dependent leader's wildest dreams even to go there.

Schaef points out (at least) two characteristics of co-dependence in general: "A major characteristic of co-dependence is being externally referented," meaning that a person finds his or her value in things, people, and situations external to himself or herself. Additionally, she notes, "the disease is built on comparison and competition."[35] The narcissist sees his or her identity in wealth, accomplishments, and other tangible objects. The As-if leader sees his or her identity in the group-ego. The Talking Head sees identity through efficiency and the bottom line. Unrecovered addicts cannot deal with their own emotional problems. Co-dependents live vicariously through someone or something else. All of them have problems dealing with emotions and view their "success" in ego-based terms.

The bottom line is that failure to deal with one's (emotional) inadequacies in a healthy way when they come up in childhood and adolescence leads to a compensatory behavior later in life. If someone has a trauma, and this trauma is not dealt with, then its effects will continue throughout life until it is, and one's emotional depth will determine the "success" rate. One can continue on one's way in life, but emotional growth has been arrested. This is the nesting ground for addiction, as well as the other personality types that we have examined. When the trauma occurred, perhaps the child or young adult did not have the emotional capacity to deal with it. Add to this an environment where a parent does not know who he or she is, and you have an accident waiting to happen.

---

[35] Schaef, *Co-dependence*, 94.

The "Eternal Child"

Though we have been speaking about co-dependency in relation to addiction, which is its typical setting in literature on the subject, it may be the case that parents, neither of whom have been affected by addiction, as the example below relates, did not recognize who they were and did not know how to hold their sufferings. In such a case, this can be the legacy for their children as well.

Br. Don Bisson, FMS, in his CD, "Recovery, Jung, and Spiritual Growth," identifies a specific type of co-dependent personality, namely, "the eternal child," (*puer aeternus* or *puella aeterna*), from the writings of Carl Jung.[36] "Eternal children" are people, who, for a variety of reasons, not necessarily addictions on their part or their parents' part, never grow up, and, by grow up, I mean emotionally and spiritually grow up. Br. Bisson offers the following qualities that such people demonstrate in their lives.[37]

1. They need to be special—rules do not apply.
2. They have an inflationary view of gifts—the reality does not mesh with the hype.
3. A "future" life is always in the offing; person cannot live in the here and now.
4. They are always on the edge of health and relationships; life occurs in the midst of danger and thrill, not day-to-day existence.
5. They always want more out of every activity and relationship, but they never expend any effort to achieve it.
6. They are needy for love from others.
7. They have no grounding—they live in their head; no connection with real people or experiences through emotional awareness.
8. They easily blame others.
9. They avoid authentic suffering.

The eternal child I refer to as the "Toys 'R' Us Kid," whose theme song

---

[36] See James Hillman, "Betrayal," 63-81, esp. 81, in *Loose Ends: Primary Papers in Archetypal Psychology* (Dallas: Spring Publications, 1975), where he mentions the *puer* as well.

[37] See Br. Don Bisson, "Recovery, Jung, and Spiritual Growth," Sherman, CT: YesNowMusic, 2008.

is: "I don't want to grow up, 'cause I'm a Toys 'R' Us kid...." We noted above that addicts have no grounding and avoid suffering/growth, and this is also true of eternal children. (See #7 and #9 above.) These are typical qualities of someone in need of recovery, but of a different sort.

As we saw above with the As-if leader, especially through avoidance of conflict, the "eternal child" never has to grow up, which means dealing with interior emotional conflicts. If such a person is in charge of a company or parish, and, because he or she is the boss or in an upper position, there is no one to demand accountability (conflict) and, therefore, growth from this person. As long as this person "maintains" the business, especially within a corporate setting, no one will be the wiser, and this person will remain where he or she is. However, no one else will grow either, and this is the problem.

In the scenario that follows, we note how the lack of challenge at any level, particularly the emotional level, leads to a general lack of depth, which has far-reaching implications.

> Michael had five children with his first wife of fifteen years, two boys and three girls. He then divorced and remarried, having no further children. Michael was intellectually gifted in school, and played and excelled at many sports during his high school and college years, but fell away from anything challenging in adulthood, athletically or otherwise. Michael taught for a government agency until retirement, a job which never challenged him. He has no close friends or relationships apart from his wife. His wife does everything for him, as his parents had done before marriage. He has no ambitions or goals. His life is predictable and stagnant. Michael ignores his doctor's warnings about his health and his morbid obesity. His two male children are addicts and have children who are gravely insecure. Social services constantly threatens to take the children away. Both of Michael's sons are also divorced.

Eternal children have no emotional depth, so they have no experience dealing with matters of depth to pass on to their children, such as when they lose a loved one or have their beliefs challenged. Eternal children lead empty lives, that is, they lack emotional depth, and this emptiness is passed on to their children. Addictions can "substitute" for the emotional vacuums that depth-less parents have produced. Michael's co-dependent parents and co-dependent wife did nothing to help Michael to grow or know himself, probably because they didn't know who they were themselves. They probably thought that marriage was about being emotionally dependent upon one another rather than helping one's spouse to individuate. Everyone now suffers the effects of codependency. It manifests in the two male children in addiction, but there were no addictions in Michael's or his wife's families. It was a condition unto itself without the presence of addiction. This is why Schaef's conclusion above is so important. Though addiction is involved in this scenario, it is a result of someone with no identity (a co-dependent) passing this condition on in a family. It takes emotional depth to develop an identity. Doing things for others is a beneficial endeavor, but when it substitutes for doing the hard work of becoming emotionally aware and gaining emotional depth, it can be counter-productive.

Unfortunately, Michael's situation is commonplace; I have met it more often than any other situation related to co-dependency in my ministry. I appreciate co-dependency as the inability to exert sufficient ego-strength so as to develop a sense of interior identity. Over time a person will simply no longer do so. Over time, as with a talent, we lose what we do not practice. "Use it or lose it" is an apt descriptor. Co-dependents live vicariously through others or through roles, but they wreak havoc on *others* by not recognizing who *they* are. Growth requires dealing with change in one's life, but constantly running from grounding, which is characteristic of the eternal child, will ensure that nothing substantive takes root, especially in one's emotional awareness.

Where Does This Come From?

Excessive computer use has had a profound impact on our behavior. The situation with one co-dependent, especially in his constant appeal to and use of technology and avoidance of human contact, is reminiscent of the circumstances surrounding the dilemma brought by some parents as they wondered about the lack of ambition of their teenage sons.

Dr. Jonathan Arnoff, a psychologist in Stockbridge, MA, had parents contacting him about their sons, who were gifted students, athletes, and musicians, but who had no initiative or inclination to leave home to develop careers or develop relationships. "I was surprised about the complaints from parents that these young men lacked desire, motivation and anxiety about taking charge of their lives," [Arnoff] said. "They were willing to live at home and not worry about or focus on their careers." "Upon further investigation," Arnoff discovered, "[the young men] were soothing themselves, defaulting to a lifestyle that involved computers and technology." His recommendation "advocates a focus on physical and psychological health through family and social relationships, education and work leading to a career, financial success and community involvement." Arnoff has spoken on "The Lost Generation of Boys" within various psychological venues.[38]

I call Dr. Arnoff's recommendation "grounding." Grounding relates the theoretical or intellectual world, and, in this case, the "virtual world" of electronic games, which may have no link to the "real" or material world, to things that actually have substance. I have personally witnessed seminarians play video games (X-Box) for hours, where I have gone to bed and then I wake up the next day to see them in the same position, still playing, as I am making my way down the hall to begin the new day. Such engagement cannot be without effect. If this thrill is not replaced with the real-life world of relationships, interactions, and experiences, then it may become an addiction, but a lack of emotional connection will have at least some consequences. Practice makes permanent. If technology rather than people become paramount, then a person's ability to interact in a human way will be affected.

In his book, *Far from the Tree: Parents, Children, and the Search for Identity*, Andrew Solomon examines various types of families with non-

---

[38] Clarence Fanto, "Local psychologist says online obsession has downside for young men," *The Berkshire Eagle*. See (as of this writing [7 February 2015]), article designation: 011114B01_art_3.xml (appeared 11 January 2014, p. B01).

typical children by conducting interviews with families about their life situations. One of the groups that he covers is the prodigy.[39] Though there are many types of prodigious gifts, the one that is most often cited is in the area of music. Solomon notes how hard work must go hand in hand with the gift received.

> Accomplishment entails giving up pleasures of the present moment in favor of anticipated triumphs, and that is an impulse that must be learned. Left to their own devices, children do not become world-class instrumentalists before they turn ten.[40]

In theological terms, Thomas Aquinas holds that "grace perfects nature."[41] However, if nature is ignored, as, for instance, a child does not practice his or her instrument, then we are all familiar with the statement: "Use it or lose it." (See the Parable of the Talents [Luke 19:11ff.], as one example among many.) One musical prodigy, now an adult, recognizes that, at an earlier age, he attempted to imagine the emotion being evoked by a piece of music, when he played.

> For some time, I was able to draw on this fantasy life of what loss would mean, what a failed romance would mean, what death might mean, what sexual ecstasy might mean. I had an amazing capacity for imagining these feelings, and that's part of what talent is. But it dries up, in everyone. That's why so many prodigies have midlife crises in their late teens or early 20s. If our imagination is not replenished with experience, the ability to reproduce these feelings in one's playing gradually diminishes.[42]

---

[39] Andrew Solomon, *Far from the Tree: Parents, Children, and the Search for Identity* (New York: Simon & Schuster, 2012). Solomon (*Far from the Tree*, 405) writes: "Prodigies are, in the eyes of many, prophetic, uncanny weirdos with little chance of lifetime social or professional success, their performances more party tricks than art.... The designation prodigy usually reflects timing, while genius reflects the ability to add something of value to human consciousness."

[40] Solomon, *Far from the Tree*, 441.

[41] Thomas Aquinas, *S. Th.* Ia, q. 62, a. 5.

[42] Solomon, *Far from the Tree*, 434.

In their youth, these children could draw upon only a limited set of emotional experiences. Their emotional maturity required that these experiences be broadened by looking outside of themselves and connecting with and reflecting on sensed natural phenomena, not virtual reality.

Robert Levin, a professor of music at Harvard, states:

> "It's hard to convey a message if you haven't learned how to pronounce the words. People who have amazing minds, but neglect their technical skills, will fail just as surely as people who are perfect at what they do but have no message. You have to take these apparently incompatible elements and make a vinaigrette of discipline and experience." ... As Pierre-Auguste Renoir said, craftsmanship has never stood in the way of genius.[43]

I believe that Dr. Arnoff is correct in his recommendation of grounding, which is also required in the case of the prodigies detailed above. But I also believe that one's peer group is important within this mix, and it can have long-reaching implications on one's development.

The Peer Group

High-school age and college-age individuals develop a peer group, that is, friends who share a common outlook or interest. One's emotional depth will determine how deep these relationships can run, but they also bear on whether one is able to make strides outside one's current environment. One's family has only so much impact; then peer groups can take up where the family left off, because of the level of trust.

I believe that Dr. Arnoff misses this important aspect in his recommendations above. Many high-school age and college-age young men and women have trouble with the transition into life on their own because of the lack of a close peer group that can help them to take steps that may require encouragement from a peer, because parental influence is no longer possible. I illustrate this point using the movie *Good Will Hunting* (1997), which I think reflects this scenario pointedly.

---

[43] Solomon, *Far from the Tree*, 420.

Summary: A janitor at MIT, Will Hunting has a gift for math and chemistry that can take him light-years beyond his blue-collar roots, but he doesn't realize his potential and can't even imagine leaving his childhood Boston South End neighborhood, his construction job, or his best friends. To complicate matters, several strangers enter the equation: a brilliant math professor who discovers, even envies, Will's gifts, an empathetic shrink who identifies with Will's blue-collar roots, and a beautiful, gifted pre-med student who shows him, for the first time in his life, the possibility of love.[44]

A conversation ensues between Will Hunting, played by Matt Damon, and his best friend, Chuckie Sullivan, played by Ben Afflack, near the end of the movie. (We will use CS to stand for Chuckie Sullivan and WH to stand for Will Hunting.) At a construction site, the two share a conversation.

CS: "How's your lady?"

WH: "She's gone."

CS: "That sucks." [Will tells how his girlfriend went to study medicine at Stanford] ...

WH: "So when are ya done with those meetin's?" [counseling sessions required by the court, given Will's proclivity toward violence to resolve disputes]

[Will disparagingly recounts how the famous MIT Mathematics professor has worked to bring representatives from various firms and government agencies to hire Will for his expertise. He wishes not to be a "lab rat."]

CS: "[You'll] probably make some nice bank, though." [Will objects more]

CS: "Better than this &*%#. It's a way out of here."

WH: "No, no.... We're gonna be neighbors."... [Will continues to speak about how his kids and Chuckie's kids will be on the same little league teams, and they will be neighbors.]

CS: "Look, you're my best friend, so don't take this the wrong way.

---

[44] Written by Damien Saunders <dvs@rainbow.net.au>, as of this writing (28 January 2015):

http://www.imdb.com/search/title?plot_author=Damien+Saunders+%3Cdvs%40 rainbow.net.au%3E&view=simple&sort=alpha&ref_=ttpl_pl_2

In 20 years, if you're still livin' here, ... still workin' construction, I'll &%#@ kill ya."

WH: "What the *%^# are you talkin' about?"

CS: "Look, you got somethin' none of us have."... [Will objects.]

CS: "No, no. Forget you. You don't owe it to yourself. You owe it to me. Because tomorrow I'm gonna wake up and I'll be fifty.... You're sittin' on a winnin' lottery ticket. And you're too chicken %#@ to cash it in. And that's %#@. Because I'd do almost anything to have what you got. So would any of these guys. It would be an insult to us. Hangin' around here is a %#@ waste of your time."

WH: "You don't know that."

CS: "Let me tell you what I do know. Every day I come by and pick you up. We have a great time. We have a few laughs, and it's great. You know what the best part of my day is? For about ten seconds, ... maybe I'll get up there and I'll knock on your door and you won't be there. No goodbye, no see ya later. And you won't be there. He just left. I don't know much, but I know that."

The scene breaks to another, where the mathematics professor is in a heated argument with the psychologist treating Will about pushing him too hard, so that Will never recovers from his attachment disorder. Will witnesses this fight, as he spies the thick file from Social Services on the psychologist's desk. The psychologist offers to let Will see the file, which has pictures of the physical abuse that the orphan, Will Hunting, had received at the hands of various foster fathers. The psychologist keeps repeating to Will that his violent behaviors are not his fault. This brings tears from Will, together with the break-through moment that the psychologist had been awaiting to assure Will of a future not conditioned by his past. Subsequent scenes have Will's friends give him a car they have refurbished for him for his twenty-first birthday, and the revelation that he will be taking a job in Boston. He thanks his psychologist for his help. The last scene of the movie has Will drop a note in the mailbox of the psychologist indicating that he will go after the girlfriend whom he had driven away emotionally, as he drives across the Mass Turnpike on his way to Stanford University to reconnect.

The ability for Will to make these breakthroughs was only possible in light of the frank discussion with his best friend, Chuckie Sullivan. In that discussion, Chuckie helps Will to appreciate that he is more than his peer group and that his peer group and environment are holding him back. His family life had been literally torture, so the peer group had become everything for him. His best friend's assertions, especially that he believed in him and that Will owed his peers nothing but his own success, was what permitted everything else to fall into place. It takes courage to venture out on one's own, and if that courage is only found through virtual reality, then it is not real. Chuckie is cutting him loose — pushing him out of the nest, so to speak, so that Will can realize his own potential, which Chuckie articulates in his own way. Parents can sometimes be substitutes for the peer group, but more often than not, that is not their role or function. Co-dependents have no courage, so they have trouble pushing their children away to realize their potential, because they don't recognize their own. Peer groups offer the buffer relationships to transition from living with a family to living on one's own. I've met many "lost" boys, and I believe the inability to connect with a strong peer group is part of the problem.

Real Life Instead of the Movies

Obviously, the drama above comes from a movie, so it is not real. However, a friend reminded me of another scenario that he has witnessed play out in his family that also bears on the future in store for those who are not endowed with a healthy sense of self, which involves boundaries.

> A couple married and had professional positions in medicine and law. They had two children, but, given their schedules, since they worked long hours, they left most of the rearing of their children in the hands of the children's grandmother. After years of tending to them, the two children viewed their grandmother as their primary care-giver, so, during college breaks they would stay at grandma's, rather than at home, since they could come and go as they pleased. She would wait on them hand and foot. She "loved" doing it.

There are three problems within this scenario: one on the part of the parents; another on the part of the grandmother; and another on the part of the children. The parents have clearly shirked their responsibility to their children to spend their "resources" on their careers. The couple is financially very well off. The grandmother needed to feel needed, which means that she is probably co-dependent. The children, given grandma's example, now look to someone who can spend all of their free time on them and address their every need. No boundary has ever been realized in this scenario. These children know no limits. One can only speculate about them, but, given this example, one has to ask the question about whether each of these children will be able to relate to a mate in a way that recognizes limits to any relationship, since no human being can provide for any other human being's every need. In order to satisfy the need for a career, the parents turned over the care of their children to the grandmother. As a co-dependent, she was willing to indulge the grandchildren in whatever they wanted and lived vicariously through them. In light of no boundaries, what will happen to these children?

Without grounding, there is no connection with what is real nor is there an ability to recognize proper boundaries. Equally so, if there is no grounding with what is real, it is difficult to connect on an emotional or human level with any of the people with whom one is attempting to interact. Unfortunately, as I have often witnessed, connections with others become opportunities not for true connections at a human emotional level, but instead connections to obtain something, such as an object or funds for a given cause. Love has become manipulation or a business transaction. Since a person is unclear about one's emotional needs, since a co-dependent does not know his or her needs, the co-dependent resorts to manipulation or bullying or some other similar behavior to obtain what one wants. This is at the personal level of one's existence.

If we look into the corporate world or parish, intimate and fulfilling encounters with people are lacking, so someone who has limited depth through co-dependence may obtain the money for the company or parish or diocese—they are skilled manipulators, but there is no satisfaction on a personal level, except through the thrill of obtaining something from someone. Thrills do not feed a person at a deep level. The co-dependent feeds the institution that promotes his or her co-dependence through superficial encounters and assistance, but the underlying emotional difficulties are never addressed. The co-dependent's behavior is celebrated and fostered by the company or Church. The unrecovered addict or co-dependent continues without recovery. Co-dependents are celebrated for their external accomplishments, but are interiorly empty. The Church or company gets its money, but there is no fulfillment at any depth, and the co-dependent system feeds back on itself. It supports its own sick way of dealing with others.

But in our discussion of the "eternal child" above, we did not give sufficient attention to the other player in the game. Given the nature of the lethargic co-dependent, who actively avoids anything that would lead to growth and usually cannot identify his or her needs, there has to be another participant in this drama, otherwise, such a person would have to fend for him or herself. But there always seems to be someone unwilling to let this happen, which leads to what I refer to as the "high-energy partner."

The High-Energy Partner

The "eternal child" cannot operate alone, because typical people do not tolerate childish behaviors, particularly in the business world or in the military. From our example above, Michael sought another spouse who would collude with his co-dependency and he found one in someone who worked in a service agency, which is a haven for co-dependents.[45] The new co-dependent, whom I will call the "high-energy partner," is the person in the couple willing to do the grunt work. This is the person who makes the decisions and otherwise keeps the household going— operations of the ego. There is no sense of a true self involved in any part of this equation. This person's energy seems endless, but the operative term is 'seems'.

Over time, two things will begin to happen. The high-energy partner will begin to resent the eternal child, since the high-energy partner has controlled every aspect of the partner's existence. Control is another function of the ego, and over time one's ability to control everything will

---

[45] Schaeff, *Co-dependence*, 85.

diminish—that's life, but neither of these individuals has been willing to accept life. The other person in the scenario is rendered helpless and wholly dependent and is, as a friend once shared, "cocooned" from the ability to damage the fantasy world of control that the high-energy person has created. Resentment will also surface in the eternal child in light of the inability to become who one was meant to be. The core of our being presses toward growing into one's true self. This process cannot be denied, so resentment will seep out, and it will show itself in cruelty, not harmonious living.

> Anna did everything for Henry. She wouldn't let him lift a finger to help her, but then she started having health issues. Henry didn't know what to do to help Anna with the housework or the cooking or the finances, which made Anna jump into a rage, when he didn't do it "right." This frightened Henry, but the real recipient of the negativity was Henry's much older uncle. A victim of their misplaced anger, he would visit periodically, often dropping in announced. Both Anna and Henry would swear and carry on, screaming at him. After allegations of abuse against the uncle, which they avoided, they had the uncle put into a nursing home and never visited him, even ensuring that he had a diagnosis of dementia, so that he would be in a locked ward.

To everyone around her, Anna is "nice," but when you see into her home, everything is different. This is the implication of not permitting someone to become who he or she is, either from the angle of the lethargic "eternal child" or from the workaholic "high-energy partner," who seems to be staying busy to avoid dealing with his or her own emotional issues. Control, grave negativity, and strange thinking—all done with a smile—are characteristic of the "high-energy partner." Schaef weighs in on the observed niceness.

> I have found that the people who are often the nicest are those who are most out of touch with their own feelings. They are nice on the outside, but often have covered up many repressed and/or unexperienced feelings and are seething underneath.... No one is always nice. No one is always even-tempered. No one is always

willing to be at another's disposal. No one is always willing to sacrifice herself or himself for others. The codependent is, however, and co-dependence is considered a disease.[46]

I would also suggest that some sort of eating disorder will be associated with the co-dependent, either anorexia (or a modified form of it) or obesity. These behaviors are used to compensate for a situation where one's identity is not valued or fostered—especially from a deeper place—so some compensation is required. Though other compensatory behaviors are possible, eating disorders have been the most prevalent forms of compensation that I have witnessed. Neither the dominant (workaholic, high-energy) nor the passive (lethargic) partner in this scenario is gender-specific; however, more often than not, I see the aftermath in a widower who has lost his wife, who can never pick the pieces up in his life. He walks around as though lost until death, because "she always did everything." This was true, and to his detriment as a person.

I believe, however, that not knowing who we are is the source of the cruelty that afflicts co-dependents, sometimes in ways that would not usually be evident.

> Greg and Jannine married. Greg developed a drinking problem over time, and Jannine became the ideal enabler. Greg literally drank himself to death with Jannine's help. Jannine also tended to their daughter Candace by doing everything for her. Candace never learned to do anything for herself. She barely finished high school, so went after men to find a "Sugar Daddy." She would let the men have their way with her and she would become pregnant. If the man wouldn't take her in to live with him, then she would abort the baby and start her search again. She did this multiple times. She left the area with friends to "make a new start," but she was unable to secure a job and ended up "borrowing money" to return to her family's home. She finally found someone who wanted their child. She married and had another child. She stayed at home and watched soap operas all day. Since she never worked

---

[46] Schaef, *Co-dependence*, 85.

and had no skills or ambition, her husband divorced her and took custody of the children. She is now on welfare and sleeps around looking for another "Sugar Daddy."

Candace's inability to do anything on her own set her up for failure from the start, thanks to her co-dependent mother. Her aborted children are some of the recipients of her cruelty. We must appreciate that there are victims to people's unwillingness to discern who they are and deal with their own sufferings whose voices might otherwise never be heard. Unless Candace gets into recovery, she will bring destruction wherever she goes.

From another perspective, we need to appreciate as well how exhausting and frustrating it is to live with people who are co-dependent. They cannot make decisions, identify their own needs, or express themselves except through manipulation, bullying, and/or passive aggression. A normal expectation within a household is that people talk over problems with behaviors or issues, and this will lead to improvement over time. Accountability is expected on the part of both parties. However, when things change for a time and then fall back to the original problematic behaviors—or something worse, it's time to recognize dysfunction. *Something is wrong with this person.* He or she is not correctable, because there is nothing to base any correction in—an identity. It is not a lack of intelligence or will power. The person has no foundation or depth or anything on which change can be built. Recognizing a child's emotional awareness and starting from scratch, and having the patience to do this, is a difficult task for anyone, but seeing a child's emotional awareness in an adult is difficult for most people to fathom. "Persons working in the chemical dependency field have found that the recovery of co-dependents and ACOAs is frequently more difficult than the recovery of the addict."[47] If professionals have trouble treating co-dependents, then there is little hope for those who must deal with these situations. I believe that this is why high-energy people and their need for control find co-dependent partners, who will give them what they are seeking. They were "made" for each other. The problem is that this

---

[47] Schaef and Fassel, *The Addictive Organization*, 189.

match was not made in heaven.

The "Hard Things"

The unwillingness to learn the lesson to do and experience the "hard things" at an emotional level early in one's life to forge one's identity leads to suffering in people's lives later on. There is also collateral damage, especially for children, who will see the example of their parents as the norm for how to deal with their sufferings.

Usually Penance Services for First Reconciliation have all of the children come to confession first. In the instance related below, families stayed together, so each individual family member would confess, then, after they were done, there would be a short interval of time before the next family came as a group. This was unusual, but permitted me to appreciate the following dynamic.

> One family waited outside the confessional. The mother came in, then the father, a "recovered" drug addict, who was engaging in lying and adultery. Their young daughter came in. She was terrified and burst into tears, but got through the process with a little coaxing.

It had never happened to me where a child became so upset about confession; this is what struck me. She was afraid of being held accountable for the trivial things that she had done. If there have been poor models in one's life with regard to dealing with one's sinfulness, such things can be turned around, but the ability to effect positive change becomes exponentially more difficult as time goes on. Nature's clock is always ticking. Opportunities for change will eventually run out, because we eventually "solidify" as human beings. Recovery programs, such as the Twelve Steps, become a way of grounding a person's life in a way that never happened earlier. But if addicts do not continue to apply "the Steps," there will be impact in their lives as well as in the lives of their family members. There can be hope, however, if a healthy person intervenes and brings children into a healthy environment and situation.

> A married woman in her thirties had a sister who was an addict,

who had two children. The woman and her husband agreed to take in the two children, ages eight and ten. The older child spoke well, whereas, the younger child mumbled sounds that were understandable only to his sister, who constantly acted as translator—they were inseparable. The woman established the rule in the house and with his teachers at school that no one was to speak for the younger child. If he wanted something, then he had to ask for it himself. Within a year's time, the child was speaking normally for an eight-year-old and had made his own friends at school. In addition, because his sister did not have to look after him, she was free to make her own friends as well.

Language skills develop during a child's early years. The younger child was arrested in his development, given his mother's inability to care for him and correct his language skills, so he relied on his sister, who did what she thought best to protect her brother. She was willing to assist him, but she lacked the requisite skill set and maturity to help him most effectively. This is not normal childhood development at any level, either for the brother or the sister. Addiction had interfered with the normal development of these children. Intervention for the younger child occurred while he was still pliable. The later the intervention, the less likely the intervention will be successful. These children were fortunate that they had an aunt willing to take them in who was also able to bring skills to bear for the children's future. We note that she had to involve the entire family and the teachers at school. This community worked together to see the child's growth realized. Had any co-dependent element surfaced, success would have been undermined, if not wholly eliminated. Co-dependents keep people dependent—*they enable*. Healthy people assist others in doing things on their own and let them take responsibility for their actions—good or bad—*they empower*.

Grown-Up, Authentic Living

People may say that they believe in God and even pray, but the proof of people's faith comes in how they conduct themselves and how their ethics and morality manifest themselves, especially in light of trauma or difficulties or sufferings in their lives. When one is working toward wealth, long life, children, and reputation, these values' association with God is elusive, which means that God may not be behind the attainment of them. However, the presence of compassion or love or true acceptance is reflective of the Presence of God, because "God is love" (1 John 4:16). If there is no love in the equation, through outreach or helpfulness, on a regular basis, God is not involved. For all those who have "made it" in society and have these "things," there are countless others who do not. As time goes on, those who have become more financially independent come to forget the help that fostered their own development, and they lose their connection with the struggle that others have undergone and continue to undergo, which means the loss of their capacity for compassion. Compassion requires emotional awareness and depth, the one commonality absent from the leadership types that we have examined.

Conclusion & Summary

What Markham brings out is that these four types of leaders: the Narcissist, the As-if leader, the Talking Head, and the Unrecovered Addict, will undermine an organization's ability to transform itself, since the energy needed for positive growth is being channeled into maintaining the unhealthy system by its leader. If an organization is complicit in carrying this out, then the outcome will be lip-service to the New Evangelization, which requires transformation to be effective. Things will continue to proceed as they always have, and the future is bleak.

It's also striking that the Narcissist has no empathy; the As-if leader has no personal identity, therefore, no connection with compassion; co-dependents have no identity or connection to compassion; eternal children avoid suffering at all costs due to no emotional capacity, and are therefore devoid of emotional depth, and Talking Heads act as though they have no emotion—practice makes permanent. These people have no compassion. I use compassion and love and mercy interchangeably. These types of people, who have no compassion, are attempting to lead communities and organizations, which must primarily be based in compassion, as the example of those being treated for cancer underscores. If there is no common denominator in love, then the community is doomed, despite lots of activities and programs that supposedly speak to the contrary. This is a clear implication and consequence of not having emotional awareness. There is no growth possible at any substantive level.

St. Paul's First Letter to the Corinthians describes precisely this point:

> 1Cor. 13:1 If I speak in human and angelic tongues but do not have love, I am a resounding gong or a clashing cymbal. 2 And if I have the gift of prophecy and comprehend all mysteries and all knowledge; if I have all faith so as to move mountains but do not have love, I am nothing. 3 If I give away everything I own, and if I hand my body over so that I may boast but do not have love, I gain nothing. 4 Love is patient, love is kind. It is not jealous, [love] is not pompous, it is not inflated, 5 it is not rude, it does not seek its own interests, it is not quick-tempered, it does not brood over injury, 6 it does not rejoice over wrongdoing but rejoices with the truth. 7 It bears all things, believes all things, hopes all things, endures all things. 8 Love never fails. If there are prophecies, they will be brought to nothing; if tongues, they will cease; if knowledge, it will be brought to nothing. 9 For we know partially and we prophesy partially, 10 but when the perfect comes, the partial will pass away. 11 When I was a child, I used to talk as a child, think as a child, reason as a child; when I became a man, I put aside childish things. 12 At present we see indistinctly, as in a mirror, but then face to face. At present I know partially; then I shall know fully, as I am fully known. 13 So faith, hope, love remain, these three; but the greatest of these is love.

Love is the greatest of values, but one must manifest it to be reflective of God's will.

As Schaef and Fassel maintain: "One must carefully check to see if the status quo was maintained when an illusion of openness and flexibility is projected."[48] Energy may be getting directed toward the wrong goals.

---

[48] Schaef and Fassel, *The Addictive Organization*, 70.

Christ may have little part to play in the grand scheme of things. This is the saddest part of this discussion. We seem to be a great distance from the Parable of the Seeds in Mark 4, but I believe that we are closer than appears. There will always be a reason for people to maintain their personal kingdoms as they are for their payoffs, in order to prevent the Kingdom of God from reigning supreme. These leadership types reflect four ways of prohibiting the Kingdom's growth. We have not explored other leadership types, nor do we maintain that these are the only models possible. These four serve to demonstrate the problem the Kingdom of God faces for its growth.

"We have to recognize that for some organizations and for some people, destroying one's life and loved ones is acceptable if one produces something useful in the society."[49] Schaef and Fassel are here talking about workaholism as a path toward death, but it is no stretch to say that organizations in general encourage such things in their employees, whether in the Church, in industry, in government, or in the military. Dying to one's false self does not mean destroying one's life. Destroying one's life is the exact opposite of living Gospel values.

We have explored several different classifications of people from the models provided by Dr. Markham as well as Anne Wilson Schaef and Diane Fassel. All of the types of people we examined find their identity in something external to themselves, not interiorly . The Narcissist sees his or her identity in accomplishment. One's value, however, never moves interiorly, so that he or she bases self-worth on comparisons with others. As-if leaders, which I would suggest are primarily co-dependents, find their identity in the group-ego. There is no independence of thought or action. Their lives are scripted by the organization, system, collective, gang, group, or family. Talking Heads see their worth in efficiency and money. Again, the basis of their self-worth is determined by an external accomplishment, but they are playing to external standards, similar in scope to the narcissist. Unrecovered Addicts are making all roads lead to avoidance of dealing with people and situations in healthy ways. They've lived their lives in unhealthy ways and they will continue to do so, co-

---

[49] Schaef and Fassel, *The Addictive Organization*, 135.

opting everyone and everything around them to avoid recovery.

As we move now to investigate the spiritual life in more depth, we should appreciate that the leadership types described above will work to sabotage others' ability to become who they are at an interior level, because it means losing control over such a person. But it also means calling attention to people's sick manner of dealing with others. The nature of these sick leaders is to formulate methods of isolation, so that people will experience loneliness, lack of connection, shunning, ostracism, and lack of support. Bernard's Law predicts no less. The funny thing is that these are the precise conditions that led to Jesus' arrest, passion, execution and resurrection. We should fear the punishments and actions of these leaders, who will attempt to protect the exposure of their illnesses. But we should not fear that God has abandoned us, even if leadership does. God can use all things for our betterment, even if it does not appear to be such. We will discuss this more in chapter fourteen, when we deal with the Book of Wisdom. We close with a statement from the monk and author Thomas Merton, who offers his appreciation in the value of saving one's soul, especially when aspects of life do not upset conscience, though they should. He writes:

> The disastrous misunderstanding: When a Christian imagines that "saving his soul" consists simply in getting himself together, avoiding those sins which disrupt his inner unity by shame, and keeping himself in one piece by self-approval. As if saving my soul were nothing more than learning how to live with myself in peace! Why is this disastrous? Because the worst evils may well have no disruptive effect on one's psyche. One may be able to commit them and live in perfect peace. Society can offer plenty of help, in quieting one's conscience, in providing full protection against interior disruption! A great deal of psychotherapy consists precisely in this, and nothing more.[50]

---

[50] Merton, *Conjectures of a Guilty Bystander*, 309.

6 METHODS OF ISOLATION

Introduction

The various leadership types discussed above will channel the group's energy in predictable directions, so that it serves the purpose of the leader in charge, which, in the cases above, undermines the Gospel message and its impact. But there is also a human toll, especially for those seeking transformational change, guidance, and shepherding. Those who have not been co-opted by the improper direction usually leave the church in question; however, there are those who hold out for change. If they remain, then they may be subject to poor treatment, but they will experience much frustration as well. They may be excised from positions of influence or neutralized in other ways. Below we will explore methods of isolation that leaders may use to ensure that their direction is realized despite attempts to block it.

The System

Closed systems do not seek change. Under Bernard's Law, individuals at the helms of such systems will engage in every official and unofficial, ethical and unethical way to ensure that their membership avoids transformational change. Leaders such as these are often entrenched so deeply and securely that their superiors turn a blind eye, since they are not up to the task of removing them or because they are themselves co-opted by the benefits such individuals deliver. (We recall the example of the abbot above, who provided financial security to the community, but who undermined all rivals.) Schaef and Fassel further state: "All systems call for behaviors and processes from those within the system that are consistent with the system. Systems subtly and explicitly reward people for exhibiting these behaviors."[51] Within a system led by one of the leadership types above, isolation and alienation will be the experience of those who do not conform to the direction that this type of leader will take, which is why we turn to a discussion of isolation.

Isolation

Shelley Weddell, in her book *Forming Intentional Disciples*, shares with us a common experience among priests and others who are devoted to transformational change: that they feel isolated from others in their communities, be they (arch)dioceses or parishes.[52] Isolation from my perspective develops from three arenas.

The first aspect is that one is operating from a deeper place in comparison with one's peers. In this case, since addicted or co-dependent people often do not recognize or acknowledge their problem—or will not address it, they view those who are looking at things in a different way as upstarts or trouble-makers, even evil or Satan. This is demonization. In light of such comments from others, explicit or subtle, a person needs to asses his or her personal worth before God. Not to have one's value determined externally by a system, no matter how noble, pigeon-holes a person into a different category. Not being a part of the group makes a person self-conscious. People may distance themselves from you, which may bring up a sense of loneliness. Loneliness is the feeling of missing the company of people. It is a human experience, not one that any person is unique in having. Persons from every walk of life are lonely: married, single, religious, or clerical. However, if one stays with this feeling for a while and "holds" it, it moves to a deeper place interiorly. This process will be more difficult for those who take their value from other people, because their interiority is not developed. However, for those who are willing to realize their value from an interior source, solitude develops.

---

[51] Shaeff and Fassel, *The Addictive Organization*, 60.
[52] Weddell, *Forming Intentional Disciples*, 28, 100, 161, 245-247.

Solitude is comfort with oneself. Solitude offsets loneliness, and it is a necessary interior move to handling growth, development, and any type of suffering, especially, in this case, isolation. Self-consciousness is a recognition that you are being singled out. If you are comfortable with yourself, then this condition will pass.

The second aspect is the sense of oneself. A person can be a part of a group, more or less, meaning that the group helps to define a person through limits and boundaries. However, one must accept these limits and boundaries as imperfect methodologies for discerning who a person is; they are not ends in themselves. The 613 commandments of Torah are meant to serve as a system of boundaries of things to do and things not to do to etch out how one should love (see Deut 6:5; Lev 19:18; Mark 11:29ff. and parr.). To love is the purpose of the Law; the commandments provide a non-exhaustive framework for realizing this. One may be dutiful in performing the commandments, but a person can still be cruel despite fulfilling the entire Law. The spirit of the law has been missed if this is the case. No transformation has occurred. "Keep the law and the law will keep you" is what the leaders described above will say. They've learned to "play the game." There's been no interior change, as is evident from numerous sources in the NT: the Parable of the Ten Virgins (Matt 25:1-13), the Parable of the Separation of the Sheep and the Goats (Matt 25:31-46), St. Paul's famous discourse on the place of love in carrying out deeds (1 Cor 13), to name but a few.[53] John the Baptist noted this in his preaching, by demanding proof of the fruit of repentance. (See Luke 3:7-18 and chapter 15 of the present work.) St. James sought the same type of demonstration of one's belief, not just lip-service (James 2:14-18). The firmer and clearer the sense of self is, the surer the commitment to Christ that's possible. A person can grow beyond the group-ego, as we saw above in the case of Will Hunting in the movie *Good Will Hunting*, but one must have the courage to do so.

The third is community. A community is where the spirit of the group-ego takes shape within a people's heart and soul; it is no longer outside, but inside and directing one's being. The value system becomes

---

[53] These selections appreciate the ability to distinguish those who are true followers from those who are not, with eternal consequences.

internalized; it is no longer mechanical. A community involves a sense of suffering, growth, and change, otherwise, the power behind human interactions is rendered innocuous and superficial. Those who "play the game" are on a different plane and so have a different type of community understanding, depending upon the leadership type and vision that they are espousing and living out. Pope Francis talks about emphasis on liturgical concerns over pastoral concerns of real people (see above), as well as emphasis on the performance of the Sacraments over evangelization (see above). The leadership types described earlier also contribute to this. Many seminarians embrace an institutional understanding of what "the Church" is, because they are looking for an identity and find it in a group-ego rather than in the mystical Body of Christ. This is not wrong; it is to be expected. But as a priest once said in a sermon, "We have to meet people where they are, but we can't leave them there." More often than not, we leave people in beginning stages of growth and believe that that is sufficient. There is little depth occurring, until internalization has occurred.

Martha Stout, a psychologist and writer, maintains that emotional connection with other people is the hallmark of the so-called "normal" individual, for instance, a significant other, one's children, or other family members or friends.[54] These connections foster loving relationships, which then lead to acting when the opportunity arises. The leaders above all have trouble with processing or denying emotion. This is the most important aspect of our study from above, since these people are not "normal"; they are sick. They lack this fundamental aspect of being human, namely, appropriate emotional response. In light of this common characteristic, when we examine what happens when someone wishes to isolate another, these same emotional connections are used as weapons. A "normal" person will wish to maintain emotional connections, thus they present clear-cut means for a manipulator to use to ensure compliance or otherwise guilt someone into doing something he or she would not normally do, as the following example illustrates.

---

[54] Martha Stout, Ph. D., *The Sociopath Next Door* (New York: MJF Books, 2005) 127-128.

A woman wanted to have regular contact with her granddaughter; however, she was estranged from her daughter, who consistently fell into addiction and unhealthy relationships. The daughter used seeing the granddaughter as a way to obtain resources from the grandmother earmarked for the granddaughter.

If we want to be a part of a group (from the perspective of an emotional connection), then we will comply with what the group wants us to do, never questioning that the ends of the leader of the group need to be investigated. As Weddell points out within another context: "Don't ever take a person's assertions for granted." My own statement is similar: "Consider the source." If a dysfunctional person is at the helm of an institution, he or she is the only one who will permit the discovery of any problems to surface, unless someone is willing to come forward despite personal risk. Such leaders are projecting a specific type of *persona*, which is healthy and appropriate. However, a dysfunctional leader will use the expression of *persona* to obfuscate the truth. It is a manipulative ploy, as Bernard's Law suggests.

If we accept each other as free persons, then we will accept the decisions that people make in their lives freely as well, but this seldom happens. If we are playing to the group, then we will attempt to make its values those that we attempt to foster in our lives. But what about when the system or group is encouraging unethical, illegal, or immoral conduct, as reports have shown both the NSA and CIA have done?[55]

Reformation-Transformation

We can have a sense that a system or group needs reformation and we can believe that it has necessary checks and balances within itself to achieve change. This is an aspect of hope. But sometimes there are situations that cannot be fixed—addictive and co-dependent systems are by their nature infected to such a degree that "fixing" will do nothing, unless the whole system goes into recovery. The structures and strictures

---

[55] See *The Baltimore Sun*, 12 April 14, p. 14; *op. cit.*, 4 April 14, p. 16; *op. cit.*, 6 April 14, p. 8; *op. cit.*, 15 December 14, p. 6, relating to the release of the report on torture by Congressional leaders.

developed over time have served to foster not just dysfunctional systemic outpourings, but an energy pool that saps the life out of its membership, as it delivers nothing back, apart from a temporary fix. The addiction or co-dependence is the prime recipient of the human resources, and fostering the system, not the persons involved, will be the prime concern for the group, though it will seldom appear in its natural form, meaning, those who wish to keep it hidden will keep it hidden, especially if they are in leadership positions. This is not the true life of mutual nurturing available from a genuine community.

Another woman shared with me a story about her young grandchild and a play date at a friend's house, which illustrates the points above. She referred to it as "Black-dog syndrome."

> Ben's parents dropped him off at his friend Scottie's house for a play date. After playing outside, they came into the kitchen, where the family's large black dog sat in a cage. The mother asked Scottie to feed the dog, so he did so, but he forgot to lock the cage door, so the dog got out of the cage and bit Ben on the hand, which required stitches. Scottie's mother was a nurse, so she called Ben's parents and told them to get over to take Ben to the Emergency Room. She had already dressed the wound before the parents arrived, but they would still need to take him to the Emergency Room. The mother told Ben's parents that the police would come; they needn't be surprised. Dog bites required that the police be called. The police questioned the parents and Ben and asked if they wanted to file charges. They said yes reluctantly. After some time passed, they found that the dog had been put down. Many children had been bitten by this dog, but only when the charges were filed, and the insurance company was involved, did the effect of the dog's behavior become fully known. The insurance company, because they would not pay out another claim against the dog's actions, insisted on the destruction of the dog as a condition of their payment of any settlement.

We should expect that the group-ego represented by "the insurance company" is a bottom-line leadership model, so handles the "dog problem" in the most "effective" manner possible.

At the human level, however, Ben now has a traumatic reaction every time he sees a large dog (post-traumatic stress disorder?). His uncles and aunts have dogs, so when he sees a dog—even one he has known for years—he remains glued to his parent's side and asks whether it is safe for him to enter a room or otherwise be a child. He needs constant reassurance in these situations. Trust was destroyed by the negligence of Scottie's parents. Now the problem is dealing with the effects of that breach of trust.

Ben's doctor says that he can get over the trauma, but it will take the reassurance of parents and others, namely, a loving home to counteract the effects of the trauma, which is something that an eight-year-old will have trouble understanding at an emotional level. "Black-dog syndrome" is a fruit of isolation. The "dog" on the loose is the dysfunctional system. Isolation attempts to keep those who question the system in a traumatized state (it's normal for the police to investigate), so that they will not report the problems to the proper authorities (press charges against a friend's family). But even then, that's only half the battle. Trauma has occurred; it is real. Ben had every right to expect that he would be in a safe environment at Scottie's house. One bite by the dog does not a pattern make, but repeated events of this kind underscore negligence in maintaining a safe environment for the people coming to Scottie's home or those in Scottie's neighborhood. Ben's trauma needs to be appreciated and witnessed as something real. He needs to be loved as he is right now, even if he pulls away from dogs whom he has known for years. His trust in big dogs has been shaken. It can only be re-established gradually, in a loving atmosphere, otherwise, it will be a source of constant fear for Ben. The inner sense of distrust that Ben is experiencing stems from being isolated. He had an expectation of safety, which was a legitimate expectation. Scottie's parents had been negligent in handling the dog, so many had been affected by their unwillingness to address this issue. The same is true with the leaders above, who do not address their emotional problems and thus inflict harm on the people around them. Isolation is not a clear-cut matter, but its purpose is to keep people second-guessing themselves, so that they don't ask questions of the system.

But Ben also serves as an example of how to mend the trauma brought about by a lack of trust, frustrated expectations, and isolation.

> Ben and his father were engaging in horse-play in the house. Their little dog, Mackie, became excited and bit Ben's father. He began to bleed profusely—there was blood everywhere. Ben's father had long-standing difficulties with even the sight of blood, so his wife yelled for him to stay conscious enough to get to the car, since she wouldn't be able to lift him up should he pass out. It was too late; he passed out on the floor. Ben became hysterical and began screaming, "My daddy's dead! My daddy's dead!"

> Ben's father heard his son's shrieks from semi-consciousness. He revived long enough to get to their car. They went to the hospital. Ben's father was stitched up, but Ben was despondent about returning home. He didn't want to go home with the dog there. The parents tried to console Ben, but he would not budge. Finally, they drove home, and Ben's mother assured him that she would find another home for their dog. She told Ben to stay in the car, while she went in to put the dog in another room, so that she could then make some calls for someone to get the dog.

> The mother looked all over the house, but couldn't find the dog. She finally looked under a bed and spied the dog at the most remote location under the bed—it was terrified. She couldn't get to it. She went out and brought her husband in to try to get the dog out. Their combined efforts yielded nothing. Ben eventually came in and stood in the doorway watching. He was the one who always calmed the dog when it became excited and got him out when he hid under the bed. He saw his parents getting nowhere, so he climbed under the bed and brought the dog out in his arms: "My poor little Mackie."

The most vulnerable player in this drama overcame his isolation through his own courage, but also through his compassion, shown even to a dog. His loving family environment made all of this possible, since he had examples who modeled compassionate behavior to him. Compassion (forgetting about ego-based concerns) conquered the fear instilled by those who put their interests ahead of the most vulnerable.

The courage to connect with a community of those who have experienced the same type of trauma—as we saw above with the cancer patients (chapter 1) or as occurs in AA and other similar meetings—

helps to combat the evil. The common experience of trauma, where the expression of compassion is possible, empowers a person to express courage in light of circumstances that are frightening, despite his or her own pain. Stout's comments from above ring true. This is also why meetings are so important for alcoholics, addicts, and others on the road to recovery. A community forged through the activity of facing the ill effects of isolation and other pain can give the necessary courage for a person to become who he or she is, the very thing that a dysfunctional community does not want to occur.

Summary

If someone is constantly looking for an outing or a party or otherwise avoiding discipline, change, growth, or commitment, beware! There's no true community possible there. The Cross of Christ is being denied. The Gospel is not being lived. Love is probably a business transaction—I'll do this for you if you do this for me. It's not a way of life. It's time to get away from this so-called community, which is probably destructive or on its way down. This sense of community and "Black-dog syndrome" have assisted us in appreciating how destructive denial of wrong-doing can be on an individual and a community in the life of an organization. From "Black-dog syndrome," we can recognize the following points:

> People denied the harm that they were inflicting on others to avoid an internal problem (the dog needed more training). The harm affected an individual through a painful, traumatizing encounter, as it also placed one dysfunctional sense of community (group-ego) against an innocent child's expectation for safety.
>
> In the grand scheme of things, the group-ego will always win out over the individual ego, unless such a person has another group-ego to appeal to for help (Ben's family) or that person is coming from a deeper place, namely, the true self.
>
> Trauma becomes a way of life for the person or persons affected (fear of previously known dogs); they have to live with it. There are no victimless crimes.
>
> A loving community (healthy family), where acceptance and truth are values, can provide the context where new growth can occur.
>
> Even additional trauma can be overcome (own dog's bite of father) as long as there is an acceptance of the traumatized person as he or she is (willingness to find a new home for their

dog).

Love or compassion or receptivity or openness must be present for modeling. It's difficult to be a trail-blazer with no models to help a person go in the emotionally healthy direction.

It takes courage for a person to step beyond trauma (he retrieved the dog under the bed).

Conclusion

There are many reasons why people will not act: fear of losing someone or something; complacency; thinking that someone else is doing something; lack of effort; unwillingness to expose oneself to scrutiny, and the list goes on. However, when someone does not do what is called for within a given situation, then there is something lacking there. In describing such a circumstance, a person called this "the Absence of the Good." Our next chapter will continue to take up this important aspect of isolation. Pope Francis writes: "We are called to bear witness to a constantly new way of living together in fidelity to the Gospel. Let us not allow ourselves to be robbed of community!" (§92). I would add, "healthy community" to the Pope's comments. It's necessary to recognize the richness of community, and the true life that it can foster. But we also need to recognize how community can be undermined as trust is destroyed. It's a vital aspect of what is required before one can better appreciate the spiritual journey in general and one's relationship with God in particular.

7 THE ABSENCE OF THE GOOD

Introduction

We continue our discussion about isolation, as we perform a close reading of an interaction between Jesus, a father, and his possessed son. The account helps us to appreciate Jesus in a different light as it also brings out other aspects of denial that will weigh in on our discussion.

Cure of a Boy with a Demon

As way of background for the story that we will examine, Jesus' Transfiguration, where he interacts with Moses and Elijah on Mount Tabor, has just taken place (Mark 9:2-10), so Peter, James and John accompany Jesus as he descends the mountain and finds his disciples and others. Elijah's reported presence on the mountain during the experience of the Transfiguration explains the question about Elijah's coming in vv. 11-13, as it connects the two episodes. Jesus and the three disciples then join the other disciples already in the scene, which is related in the following verses in Mark's Gospel.

The Absence of the Good

> Mark 9:14 When they came to the disciples, they saw a large crowd around them and scribes arguing with them. 15 Immediately on seeing him, the whole crowd was utterly amazed. They ran up to him and greeted him. 16 He asked them,

"What are you arguing about with them?" 17 Someone from the crowd answered him, "Teacher, I have brought to you my son possessed by a mute spirit. 18 Wherever it seizes him, it throws him down; he foams at the mouth, grinds his teeth, and becomes rigid. I asked your disciples to drive it out, but they were unable to do so." 19 He said to them in reply, "O faithless generation, how long will I be with you? How long will I endure you? Bring him to me." 20 They brought the boy to him. And when he saw him, the spirit immediately threw the boy into convulsions. As he fell to the ground, he began to roll around and foam at the mouth. 21 Then he questioned his father, "How long has this been happening to him?" He replied, "Since childhood. 22 It has often thrown him into fire and into water to kill him. But if you can do anything, have compassion on us and help us." 23 Jesus said to him, "'If you can!' Everything is possible to one who has faith." 24 Then the boy's father cried out, "I do believe, help my unbelief!" 25 Jesus, on seeing a crowd rapidly gathering, rebuked the unclean spirit and said to it, "Mute and deaf spirit, I command you: come out of him and never enter him again!" 26 Shouting and throwing the boy into convulsions, it came out. He became like a corpse, which caused many to say, "He is dead!" 27 But Jesus took him by the hand, raised him, and he stood up. 28 When he entered the house, his disciples asked him in private, "Why could we not drive it out?" 29 He said to them, "This kind can only come out through prayer."

The disciples are embroiled in an argument with the scribes, the group of Pharisees who were learned about the ins and outs of the Law. In light of Jesus' arrival, the crowd runs from the argument and goes to meet Jesus: "They were utterly amazed," at what, we are not told, but that Jesus simply comes on the scene seems to be sufficient. Jesus inquires about what the argument is about. There is a father who has brought his son to Jesus' disciples to have them exorcise a demon from him. The demon makes the boy mute as it also throws him down, makes him foam at the mouth, grind his teeth, and become rigid. The disciples are unable to expel the demon. At this statement, Jesus says, "O faithless generation, how long will I be with you? How long will I endure you? Bring him to me."

We can see a different side of Jesus in this passage. He is taking everyone to task for their lack of faith. He is even despairing of having to be around the people. "How long will I [or must I] be with you? How long must I endure you?"

Have you ever become exasperated when someone you are helping or explaining something to just doesn't get it? Do you lose your patience? Have you faulted yourself, even thinking that it was sinful to lose your patience? But if we were to approach things under the heading, "What would Jesus do?" then we can see canonized right here in this passage that Jesus is not only upset, but calls a spade a spade: "O faithless generation." The disciples couldn't accomplish the exorcism, so the scribes are questioning their ability to effect anything. The scribes are the nay-sayers. Nothing ever works, because they can't envision it working. "Seeing is believing," not faith. But they aren't the only ones in the picture. The people are amazed at Jesus' presence, but there's no faith when he's not present. But we still see other things.

When they finally bring the boy to Jesus, the father describes the boy's story to him. The boy falls down into a convulsion and begins to foam at the mouth, because the demon recognizes Jesus and so presumably demonstrates its power over the boy. Jesus questions the father regarding how long this has been taking place, and the father responds that it has been happening since childhood. He further elaborates that the boy's life has been endangered, since the demon sends him into fire and water, which could have proved fatal.

The father then pleads for Jesus' compassion for help for his son, and says, "If you can do anything…" Jesus' ire is up, which is clear from his next statement: "*If you can!*" This reaction follows in the same vein as his earlier appreciation about the lack of faith present in the disciples, who could not expel the demon; in the scribes, who are arguing about the disciples' inability to do anything; in the crowd, who has abandoned the disciples and scribes for the amazement that Jesus brings; and now in the father who wonders even whether Jesus can deliver! But Jesus responds: "Everything is possible to one who has faith." Jesus is not just any other person with whom the father has interacted before. He is clearly someone different who demands a different reaction, and he gets it: "Then the boy's father cried out, 'I do believe, help my unbelief!'" A crowd begins to form, so Jesus, to avoid a spectacle, expels the demon with the words: "Mute and deaf spirit, I command you: come out of him and never enter him again!" The demon takes its toll on the boy, as it makes the same boy who was mute, shout and go into convulsions. The boy becomes like a corpse, as the bystanders attest. But Jesus demonstrates that this is not the case and that he is very much alive. He takes him by the hand, raises or helps him up, and he stands, demonstrating that he is not dead. There is no recorded reaction to the event, except that Jesus enters someone's home. The excitement is over.

At this point the disciples ask why they could not expel the demon. Recall that Jesus had given them authority over demons as he sent the Twelve out to preach in Mark 6:7. The Kingdom of God is mightier than the Kingdom of Satan; however, the disciples wonder about this particular case. Jesus tells them that this type of demon can only be expelled through prayer, that is, deep communion with God. Jesus must be in that state, since he does not withdraw to pray, as he does frequently (Mark 6:46; 14:32; Luke 5:16; 6:12; 11:1), but instead assesses the situation, talks with the father, and then acts in light of the facts. Since Jesus seeks to leave this place incognito, we can appreciate that he is not interested in doing anything more in this locale where the people have no faith and upset the Lord. Even his own disciples, who must recognize some sort of authority within themselves, discover that their level of faith is hard-pressed to fend off the negative influence of the context in which they find themselves.

Context

Our context matters, meaning, if we are in the right environment it can help us on our way to realizing who we are. It can be a propellant to success or awareness or goodness. But it can also bring us to a point where we doubt ourselves, those around us, and even God. This was the case here. Most of us are susceptible to our contexts, even Jesus. Recall how Jesus was only able to effect a few healings so lacking was the faith "in his native place." (See Mark 6:2-6.) I believe that only exceptional people are able to overcome their contexts in such a way as to realize their potential despite them. But how can this context notion work and how does it relate to the theology of isolation that we have been discussing?

A woman spoke with me about a ministry that she often participates in and helps with: Rachel's Vineyard Retreats. These retreat experiences help women (and sometimes men) come together to reconcile with their aborted children and others in light of abortions they have procured. It's an intensely soul-searching and healing experience. I've never attended one, but this woman has described the events in great detail. In one conversation with her, she pointed out how she found that women who have been abused or molested in their homes, which is a common occurrence with such women, do not have trouble dealing with the fact of the abuse or their molester, who is oftentimes their father, uncle, or some other close family member. The problem comes in processing the role of the mother or mother figure, who knew that the molestation or abuse was taking place, yet looked the other way and did nothing. What was this about? How do we name this type of experience? What do we do with the complicity of a mother?

The woman describing this situation with the mother referred to the experience as "the absence of good." Upon hearing this expression, my heart fluttered, because I knew that I was hearing truth. I knew that I was hearing words from God. We might call this lack of action on the part of the mother a "sin of omission," but I believe that "absence of the good" captures the sense of what was going on more poignantly. A priest with whom I shared this account also said that the qualities were reflective of a definition for evil. I do not discount these other descriptions, but I will use the "absence of the good" to convey the sense of an expectation for a trusted figure to protect who does not deliver. This is deeply wounding.

The story about the deaf-mute boy reveals that, when we're confronted with people who claim to be able to help us—this time with the disciples and the scribes, which leads to an argument—we can lose our faith. We're drawn into a downward spiral, because neither Jesus' disciples nor the scribes had the right response, and everybody knew it. No one cured the boy. I'm sure that the father had sought out every possible option to address his son's condition, as any parent would, but time after time he met with no results. This can be debilitating. His initial reaction to Jesus is understandable in light of his search for a cure for his son, especially having interacted with the disciples of this preacher and so-called miracle-worker. "If you can do anything..." is said not with malice; it's said because of hopes dashed countless times.

But this is also the power of the absence of the good. We have an expectation that certain people in our life are going to deliver for us, especially at those times when we need them most. Admittedly, this is an expectation associated with a societal or cultural role, but its impact is hard to deny. It is the exceptional person who is able to maintain faith in God, despite the debilitating nature of the absence of the good.

If we have experienced trauma at the level of black-dog syndrome or the absence of the good, we need to take stock in what we are looking at or we might condemn ourselves and lose faith in God. When we lose someone through death or something similar, mourning is a time when we fixate on the hole in our heart, if you will, but the grieving process helps us to appreciate not that there is no hole, but that we can live despite the hole, and we need not be fixated on the hole in order to live our lives. Elizabeth Kübler-Ross offers the following five stages of loss and grief, from her book *On Death and Dying*, which may occur all at once, in or out of sequence, or not at all, during this important process.

> Shock/Denial and Isolation
> Anger
> Bargaining
> Depression
> Acceptance—fit into life.

However, the point of these stages is for a person to integrate the hole or absence into one's life, the absence of the person, seeing life as a whole experience, and not only emphasizing what one does not have.

For the women who attend a Rachel's Vineyard Retreat or those who were sexually abused by priests or others, the exploitation is one thing, but the expectation of someone who is associated with protecting them or "doing the good" is not something that anyone should lower standards about. We should recognize that the wounds brought about by people and institutions who did not do the right thing, have seriously debilitating consequences. It brings down a person's level of faith and trust in human beings, and, like or not, our sense of God is based on these natural experiences, so, by analogy, it also beings down our sense of God, so our faith and trust in God may also suffer.

Mourning the Absence of the Good

We must recognize that there are certain expectations in life that can cause severe trauma when they do not happen in expected ways: If a parent buries a child, which includes abortion; if a marriage fails; if a parent betrays a significant trust, as with a mother's complicity with another family member's abuse, these are all instances of where our expectations of trust are undermined. We must first of all affirm within ourselves that these expectations were right and good! We were not at fault, despite others' attempts to suggest otherwise. We cannot permit "the crowd" to silence us. But we must also acknowledge the loss of this aspect of our lives. It's something that's intangible, so it is all the more difficult to recognize, but name it we must—it's *the absence of the good*. We need to mourn it, so that we do not fixate on it for the rest of our lives, as it saps our energy, but, instead, we need to recognize that such absences cause deep hurt. We need to reorient our focus over time, so that this wound fades to the background—appreciating that it will never go away. Our attention must be drawn to the present, where we set about living our lives, despite the hole, but in wholeness and holiness.

I used this process to develop another exercise for my own situation, which I had to address from my own past.

> I wrote an angry letter to a Vocation Director in my early twenties, due to my perceived sense of injustice on his part. In light of my letter and unbeknownst to me, he placed me on a national "Alert List," which followed me for more than twenty years. (I may even now be on the list.) In making inquiries about becoming a priest, I met priests who knew about the Alert List and acted on it, so

sometimes they would string me along, but they would cut off contact at a certain point without reason. Others were willing to work with me despite the list. Only one priest revealed that I was on this list, though he wouldn't elaborate, but at least he told me. The Vocation Director for the Archdiocese of Baltimore read me the letter during the feedback session from my psychological evaluation with the psychologist who performed it. The letter to the Vocation Director was strongly worded, but I don't regret writing it. Was this letter worth twenty years of punitive damage? I don't think so. It's not enough simply to say: "Get over it." That's obvious. How one gets over it is not so clear. So I made this prayer my Lenten discipline, namely, to mourn the "absence of the good" in these circumstances and others throughout Lent. The things which I had typically done year after year for Lent fell into the background as I deliberately spent five minutes each day in prayer with the Lord, praying for help to mourn this absence of the good.

My own healing is largely contingent upon a deep examination of this matter in my life—holding it with God for longer and longer periods, since resentment can sap our energy. I find that resentment is reflective of an interior energy awaiting affirmation. In my case, I was wondering if it was appropriate on my part to expect good from others, especially, though not exclusively, from vocation directors, priests, and bishops. And the answer was: Of course, it is appropriate. I am not judging anyone else; I am getting in touch with my yearning for the good, which did not materialize. Attending to this resentment and frustration was necessary for me, so that I could move on and have the energy to live a fuller life.

Pope Francis writes: "The Christian ideal will always be a summons to overcome suspicion, habitual mistrust, fear of losing our privacy, all the defensive attitudes which today's world imposes on us" (§88). His Holiness is correct as far as he goes, but healing is necessary for moving beyond the absence of the good that we experience. In recognizing further healing, we cannot blame anyone else. Instead, I can appreciate that, like myself, others do not have the capacity for the good, probably because others have not exemplified good to them or they have placed too much faith in an institution, which may be greater than its adherents, but still is less than perfect. This is not their fault, though an openness to awareness over time is necessary for everyone. It is also necessary to recognize that those who had been vocation directors for longer periods were much more open than were those who were just beginning in their positions. People new to posts generally want to make a good impression (ego-based), whereas, those who have been in a position for a while no longer need to prove anything to others (true self-based), as long, of course, as they are healthy people. Time brings about its own awareness as well, if we are open to it.

If our value system is fixated on right and wrong, we are still within the realm of the ego. I, like everyone else, have to let my ego fall into the background, so that my true self can flower. "All the defensive attitudes which today's world imposes on us" must fall away, so that "it is no longer I who live, but Christ who lives in me" (Gal 2:20). Christ is our true self, but we will fight tooth and nail to ensure that this does not take place, but we cannot lose the sense of how the absence of the good or other's example of avoiding crosses can have an impact on each of us. Not dealing with this can lead to grave consequences for ourselves and others.

> A couple in their late seventies recounted their activities at the parish, where they were constantly being put off and excluded. Whenever speaking with them it seemed as though listeners were being held hostage. They couldn't get over their hurt and resentment. They were bringing others down. When one of them became ill, they hid the illness, since sickness meant weakness, which is something that the ego does not deal well with. They avoided dealing with the healing that they needed, because they had no other example to follow nor was there promotion of Gospel values which could counteract the pain and hurt that they were experiencing.

Leaders provide the tools to those whom they lead in order to grow into the persons whom God wishes them to be. This is true of parents as it is also true of every other organization or system. When this does not occur, there are grave consequences.

Conclusion

Our hurts and difficulties have to be named, if only through the phrase "the absence of the good." By not naming these experiences, we become paralyzed interiorly and we unwittingly collude with Bernard's Law, which ensures that there is maneuvering room for others to engage in unethical, immoral, or illegal behaviors. But others can only offer us so much in terms of their experience. We need to experience things for ourselves. The father wanted his son to be freed from the power of the evil spirit. No one had been able to help him, not the scribes and Pharisees, not Jesus' disciples, not anyone else whom he most assuredly contacted for help. But it is difficult to plod new ground, where no one has gone before, when all of our hopes for help have been dashed. We should assume that everyone was well meaning, doing the best that they could, but being defeated time and time again weighs on everyone—even Jesus. Context matters. But this account invites all of us to look at our beliefs and expectations again. People with limited perspective can weigh us down. We need to deal with Jesus directly, otherwise, we will avoid what Jesus offers to each of us personally and individually. We all come from different contexts, but we are all invited to make things personal with Jesus. There is a cost to this process. We cannot avoid it, nor should we deny it. The absence of the good can have a debilitating power over us, because our context determines our values, but the Presence of the Good can help us look to God to recognize the absence and hold it with God.

8 EXPECTATIONS AFFECT OUR RELATIONSHIP WITH GOD

Introduction

The Raising of Lazarus from the dead is a story unique to the Gospel of John. Though Jesus performed several resuscitations, such as the son of the widow from Nain (Luke 7:11-17) and Jairus' daughter (Mark 5:22-43 and parr.), Lazarus is someone who has already been in the tomb, and, therefore, dead for four days. But this account offers us much more than the uniqueness of Lazarus' resuscitation. The exchanges between Jesus and others help to inform us about what blocks us from new life. Additionally, the story of Jesus' interaction with blind Bartimaeus offers other perspectives into what blocks new life from being realized. Both accounts suggest unlikely sources of discouragement and limitation, which is why their exploration is so important as we continue to discover various sources for blockages to new life.

The Raising of Lazarus — John 11:1-43

> John 11:1 Now a man was ill, Lazarus from Bethany, the village of Mary and her sister Martha. 2 Mary was the one who had anointed the Lord with perfumed oil and dried his feet with her hair; it was her brother Lazarus who was ill. 3 So the sisters sent word to him, saying, "Master, the one you love is ill." 4 When Jesus heard this he said, "This illness is not to end in death, but is

for the glory of God, that the Son of God may be glorified through it." 5 Now Jesus loved Martha and her sister and Lazarus. 6 So when he heard that he was ill, he remained for two days in the place where he was. 7 Then after this he said to his disciples, "Let us go back to Judea." 8 The disciples said to him, "Rabbi, the Jews were just trying to stone you, and you want to go back there?" 9 Jesus answered, "Are there not twelve hours in a day? If one walks during the day, he does not stumble, because he sees the light of this world. 10 But if one walks at night, he stumbles, because the light is not in him." 11 He said this, and then told them, "Our friend Lazarus is asleep, but I am going to awaken him." 12 So the disciples said to him, "Master, if he is asleep, he will be saved." 13 But Jesus was talking about his death, while they thought that he meant ordinary sleep. 14 So then Jesus said to them clearly, "Lazarus has died. 15 And I am glad for you that I was not there, that you may believe. Let us go to him." 16 So Thomas, called Didymus, said to his fellow disciples, "Let us also go to die with him." 17 When Jesus arrived, he found that Lazarus had already been in the tomb for four days. 18 Now Bethany was near Jerusalem, only about two miles away. 19 And many of the Jews had come to Martha and Mary to comfort them about their brother. 20 When Martha heard that Jesus was coming, she went to meet him; but Mary sat at home. 21 Martha said to Jesus, "Lord, if you had been here, my brother would not have died. 22 [But] even now I know that whatever you ask of God, God will give you." 23 Jesus said to her, "Your brother will rise." 24 Martha said to him, "I know he will rise, in the resurrection on the last day." 25 Jesus told her, "I am the resurrection and the life; whoever believes in me, even if he dies, will live, 26 and everyone who lives and believes in me will never die. Do you believe this?" 27 She said to him, "Yes, Lord. I have come to believe that you are the Messiah, the Son of God, the one who is coming into the world." 28 When she had said this, she went and called her sister Mary secretly, saying, "The teacher is here and is asking for you." 29 As soon as she heard this, she rose quickly and went to him. 30 For Jesus had not yet come into the village, but was still where Martha had met him. 31 So when the Jews who were with her in the house comforting her saw Mary get up quickly and go out, they followed her, presuming that she was going to the tomb to weep there. 32 When Mary came to where Jesus was and saw him, she fell at his feet and said to him, "Lord, if you had been here, my brother would not have died." 33 When Jesus saw her weeping and the Jews who had come with her weeping, he became perturbed and deeply troubled, 34 and said, "Where have you laid him?" They said to him, "Sir, come and see." 35 And Jesus wept. 36 So the Jews said, "See how he loved him." 37 But some of them said, "Could not the one who opened the eyes of the blind man have done something so that this man would not have died?" 38 So Jesus, perturbed again, came to the tomb. It was a cave, and a stone lay across it. 39 Jesus said, "Take away the stone." Martha, the dead man's sister, said to him, "Lord, by now there will be a stench; he has been dead for four days." 40 Jesus said to her, "Did I not tell you that if you believe you will see the glory of God?" 41 So they took away the stone. And Jesus raised his eyes and said, "Father, I thank you for hearing me. 42 I know that you always hear me; but because of the crowd here I have said this, that they may believe that you sent me." 43 And when he had said this, he cried out in a loud voice, "Lazarus, come out!" 44 The dead man came out, tied hand and foot with burial bands, and his face was wrapped in a cloth. So Jesus said to them, "Untie him and let him go." 45 Now many of the Jews who had come to Mary and seen what he had done began to believe in him.

From the outset, Jesus makes clear that there's going to be something more to this story than meets the eye when he notes that Lazarus' illness is not to end in death (v. 4a), though Lazarus, nonetheless, dies (vv. 12, 14). It is so that "they would see the glory of God" (v. 4b), that is, Lazarus' illness is going to be an opportunity for God to manifest himself in some way. This will actually be the culminating sign or miracle that prompts "the Jews" to conspire against Jesus so as to put him to death (vv. 49-50). Because of it, Jesus goes into hiding (vv. 53-54).

Martha's Belief (vv. 20-27)

We note that Martha and Mary are grieving over the death of their brother, Lazarus. The exchange that Jesus has with Martha is most telling (vv. 20-27), since it speaks of faith.

Martha believes that Jesus has power over life (v. 21)—at least to some degree, since he is known to be a miracle-worker, especially with regard to healing the sick. The many exorcisms and cures that Jesus has performed are evidence of this. Martha is open, even after her brother's death, to a miracle (v. 22), but she falls short of the fullness of faith that this account is looking for. Martha believes that Jesus can ask God for favors, because he holds a special place before God. She sees him as a holy man. We also recognize her belief in the general resurrection at the end of time: "I know that [Lazarus] will rise again in the resurrection at the last day" (v. 24). (See Dan 12:1-3.) Additionally, the titles she uses to describe Jesus: "the Christ, the Son of God, he who is coming into the world" (v. 27), are correlative titles for the Messiah, the anointed figure, God's messenger, who would inaugurate a period of God's rule over his people culminating in an eschatological occurrence. In other words, Martha's faith is limited, as is ours. She can recognize who Jesus is from certain perspectives, but not from the full sense of what Jesus is asking. After all, she has seen her brother die, yet Jesus maintains: "He who believes in me shall never die" (v. 26). She's already seen that this is not the case. How can she believe anything else? Her experience, not her faith, is leading her in a specific direction. We do the same.

Mary's Belief (vv. 28-37)

We already heard from Martha her belief that had Jesus been present, Lazarus would not have died. Mary makes a similar claim, "Lord, if you had been here, my brother would not have died" (v. 32). We also hear of something similar from the crowd consoling Mary: "Could not he who opened the eyes of the blind man have kept this man from dying?" (v. 37). All of them view death as the final chapter, as they also view Jesus as a miracle worker who can forestall death. But once death has occurred, there is nothing more that Jesus can do. And yet, from the outset of the passage, we realize that Jesus recognizes the situation with

Lazarus only too well, and so that we do not lose the irony: "When [Jesus] heard that [Lazarus] was ill, he stayed two days longer in the place where he was" (v. 6). We are reminded: "This illness is not unto death; it is for the glory of God, so that the Son of God may be glorified by means of it." Martha, Mary, and the crowd have given up any hope in light of Lazarus' death. If Jesus could not save him before he was entombed, he is gone until the Resurrection on the last day.

In vv. 38-44, we hear again of Martha's lack of hope in anything beyond death. She recognizes the normal course of events with regard to a dead body, especially that it will have a stench when left to rot in a tomb (v. 39).

But this story turns out not to be about a corpse in a tomb, as much as it is about the power of Jesus and his ability to bring back a beloved disciple from the dead. He deliberately ensured that Lazarus died—what a thing to do to a friend, right? There's no codependence on Jesus' part. He didn't step in to save the dying Lazarus. Jesus is of singular purpose—to manifest the glory of God. The people in the story: Martha, Mary, and the crowds there to console them could not see the end in sight, but Jesus pulled it out in the end. All of them had some level of faith objectively clear: Messiah, Resurrection on the last day, miracle worker, but they were all limited. Did they believe in Jesus for who he was or for how they perceived him and through their own expectations? They had been fixated on what Jesus could do for Lazarus, which was understandable. No one likes to lose a loved one. But that belief got in the way of seeing Jesus for who he was—"the resurrection and the life," that is, as the source of both.

In John's Gospel we read:

> John 10:17 This is why the Father loves me, because I lay down my life in order to take it up again. 18 No one takes it from me, but I lay it down on my own. I have power to lay it down, and power to take it up again.

Jesus has life in himself—life which he has received from the Father. This is the underlying point of this story—to demonstrate this fact. At the end of the story, Jesus invites Lazarus out of the tomb, but first he says: "Take away the stone." The stone symbolizes the block that stands in the way of each of us that prohibits us from recognizing new life or a different way of looking at people and things. Martha, Mary, and the people there to console them had one set of beliefs, and these beliefs limited them from seeing Jesus, the source of life, in their midst. What other sorts of blocks stand in the way of recognizing Jesus for who he is and also recognizing that he has power to give life?

As we consider the Raising of Lazarus, a few questions come to mind.

1. Have you ever felt as though Jesus had left you to die in some circumstance? With some relationship? With your self?
2. Did you ever think that God was calling you to a deeper faith, not in dogmas, like the resurrection on the last day, but as an invitation to accepting God for Who He Is? Remember what Jesus said on Good Friday: "My God, my God, why have you forsaken me?"
3. Do you recognize that you are limited by your beliefs, so that you do not see Him as He is, but, instead, attempt to hem him in, so that he cannot deliver for you?
4. Are you fighting the Lord's call to unbind you from an immature or unenlightened sense of self?
5. Do you have a preconceived notion about faith, so that God could deliver and unbind you, but you would be so fixated on what you didn't have, like your brother Lazarus, that you'd miss what you did have, like the Source of Life in your midst?
6. Are you wrapped up in the conclusion?

This is one account in the Scriptures that helps us to appreciate that even beloved disciples like Martha and Mary do not understand everything that Jesus is inviting them to appreciate. They are limited by their beliefs, as we all are. Their beliefs are good and true and have left them right in front of Jesus. The question is whether we are willing to permit Jesus to take away the stone or stones that block us, which involves knowing Jesus as he is, so that, in turn, we can know the freedom that Jesus invites us all to experience.

Bartimaeus the Blind (Mark 10:46-52)

Another interaction with Jesus that illustrates limitations placed on belief comes from Bartimaeus the Blind and his wish to be healed of his blindness. The story follows:

> Mark 10:46 They came to Jericho. And as he was leaving Jericho with his disciples and a sizable crowd, Bartimaeus, a blind man, the son of Timaeus, sat by the roadside begging. 47 On hearing that it was Jesus of Nazareth, he began to cry out and say, "Jesus, son of David, have pity on me." 48 And many rebuked him, telling him to be silent. But he kept calling out all the more, "Son of David, have pity on me." 49 Jesus stopped and said, "Call him." So they called the blind man, saying to him, "Take courage; get up, he is calling you." 50 He threw aside his cloak, sprang up, and came to Jesus. 51 Jesus said to him in reply, "What do you want me to do for you?" The blind man replied to him, "Master, I want to see." 52 Jesus told him, "Go your way; your faith has saved you." Immediately he received his sight and followed him on the way.

Jesus's reputation had become known to Bartimaeus, though we do not know to what extent. Similar to Martha, Mary, and the Jews who were consoling Mary, however, Bartimaeus seems to have recognized Jesus as a miracle-worker or healer. Since Bartimaeus ultimately asks Jesus to make him see, this seems a fair assumption.

But Bartimaeus must also believe that Jesus is a descendant of David, since he calls out to him as: "Son of David" twice in vv. 47 and 48b. The blind man is sitting by the roadside begging, because he would have no way of making a living for himself otherwise. People would be moved to offer him alms on occasion. He would be viewed as a marginal figure at best and impure, even sinful, at worst (see John 9:2, 34).

But the blind man, Bartimaeus, is set alongside "the many" who rebuke him for calling out to Jesus (v. 48). "The many" attempt to keep him quiet, but their rebukes do not discourage him from trying again to get Jesus' attention: "Son of David, have pity on me" (v. 48c). Jesus asks others to call him over (v. 49a). In light of Jesus' summons, those who were once telling the blind man to keep quiet are now encouraging him to go to Jesus. Things have turned around, as they tell him, "Take courage; get up, he is calling you" (49b). The blind man is not the one who was lacking courage, since he yelled out to Jesus despite the discouragement from the nay-sayers. We should also note that Bartimaeus has nothing to lose. He is on the edge of society, dependent on others' generosity. He has had little control over his life since he was blind. We read that: "He threw aside his cloak, sprang up, and came to Jesus" (v. 50). He was excited about going to see Jesus, even "[springing] up." The people who invite him to "take courage" recognize that a change is possible, but they have probably never been in a position like Bartimaeus'. They have something to lose.

Though it may be obvious to everyone that a blind man would want to see, Jesus does not presume to know what Bartimaeus wants from him, and Jesus asks him what he wants him to do for him (v. 51a). Bartimaeus tells Jesus: "Master, I want to see" (v. 51b). The blind man recognizes that Jesus is in charge and calls him, "Master," as he also shares with him that he wants to be able to see. Jesus affirms that Bartimaeus has faith in him, since he has come seeking healing. Jesus sends Bartimaeus on his way: "Go your way; your faith has saved you." "Saved" and "healed" are correlative terms in Greek, so the healing and saving go together. We learn that Bartimaeus immediately receives his sight and he follows Jesus on his way.

The nay-sayers do not want Bartimaeus' yelling after Jesus to detract from their experience of him, since the event seems packed with such energy that it stirs even the marginal figure of Bartimaeus. But Bartimaeus is not a part of the crowd mentality. He may be at the crowd's mercy in terms of receiving alms, but he is looking for a way to be whole, which, in turn, will help him to be free from dependence on others. Bartimaeus seeks Jesus' pity, as he would an alms, but he recognizes that Jesus offers something considerably more valuable and life-changing. "The many," and their concern to be aligned with the "way things are," lose track of their true needs, because of their concern to be in line with what the crowd asks of them—conformity and silence.

Those who do not benefit from being a part of the crowd will be least likely to follow its conventions, as is true with Bartimaeus.

This account, then, invites us to take our needs to Jesus, despite the discouragement of the crowd, so that we can present them to him ourselves. In doing so, however, we should not presume that Jesus knows what needs we are asking him to address. He invites us to articulate our needs, not so much for his benefit, but so that we can understand what we consider important in our lives. Jesus is portrayed as knowing people's thoughts (Matt 9:4 and parr.), so we should recognize that the invitation to articulate one's needs is for us, not for him. The question is whether we think it necessary to follow the crowd and its discouragement, or recognize our needs and ask for Jesus' mercy? The crowd is not Jesus nor does it validly represent his wish for us. The choice seems clear here, but in actual practice the choice is anything but simple, and often requires the courage that the crowd in the end encouraged for Bartimaeus, who seemed already to have it. The crowd was recommending something that it did not have.

Conclusion

These two accounts bring out several points. First, the Raising of Lazarus underscores the need to appreciate that our learned beliefs, as true as they may be, leave us hanging in light of a full encounter with Jesus that we must do for ourselves. Jesus is the source of life, but if we are fixated on what Jesus didn't provide in terms of saving someone who has died— perhaps a loved one of our own, we might lose track that he is the Resurrection and the Life. Expectations of Jesus as a miracle worker and Messiah can take us only so far. Experience of Jesus as the source of Life leads us well beyond such expectations. The marginalization of people can help them to see what others, enmeshed in society or culture or a system, cannot see: Jesus can heal blindness. But we must be able to articulate our needs to Jesus, and the first is to see that we are blinded by our own (limited) beliefs. Jesus wishes to heal, but he will not presume to know which need requires healing. These lessons lay the foundation for appreciating how isolation can undermine one's faith in the reality of Jesus' Presence, when we place too much value either in a belief system or in the injunctions of the crowd or group. I once heard a psychologist say: "Only you can identify your needs." It seems that Jesus conducts his affairs under the same heading.

9 STAGES OF GROWTH

Introduction

My intent with the foregoing chapters was to identify aspects of our lives that can stand in the way of growth. Leaders and their particular difficulties can arrest our ability to move forward in our spiritual lives. People attempting to isolate or shun us might cause us not to identify our needs, spiritual or material, and seek to fulfill them, as they also might cause us to withdraw our request to have our needs fulfilled and believe that someone else knows better than we do what our needs are, presuming, of course, that we are mature enough to recognize them. Additionally, identifying our needs and expectations, then having them deliberately undermined through the absence of the good, is also something that can make us believe that we do not know ourselves at an interior level, especially if this happens in our formative years. In the last chapter we explored how some expectations about Jesus only take us so far in appreciating what he offers to us as he is as a person, since our beliefs do not encapsulate the fullness of his person, any more than any (auto)biography can for anyone else. (See John 21:25.) All of these efforts attempt to restrain our taking the initiative to do the hard work of discernment about our true selves and the world in which we live. This is the process of individuation, the best weapon against any sort of outside force that is brought to bear to undermine us and keep us under someone or something else's control.

We move now to a discussion of the general stages of life, which will offer us a way of discerning two major turning points in our lives that can offer us a way of understanding what is going on in people's lives and what happens when we deny these organic processes.

Stages of Life

Carl Jung, eminent psychiatrist and prolific writer, proposed four stages of life that everyone goes through, if, of course, they live long enough. He is primarily interested in the problems that develop at mid-life, so collapses the beginning of life (childhood) and the end of life (old age) as reflecting few to no interior problems.[56] To facilitate discussion, we are reducing the stages to three: the Stage of the Ego, the Stage of the True Self or Authenticity, and the Stage of Surrender, which we will treat only cursorily.[57]

The Stage of the Ego involves values that we have discussed at length in previous chapters, which we have rendered in short-hand from the bible as: wealth, long life, children, and reputation. Power, prestige, and status could also be used, or: what I have, what people think (of me), and what I do (for a living). All of these reflect values external to our inner selves. In the first stage of life we work toward achieving or acquiring these values, especially through roles that we live out, such as mother and father, plumber, priest, doctor, and a host of others. These achievements are outside ourselves, but may influence who we become as people. At mid-life (around 40's and 50's), human beings generally enter a new phase of life, where energy is redirected at the organic level, meaning that it is innate to the human condition that we change at this point in our lives.

Mid-life is usually the time when we turn inward as our ego falls to the

---

[56] Carl Jung, "The Stages of Life," pars. 749-795, from *The Structure and Dynamics of the Psyche. Collected Works*; vol. 8, in Joseph Campbell, ed., *The Portable Jung* (New York: Penguin Books, 1971), 22.

[57] These summaries are my own understanding of Jung's presentation, as limited as that is.

background. Ego-based values are no longer high on the list of priorities. Instead, the questions involve: Who I am, what I have (in terms of interior and intangible resources, for example, integrity), and what God thinks, are a summary of the type of thinking at this stage in life. There are no comparisons with others, since the discernment of the true self comes in reflecting on what is within. This is unchartered territory. One's physical and other limitations become clearer. A person accepts himself or herself, warts and all. A person is capable of compassion toward oneself, and can thus share this with others. Roles fall away. For women, menopause is a clear indicator of a change to one's physical body. Though not as obvious or pronounced, male menopause will often involve a shift in physical functionality as well. For both genders, the direction of one's energy changes, and the ego is no longer one's primary focus. The following example is the most dramatic example that I have encountered of this type of change occurring in someone's life.

> A woman, 46, came for a meeting to discuss a recent change in her life that she wondered about, since she thought that there was something wrong with her. She had always been a fiercely "in your face" person, protecting the interests of her husband and children, as well as her own. But she woke up one day recently and she didn't feel the need to be aggressive in any way. It was as though that "need" had disappeared from her life. She also had recently been teaching about morality as a catechist in her parish and she recognized her own lack of moral integrity as she taught the subject matter. In light of these experiences, she had a new perspective on what she did and was examining her life with a new-found vigor.

Several things are evident from this account. First, the woman is 46. She was aggressive in her dealings with other people, but this abruptly stopped. Her age and this incident suggest that she is experiencing mid-life. Second, she is seeking something deeper with regard to her sense of morality. She recognized that she had not been leading a moral life, as least in some ways, and her teaching had demonstrated that this was the case to her. Her openness to feedback underscores her willingness to change, as her willingness to follow the law of God more authentically is what gives this Stage its name. Her movement to the Stage of Authenticity is interior on all fronts. She also does not feel the need to maintain her role as mother. She is being who she is without the need to protect her children as ego-extensions. There is nothing wrong with this woman. Everything is right as she acknowledged a change and sought someone out to help her to recognize what was going on.

We need to understand that we can undercut the process of moving from one stage to another, which means that we resist going interiorly. However, the energy is different from one stage of life to another. If someone denies the movement or is ignorant of it, then that person will redirect energies to areas of life that should have been left behind. It is not surprising that couples will divorce when children leave home after college or otherwise set up housekeeping themselves and then marry again and have additional children. They are repeating the first stage of life, whereas growth invites them to move interiorly and leave the production and maintenance of ego-extensions behind. I would suggest that the energy that they are redirecting counter to the flow of their lives will damage themselves as well as the people around them. It will also take them more energy to do the things that they are doing.

> A nationally recognized physician called a former classmate to let him know that he was going to be a father again at 64. The friend wondered about this, since he knew that the physician had been twice divorced and had five children. "Oh, I'm having a baby with my 30 year-old girlfriend."

The physician is chronologically at the Stage of Surrender, but he has initiated the Stage of the Ego once again.[58] No one has invited this physician to recognize a further stage of life, probably because he is

---

[58] Jung ("The Stages of Life," 14) writes: "Just as the childish person shrinks back from the unknown in the world and in human existence, so the grown man shrinks back from the second half of life. It is as if unknown and dangerous tasks awaited him, or as if he were threatened with sacrifices and losses which he does not wish to accept, or as if his life up to now seemed to him so fair and precious that he could not relinquish it."

"successful" in his career. He garners top pay for his services and he is highly respected in his field. He is looking for yet another opportunity not to grow in his understanding of fatherhood, so he is having another child and following the "trend" of avoidance of marriage, which means no solid commitment. From the outside looking in, this physician's life seems to be ideal, since he has a "trophy" mate and can demonstrate that he still has what it takes through "producing" a baby at 64. The physician is denying the invitation to interiorize at this stage. By this denial, he will cause damage to those around him as well as to himself.

For those around retirement age (meaning 65 as a general cultural figure), the movement of one's life tends toward surrender, that is, acceptance of what comes one's way, hence the name: Stage of Surrender. For example, someone learns that he or she has cancer. This person may undergo treatment for the cancer. If the cancer recurs after the initial treatment, this same person may forego treatment and may "surrender" to the inevitable outcome of not treating the cancer. Such people exhibit a new-found freedom and sense of life in their surrender to the inevitability of death. This reflects the Stage of Surrender.

Most people in our culture are not accepting the stages of the journey as they present themselves; they are working to maintain what they have, especially in the Stage of the Ego, for as long as they can. The problem is that it is innate to our development as persons. We can put it off through various means, such as divorce and remarriage, plastic surgery, or a host of other ways. But those who defy this process will wreak havoc: Not might, not could, but *will* wreak havoc on themselves and others. Instead, people serve ego-based concerns disconnected from God and pretend that they are "good" people. As we will see in a later chapter, true goodness needs to take root within a person on his or her own; it cannot be the actions of the group-ego. Individuation, which occurs most profoundly in the Stage of Authenticity, is a necessary characteristic of someone, especially a leader, for any community wishing to experience transformative change. But before that leader is identified, other aspects of the journey into the Stage of Authenticity need to be discussed, especially as these stages relate to the topic of isolation, to which we now return.

Isolation Revisited

Those who have moved from the Stage of the Ego to the Stage of Authenticity—cleric or lay—will find themselves isolated, because this is figuratively the "narrow gate" that leads to the Kingdom, and Christ said that they are few who take it. (See Matt 7:13-14.) Such a journey places a person in a frame of reference so foreign to the group-ego that it can only be communicated with difficulty, through many trials and mixed success. Isolation provides a necessary prerequisite for becoming oneself apart from the group, which is individuation, and is a necessary prerequisite for growing in the spiritual life. The group can only take us so far; we must walk our own journey of faith. People around us with similar inclinations are wonderful and can offer support. But we must realize that, most of the time, we hear the Word most often in the midst of the group-ego first, since we seek meaning, which is something beyond ourselves. But as time goes on, and we make the Word a part of ourselves, our individual understanding helps us to grow in our own way with the Word as it takes root within us. This is how Sherry Weddell, in her book, *Forming Intentional Disciples,* describes the isolation and loneliness that those who take up "forming intentional disciples" experience.

> I have already talked about the isolation that can lead to Catholics who are spiritual seekers to leave the Church. But what few people seem to understand is how debilitating spiritual isolation can be even for highly committed Catholics who are disciples. Many priests and lay leaders who are disciples and who long to evangelize experience a devastating isolation. At least half of the leaders who attended one Making Disciples seminar a few years ago expressed profound loneliness. They were from twenty-two dioceses all over the United States and Australia. They told us over and over again how isolated they were back home and how incredibly healing it was to be able to talk to other Catholics who cared about the same things they cared about.... The reason for their desperate air was always the same: the lack of a community of spiritual friends with whom they could walk the path of

discipleship.[59]

Those in the Stage of the Ego will not understand the perspective of those who have passed into the Stage of Authenticity. If their numbers and/or influence are greater than the sense of the Stage of Authenticity, then they will "win out" in ensuring that the community as a whole does not move to a deeper level. Those in the Stage of Authenticity will be isolated. Transformation can only occur when there is a sufficient number of those in the Stage of Authenticity to effect the change.

According to Bernard's Law, those who lead ego-based lives (Stage of the Ego) will continue to lead such lives for as long as any of the following is the case:

1. The critical mass of people in their environment remains at the Stage of the Ego or
2. People are not invited to pursue something deeper or
3. People recognize that they have put off the movement to the new Stage and can't squeeze anything else out of the Stage of the Ego for themselves or their ego-extensions (children, grandchildren, family members, friends, etc.).

Only when critical mass gains a footing, achievable first and foremost through leadership, will values of Authenticity become normative. Confrontation and conflict are reflective of any sort of growth. Obfuscation, avoidance, passive aggression, and appeal to institutions and rules are manifestations of a system that is avoiding growth and, therefore, remaining in the Stage of the Ego. If everything seems to be functioning without any evident conflict, there is something wrong, since "Jesus says, 'I have come not to bring peace, but division'" (Luke 12:51). We should recognize that division involves isolation. Anyone who is going against the flow in any area of society or in any community should expect to be isolated.

Spiritual Needs Not Being Met

Weddell offers some sobering statistics about departures from churches of people's youth: "Approximately 53% of American adults have left the

---

[59] Weddell, *Forming Intentional Disciples*, 245-246.

faith of their childhood at some point; 9% have left and returned."[60] She goes on to say that "Catholics who become Protestants say that their strongest reason for doing so was 'that my spiritual needs were not being met.'"[61]

If churches are fostering the Stage of the Ego, which requires little transformation and applauds egotistical values—all achievable without God—then why would anyone intent upon real growth in the Spirit of God be fed in any substantial way? Those who are seeking real spiritual growth do not relate to such a place or community, so they leave, and those left, without any corrective action, will continue to believe that they are "doing God's work," when God is not necessarily involved.

If we're looking for a religious personage to make us feel good about ourselves, rather than inviting us to recognize how we've avoided growth for ourselves, damaged others and the world, then any church or mosque or synagogue will do, since they all point to the same ego-centered values.[62] The problem is that over time this will not satisfy anyone at anything but a superficial level. But in light of week after week of no substance in sermons and other programs, most people will become complacent, stop caring, and stop offering their time, talent, and treasure. Those seeking more nourishment will depart this so-called community in order to find something more nourishing. This revelation is not surprising, nor is the sobering reality that volunteerism is plummeting in parishes—at least in the ones where I have served.

The "programs" being offered in churches do not help people to deal with their inner darkness nor do they bring anyone into deeper meaning, as, for instance, through an encounter with the Eucharistic Ritual or other non-linear events, in a word, Mystery. Depth is required for such encounters with Mystery to be truly nourishing. Commitment and community, which involves intimacy and the true self, go hand in hand. When institutions seek financial resources through deliberate asking and

---

[60] Weddell, *Forming Intentional Disciples*, 19.

[61] Weddell, *Forming Intentional Disciples*, 28.

[62] See "the Elements of Sermonizing Style," in *The Wall Street Journal*, 12 September 2014.

little preparation of a spiritual nature, a red flag goes up in my mind and in the minds of many parishioners. True commitment to God fosters a sense of stewardship. If you need to ask, then you are a bankrupt community, and no matter how much money you collect, it will never satisfy the bottomless pit idolatry creates.

> *The presence of a significant number of disciples changes everything*: a parish's spiritual tone, energy level, attendance, bottom line, and what parishioners ask of their leaders. Disciples pray with passion. Disciples worship. Disciples love the Church and serve her with energy and joy. Disciples give lavishly. Disciples hunger to learn more about their faith. Disciples fill every formation class in a parish or archdiocese. Disciples manifest charisms and discern vocations. They clamor to discern God's call because they want to live it. Disciples evangelize because they have really good news to share. Disciples share their faith with their children. Disciples care about the poor and about issues of justice. Disciples take risks for the kingdom of God.[63]

Personal relationship and personal commitment work together. If, however, there is no leadership to direct a person or a community to foster these aspects, then there is little hope of growth in any substantive way.

> Widespread neglect of the interior journey of discipleship has unintentionally fostered an immense chasm between what the Church teaches is normal and what many Catholics in the pews have learned to regard as normal. Many lifelong Catholics have never seen personal discipleship lived overtly or talked about in an explicit manner in their parish or family. It is difficult to believe in and live something that you have never heard anyone else talk about or seen anyone else live. It is also very difficult to openly hold a minority opinion or speak of a minority experience in the midst of a group that does not understand.[64]

---

[63] Weddell, *Forming Intentional Disciples*, 80-81. Emphasis hers.

[64] Weddell, *Forming Intentional Disciples*, 57.

Part of the preparation for any Sacrament should involve discerning one's sinfulness, namely, the selfish ways of interacting with others that are detrimental to other people and, ultimately, ourselves—Original Sin. The movement inward is not an easy one, nor is it something that most people will do without encouragement and guidance. If a person is embedded in the ways of the world and doing what everyone else is doing (ego-based), then how can such a person recognize anything as "sinful," unless someone helps that person to look at things from a different perspective, namely, in light of Christ as Savior. If someone does not recognize his or her need for a Savior, then why would a Sacrament be more than an empty ritual to that person?

"It is difficult to openly hold a minority opinion," as we related above. This is what trail-blazers do, but they have a firm hold on who they are: they live in the Stage of Authenticity. Holding suffering is a necessary prerequisite for making any lasting change in one's life, because it is important to the human person. If someone is constantly appealing to the group-ego or otherwise sees no subjective relevance to the spiritual journey, then individuation at a deep and lasting level will not occur. If resistance is too powerful, change cannot take place at the individual or community level.

Christ as Savior

> The Church has reiterated time and again that: the "good news" is directed to stirring a person to a conversion of heart and life and the clinging to Jesus Christ as Lord and Savior; to disposing a person to receive baptism and the Eucharist and to strengthen a person in the prospect and realization of new life according to the Spirit.[65]

Those who are fearful of venturing beyond their current frame of reference and experience will attempt to quash others who have gone beyond them. This is the nature of the isolation that we are discussing, and it will be the experience of anyone who takes the life of faith and the spiritual journey seriously.

---

[65] Weddell, *Forming Intentional Disciples*, 61.

A couple of years ago a friend was being trained as a catechist in a large archdiocese. She was solemnly informed in a class on spiritual growth that "one day you just wake up, and you're different." This very common myth in Catholic culture is, to put it gently, false. How do we know? Because it is false in absolutely every other area of adult life.[66]

Weddell is correct about this point. The woman above who, at 46, was entering the Stage of Authenticity, *sought out someone to talk with about her experience in order to understand what was going on within her.* Because of its uncommon nature, movement into the Stage of Authenticity is something that affects a person deeply, but if such a person is not invited to recognize what is going on, then that person may return to fostering values from the Stage of the Ego, because everyone else seems to be working in this direction. This is a vicious circle, where fulfillment and happiness are elusive.

Without the guidance of someone familiar with the spiritual journey, this person and others like her would be encouraged through ignorance *not* to grow. (See the story of Bartimaeus above.) Discouraging growth denies the organic nature of the human experience, which is directly linked to the spiritual journey. Undermining the call to growth will have devastating consequences on all of humanity. I believe that this is usually done in ignorance, not deliberately, but the impact is still real.

Repentance

Again in her book, Weddell quotes an Orthodox priest about the need for repentance, and I believe that his comments on spiritual preparation are sound:

> Having neglected repentance in my life, I am indifferent to it in yours.... Because we neglect repentance and the spiritual formation of laity as disciples, we essentially ask people to carry burdens that are beyond their strength. Without an awareness of the gifts Christ has given them personally in baptism and without

---

[66] Weddell, *Forming Intentional Disciples*, 64.

the proper spiritual formation in the exercise of those gifts—and this includes an ethical formation in the limits that these gifts impose on my will—is it any wonder that people fail? We cannot ask even good and talented people who are not yet disciples to undertake the works appropriate only to apostles. And yet we do this all the time.[67]

Repentance is not just sorrow for sins, but a recognition of the inner cause of one's darkness, and the need for a Savior to take its damaging effects away. *What we are not aware of, we cannot control. What we cannot control is in control of us.* After a sermon on the need to accept one's burdens, which would lead to an opening to compassion, a woman wrote the following:

> Well, the [homily] on "burdens" really got to me. Here I thought I led such a charmed life with no burdens, until [the priest's] comment about everyone having burdens. That made me search for mine. And yes, [the priest] [was] right! I *did* find some, but decided it was so much better not digging them up.[68]

This is precisely the blockage to Weddell's discipleship or transformation or compassion or however else you may wish to characterize it. In the process of "digging up" their own burdens, resentments, hatreds, prejudices, etc.—in a word: darkness—people come to appreciate the burdens of others in a real way and possibly how to help to relieve them. The suggestion that our darkness never influences our thoughts and actions is ridiculous. It isn't a matter of whether it will come up; it is a matter of when. Unless a person faces such things, that person will not experience the next stage of life and will be spiritually crippled. Spiritual maturity is directly tied to one's emotional maturity.

Revisiting Community

It takes a close personal relationship with Christ to remain alive with His

---

[67] Weddell, *Forming Intentional Disciples*, 90-91.
[68] Personal e-mail, Sept 2014. Emphasis is in original.

spirit and fruitful within an inauthentic community.

> In the absence of a discipleship-centered Christian community, even the most independent and committed Catholics cannot flourish, and they begin to wither—and even leave.[69]

If someone is genuinely committed to the spiritual journey, but there is no community to support that person, then the resistance inherent to a community that has not passed into the next stage of life will not be able to sustain the committed individual. It takes a unique person to be able to rise above such a negative and life-depleting situation. Such a person needs to recognize that it may be time to cut one's losses and retreat, because, as the Parable of the Ten Virgins (Matt 25:1-13) reveals to us, those who do not have a sufficient amount of internal resources can bring down those who do. This is why (unrecovered) addicts and co-dependents are so dangerous, since these people cannot stand on their own or bear their crosses. Deficient leaders are those who do not empower others to develop such resources.

Interestingly, Weddell recounts the story of a young man who became a Dominican: who "summed up his experience of discernment this way: 'It was a real choice. You made being a lay apostolate sound so interesting'"[70] I was struck by her narration of this circumstance, because the young man noted how interesting the lay apostolate sounded, but he became a Dominican, a priest in a religious community. There was no community to receive him, so he joined one that was ready-made.

> If we focus on making disciples and equipping apostles first, the rest will follow. We won't have to worry about our institutional gaps. The disciples and apostles we form today will find and sustain our institutions and structures tomorrow, and the Holy Spirit will gift and inspire them to do things that we have never dreamed of. What we are called to do is to truly see and then make disciples of the anointed ones who are wandering in and out of our

---

[69] Weddell, *Forming Intentional Disciples*, 245.

[70] Weddell, *Forming Intentional Disciples*, 95.

parishes right now.[71]

I agree with Weddell's conclusion, but I also believe that she has lost sight of the need to see isolation in its proper context. Isolation builds individuals who in turn recognize who they are. By recognizing who you are in light of God, you become your fullest reality. "Be still and know that I am God" (Ps 46:11). This basis is where compassion can grow — first with one's self, then with others. Avoidance of isolation limits one's ability to individuate. Individuation is not a pleasant experience, but it helps to bring about one's true self, which is needed against the forces of the group-ego that attempt to stand in the way of our ability to be who we are.

Conclusion

There is ambivalence in isolation. It can cause a person to recognize who he or she is in light of the group-ego, but it can also be a lonely situation in life. I recognize that people may leave communities because they are not intentional disciples, but this is symptomatic of the spiritual life, not because another community has it all together necessarily. Weddell quotes Pope Benedict XVI's comments from his inaugural homily:

> If we let Christ enter fully into our lives, if we open ourselves totally to him, are we not afraid that he might take something away from us? Are we not perhaps afraid to give up something significant, something unique, something that makes life so beautiful? Do we not then risk ending up diminished and deprived of our freedom?[72]

We can experience being "diminished" if we see ourselves through the group-ego and we separate from it. However, the organic process of becoming ourselves leads us into a different, more authentic way of life. This is a frightening undertaking. But it is the experience of the hard things that most people will ignore when it comes to the reality of the Gospel.

---

[71] Weddell, *Forming Intentional Disciples*, 96.

[72] Weddell, *Forming Intentional Disciples*, 157.

Matt. 10:35 For I have come to set a man against his father, a daughter against her mother, and a daughter-in-law against her mother-in-law;

Matt. 19:29 And everyone who has given up houses or brothers or sisters or father or mother or children or lands for the sake of my name will receive a hundred times more, and will inherit eternal life.

The Stage of Authenticity brings us to a reality deeper than ego-based concerns. This is a tough sell for most, but it is the demand of the Gospel. Who has the courage to go after it?

Matt 13:44 The kingdom of heaven is like a treasure buried in a field, which a person finds and hides again, and out of joy goes and sells all that he has and buys that field. 45 Again, the kingdom of heaven is like a merchant searching for fine pearls. 46 When he finds a pearl of great price, he goes and sells all that he has and buys it.

A parable from Fr. Anthony De Mello also illustrates this point before we turn our attention to a discussion of discipleship and its implications.[73]

The sannyasi [an ascetic] had reached the outskirts of the village and settled down under a tree for the night when a villager came running up to him and said, "The stone! The stone! Give me the precious stone!"

"What stone?" asked the sannyasi.

"Last night the Lord Shiva appeared to me in a dream," said the villager, "and told me that if I went to the outskirts of the village at dusk I should find a sannyasi who would give me a precious stone that would make me rich forever."

---

[73] Anthony De Mello, *The Song of the Bird* (New York: Image, 1984), 140-141. The story there is entitled, "The Diamond."

The sannyasi rummaged in his bag and pulled out a stone. "He probably meant this one," he said, as he handed the stone over to the villager. "I found it on a forest path some days ago. You can certainly have it."

The man gazed at the stone in wonder. It was a diamond, probably the largest diamond in the whole world, for it was as large as a person's head.

He took the diamond and walked away. All night he tossed about in bed, unable to sleep. Next day at the crack of dawn he woke the sannyasi and said, "Give me the wealth that makes it possible for you to give this diamond away so easily."

10 DISCIPLESHIP AND PETER

Introduction

We begin this chapter by appreciating what Sherry Weddell means by "forming intentional disciples." In her treatment of "discipleship," Weddell identifies five stages that comprise the conversion process. Stages four and five include the movement from "spiritual seeking" to "forming intentional disciples."

> 4. Spiritual seeking: the person moves from being essentially passive to actively seeking to know the God who is calling him or her, if you will, "dating with a purpose" but not yet marriage. 5. Forming Intentional Disciples: this is the decision to "drop one's nets," to make a conscious commitment to follow Jesus in the midst of his Church as an obedient disciple and to reorder one's life accordingly.[74]

Here we can see that Weddell bases her imagery on the story of the call of Peter and Andrew, whereby Jesus joins Peter in his boat and tells him to lower his nets after a night of fishing that yielded nothing. Peter does so, which delivers him and his partners a great catch of fish. (See Luke 5:4-11. Cf. John 21:1-11.) Peter then falls down at the feet of Jesus and says, "Depart from me, Lord, for I am a sinful man." (Luke 5:8). This passage is unique to Luke's Gospel, but the image is apt as a metaphor

---

[74] Weddell, *Forming Intentional Disciples*, 130.

for discipleship.

Though we quoted Luke above, given Weddell's imagery, I choose to use the Gospel of Matthew as our starting point as we work our way through many of the times when Peter is mentioned, since he is the premier and archetypal disciple. His portrayal in Matthew's Gospel includes the passage unique to Matthew related to the keys (16:18). I believe that this statement is important in understanding Peter in full. As we make our way through the Gospel of Matthew, we will use only a short phrase to help the reader to recall the episode in the Gospel. We will have reason to look outside the Gospel of Matthew for other aspects of discipleship later on in our inquiry, since I believe these passages also need to be addressed to appreciate Peter and his discipleship in a fuller sense.

Discipleship and Peter through Matthew's Gospel

Jesus has been teaching the people and, as he walks along the shore, he sees some fishermen in their boats.

> Matt. 4:18 As he was walking by the Sea of Galilee, [Jesus] saw two brothers, Simon who is called Peter, and his brother Andrew, casting a net into the sea; they were fishermen.

Jesus took men into his company who, for all intents and purposes, were ordinary people with ordinary lives and typical jobs for the time period. The point, however, is that these men were invited to follow Jesus and they did. They went around with Jesus and listened to his teachings, as disciples would for a teacher or rabbi of the period. Jesus was an itinerant teacher, meaning that he moved from place to place. He also performed miraculous healings. These men began making up Jesus' inner circle of disciples.

> Matt. 10:2 The names of the twelve apostles are these: first, Simon called Peter, and his brother Andrew; James, the son of Zebedee, and his brother John....

We note that Simon is surnamed Peter. He is the first in the list of "the Twelve," which means that he is most prominent, not just another name in the list. This is important. Commentators argue about the place of Peter in relation to claims related to the Bishop of Rome or Pope, but none argue that he was not the lead disciple. Davies and Allison, major commentators on the Gospel of Matthew, assert that he was in a category by himself.[75]

During another episode, when Jesus walks on water, Peter asks the Lord to invite him to walk with him, too.

> Matt. 14:28 Peter said to [Jesus] in reply, "Lord, if it is you, command me to come to you on the water." 29 He said, "Come." Peter got out of the boat and began to walk on the water toward Jesus.

Peter walks on water as well, but his faith is not sufficient to keep him afloat. Jesus chides him for his lack of faith, "O you of little faith, why did you doubt?" (14:30).

In another episode, when Jesus asks who people say that he is,

> Matt. 16:16 Simon Peter said in reply, "You are the Messiah, the Son of the living God."

Jesus praises him for this identification. In light of it, Peter is given a prominent place in the church (assembly of believers) for this assertion, because he has received this revelation from God, according to Jesus himself.

> Matt. 16:18 And so I say to you, you are Peter, and upon this rock I will build my church, and the gates of the netherworld shall not prevail against it.

The play on words here is between Peter's name and the word for 'rock',

---

[75] Their argument is persuasive and well researched. See W. D. Davies and Dale C. Allison, Jr., *The Gospel according to St. Matthew* (ICC; 3 vols.; Edinburgh: T & T Clark, 1991), 2. 647-652.

presumably in Aramaic.[76] However, when Jesus talks about being turned over to the chief priests and executed, just a few verses later, Peter takes the Lord aside and begins to rebuke him.

> Matt. 16:21 From that time on, Jesus began to show his disciples that he must go to Jerusalem and suffer greatly from the elders, the chief priests, and the scribes, and be killed and on the third day be raised. 22 Then Peter took [Jesus] aside and began to rebuke him, "God forbid, Lord! No such thing shall ever happen to you." 23 He turned and said to Peter, "Get behind me, Satan! You are an obstacle to me. You are thinking not as God does, but as human beings do."

Jesus recognizes that Peter's concern does not come from God, whereas his earlier identification of Jesus did. Jesus' destiny is to be rejected by the Jewish establishment and to die. Jesus calls Peter, "Satan," that is, one who leads another to sin, in this case away from Jesus' destiny and the reason he came into the world.

A short time later, Jesus takes special disciples up a mountain.

> Matt. 17:1 After six days Jesus took Peter, James, and John his brother, and led them up a high mountain by themselves.

The intimates of Jesus are taken with him to see the Transfiguration on the mountain. Peter is included in the list of those who are intimates with Jesus.

Later, Peter asks Jesus about forgiveness.

> Matt. 18:21 Then Peter approaching asked him, "Lord, if my brother sins against me, how often must I forgive him? As many as seven times?"

Peter is used as a foil to ask Jesus about forgiveness, which Jesus says must be practiced endlessly. One should always be ready to forgive.

---

[76] An approximation in French reflecting the play on words might be: "Tu es Pierre, et sur cette pierre je bâtirai mon église."

In another episode, Peter asks what reward there is for him and the disciples who have given everything up for him.

> Matt. 19:27 Then Peter said to him in reply, "We have given up everything and followed you. What will there be for us?"

Peter notes that he and the other disciples have given everything up to follow him. Jesus tells them that they will receive great rewards both in this world and the next for what they have given up.

Time ensues, and in chapter 26, Jesus and the disciples make preparations for the Passover. At Jesus' Last Supper with the disciples, he tells them that one of their own number will betray him.

> Matt. 26:33 Peter said to [Jesus] in reply, "Though all may have their faith in you shaken, mine will never be."

> Matt. 26:35 Peter said to him, "Even though I should have to die with you, I will not deny you." And all the disciples spoke likewise.

Peter and the other disciples claim that their faith in Jesus will never be shaken. Nonetheless, Jesus subsequently takes Peter and others into the Garden of Gethsemani as he contemplates what will transpire in the coming hours: his arrest, passion, and death.

> Matt. 26:37 [Jesus] took along Peter and the two sons of Zebedee, and began to feel sorrow and distress.

> Matt. 26:40 When he returned to his disciples he found them asleep. He said to Peter, "So you could not keep watch with me for one hour?"

This is where things begin to fall apart for Peter, the disciple. Peter could not keep his eyes open, though this is the pivotal night of Jesus' existence and journey. Though Peter has celebrated the Last Supper with Jesus, he does not recognize the significance of what has taken place. He and the others abandon Jesus, when the soldiers come to take him away.

He does, however, follow along to see what will happen to Jesus.

> Matt. 26:58 Peter was following him at a distance as far as the high priest's courtyard, and going inside he sat down with the servants to see the outcome.

> Matt. 26:69 Now Peter was sitting outside in the courtyard. One of the maids came over to him and said, "You too were with Jesus the Galilean."

> Matt. 26:73 A little later the bystanders came over and said to Peter, "Surely you too are one of them; even your speech gives you away."

> Matt. 26:75 Then Peter remembered the word that Jesus had spoken: "Before the cock crows you will deny me three times." He went out and began to weep bitterly.

Peter denies Jesus three times, though he claimed in 25:33 and v. 35 that he would be faithful to him even to death. That didn't happen. This was one of Jesus' intimate disciples, who was there with him at even the most important moments during his ministry. He was the insider's insider; this is what is remarkable about Peter and his actions. He has given up everything, as he claimed in 19:27, but the question is whether he has actually placed his faith in Jesus. This is a different question. His faith did not support him on the water, and his vision of Jesus' future had Jesus call him Satan. There is very little evidence in the episodes above that suggest that Peter had a lot of faith in the reality of Jesus' mission, though he had been Jesus' intimate disciple.

Paul's Letter to the Galatians

If we now move from the Gospel of Matthew to Paul's Letter to the Galatians, we find that Christ's passion, death, resurrection and ascension—perhaps fifteen or so years—have passed. We next hear of Peter (Cephas=Aramaic for Peter) in Jerusalem, when Paul visits him there after his conversion.

Galatians 1:18 Then after three years I [Paul] went up to Jerusalem to confer with Cephas [Peter] and remained with him for fifteen days. 19 But I did not see any other of the apostles, only James the brother of the Lord. 20 (As to what I am writing to you, behold, before God, I am not lying.) 21 Then I went into the regions of Syria and Cilicia. 22 And I was unknown personally to the churches of Judea that are in Christ; 23 they only kept hearing that "the one who once was persecuting us is now preaching the faith he once tried to destroy." 24 So they glorified God because of me.

We next find Peter (Cephas) in Antioch (modern-day Turkey), where he has been ministering to Gentiles, that is, non-Jews.

Gal. 2:1 Then after fourteen years I again went up to Jerusalem with Barnabas, taking Titus along also. 2 I went up in accord with a revelation, and I presented to them the gospel that I preach to the Gentiles — but privately to those of repute — so that I might not be running, or have run, in vain. 3 Moreover, not even Titus, who was with me, although he was a Greek, was compelled to be circumcised, 4 but because of the false brothers secretly brought in, who slipped in to spy on our freedom that we have in Christ Jesus, that they might enslave us — 5 to them we did not submit even for a moment, so that the truth of the gospel might remain intact for you. 6 But from those who were reputed to be important (what they once were makes no difference to me; God shows no partiality) — those of repute made me add nothing. 7 On the contrary, when they saw that I had been entrusted with the gospel to the uncircumcised, just as Peter to the circumcised, 8 for the one who worked in Peter for an apostolate to the circumcised worked also in me for the Gentiles, 9 and when they recognized the grace bestowed upon me, *James and Cephas and John*, who were reputed to be pillars, gave me and Barnabas their right hands in partnership, that we should go to the Gentiles and they to the circumcised. 10 Only, we were to be mindful of the poor, which is the very thing I was eager to do.

Here we note that James, the brother of the Lord, appears first in this list (v. 9). It seems that in the course of the last fourteen years, James, a relative of the Lord, took over as head of the Church in Jerusalem. Peter has been reduced in prominence, as far as this list and the ensuing episode convey. The issue represented here is over whether a Christian must follow the Mosaic Law in order to be a Christian. In sum, do you have to become a Jew first in order to become a Christian? James and what is known as "the circumcision party" say yes, whereas, Paul says no. This is what Paul is addressing below, as the episode above now continues. Some time has elapsed.

> Galatians 2:11 And when Cephas came to Antioch, I opposed him to his face because he clearly was wrong. 12 For, until some people came from James, he used to eat with the Gentiles; but when they came, he began to draw back and separated himself, because he was afraid of the circumcised. 13 And the rest of the Jews [also] acted hypocritically along with him, with the result that even Barnabas was carried away by their hypocrisy. 14 But when I saw that they were not on the right road in line with the truth of the gospel, I said to Cephas in front of all, "If you, though a Jew, are living like a Gentile and not like a Jew, how can you compel the Gentiles to live like Jews?"

Peter (Cephas) was not willing to stand up to James and the circumcision party, so Paul was left on his own—isolated. Paul's understanding eventually wins the day, as the Acts of the Apostles demonstrates, but not without a lot of acrimony and discussion. This is the first issue of the Church, but Peter is on the wrong side—at least for a time. His portrayal here is less than inspiring.[77]

---

[77] The Acts of the Apostles, where Peter is featured as the main character in chaps. 1-5, 8-12, and 15, is not considered in our discussion above. The portrayal of Peter in Acts reflects a different person from the episodes above. It is so different that one would have to reconcile this different character with those above, and this is not an easy task to accomplish. The Peter portrayed in Acts has confidence in face of

The Gospel of John

In the Gospel of John, Jesus asks Peter three times whether he loves him. This is generally understood to be a rehabilitation of Peter in light of the three denials that Peter made when asked if he was Jesus' disciple. We pick up the questioning at the third question from Jesus.

> John 21:17 [Jesus] said to him the third time, "Simon, son of John, do you love me?" Peter was distressed that he had said to him a third time, "Do you love me?" and he said to him, "Lord, you know everything; you know that I love you." [Jesus] said to him, "Feed my sheep. 18 Amen, amen, I say to you, when you were younger, you used to dress yourself and go where you wanted; but when you grow old, you will stretch out your hands, and someone else will dress you and lead you where you do not want to go." 19 He said this signifying by what kind of death he would glorify God. And when he had said this, he said to him, "Follow me."

Verses 18-19 describe how Peter ultimately meets martyrdom for the faith; he will "stretch out [his] hands," presumably being taken into custody and led by someone else to his execution for the faith.

Summary

The point of these scriptural citations, as selective as they are, and the comments that correspond to them, is that Peter went through a development in his life. While Jesus was on the earth, Peter was picked as the leader of the Twelve. He made assertions about his faith, loyalty, and his willingness to give his life that never panned out, except at the very end. He wondered what his discipleship was going to deliver for himself and the other disciples, since they had given up everything. He denied Jesus three times, but, even more than that, he misunderstood that

---

authority, though he is still described as being uneducated (4:8, 13). This is feasible, in light of the resurrection and the confidence that such faith instilled, but it seems not to be consistent with the rest of the New Testament witness.

the cross was a necessary part of Jesus' journey, mistaking human ways for God's ways. In his later years (John 21:18: "when you grow old"), he will be a martyr, and thus pay the price with his life for his testimony to Christ. Looking at the initial call in isolation might suggest to someone that Peter was already committed to Jesus in a major way. Materially it seems that he and the other disciples were committed, since he says so. However, Peter's example shows that he lost his prominence and any authority he had in Jerusalem to James and the circumcision party. Paul was the one who was willing to take the heat for ministry to the Gentiles. Both Barnabas and Titus were unwilling to side with Paul against Peter, James, and the circumcision party. This does not paint the best picture of Peter, but I would suggest it is far more representative than an idealistic one, because it is messy and human.

If we examine what discipleship entails through the life of Peter, and not just through a metaphor of "dropping nets," we can appreciate that his lifetime commitment went through several different stages, all of which make us question Peter's true intent, until his demise in martyrdom. He was physically in the presence of the Lord Jesus for the duration of his ministry. He had an intimate relationship with him; he was arguably the closest disciple, apart from the Beloved Disciple of John's Gospel. (See John 13:23; 21:17.) He experienced the Risen Lord and even had his own experience of him, according to the tradition known to Paul (1 Cor 15:5) and Luke (Luke 24:34). But even after all this, he was willing to go along with James over Paul, when it came to the Gentiles. Time shows that Paul's understanding would become the way of life for non-Jewish Christians.

Weddell quotes "the Great Commission" at the conclusion of Matthew's Gospel:

> Matt. 28:19 Go, therefore, and make disciples of all nations, baptizing them in the name of the Father, and of the Son, and of the holy Spirit, 20 teaching them to observe all that I have commanded you. And behold, I am with you always, until the end of the world. Amen.

Emphasis on the Great Commission involves obtaining additional members for the Church, but any depth of faith is missing. Peter didn't seem to have faith at the level of a willingness to suffer until the very end. Unless someone is willing to delve into the depths of one's being and recognize a true "cost" or cross involved with a choice that a person makes, then one's assertions will be empty. Denial will be constant. Discipleship will be nebulous. The archetypal disciple Peter seems to show that discipleship alone doesn't take us to the Kingdom. Something important is missing from the equation.

Something Missing from Discipleship

In the last chapter we looked at a quote from the blog of an Orthodox priest, Fr. Gregory, who reflects on discipleship. The lines of the blog following the quote from the last chapter help to identify what I believe is missing in the equation.

> Putting aside for a moment the bad theology this implies, at least in the short time our neglect of repentance works well enough for the parish. The doors stay open, the lights stay on, the services are celebrated and life isn't really all that bad. Or at least, it isn't all that bad until the person (or parish!) is exhausted. When this happens, when exhaustion takes hold and I am no longer able to do the things I have identified with being Christian, I suffer a crisis — I wonder what, if anything, it means to be an Orthodox Christian. And if the only answer I get from my priest or brothers and sisters in Christ is to "try harder" or "do more" (even if that more is prayer), I'm likely to become discouraged. Yes, because I'm basically a good and sincere person, I might try harder for at least a little while. But the problem isn't a lack of effort but a lack of direction *(harmatia*, literally "missing the mark" or sin); my suffering is teleogical [relating to the end], not functional. Give me more to do and I will eventually withdraw emotionally assuming I don't simply walk away.

I would suggest that Fr. Gregory is getting to the heart of the issue at hand: there is no depth, because people are not looking at their true state of sinfulness. Granted, they probably haven't murdered anyone, but have they come to grips with the fact that they have damaged other people along their journey? Addicts and co-dependents damage people by not providing an example of holding one's sufferings. If one cannot hold one's sufferings, a person cannot "take up his or her cross." A basic tenet of the Christian faith is being denied. A relationship with anyone is about recognizing how one does not measure up, misses the mark of anyone's expectation. This is true human interaction. Jesus was willing to accept Peter as he was, but Peter had not done the same with his own self. That is the nature of the problem.

> This doesn't mean that those who are disciples, much less those who are apostles, of Christ don't get fatigued and discouraged; it doesn't mean they don't confuse doing with being or vocation with activity. They certainly do. The difference though is that they have the habit of repentance. It is *metanoia*, a change of heart, a re-direction of my life, that is needed. They know already what it is to be saved from sin; they know that following Christ, conforming their lives to His, requires that they turn continually from sin in their own lives. For the disciple and the apostle, the exhaustion and frustration that we all experience is not simply a physical, psychological or social experience. While it is certainly this, it is something that is understood in Christ.

Our undoing comes in the recognition that, more often than not, our actions can be devoid of any connection with God or Christ. We assume wrongly that just because a baptized person does something that that deed is Christian. That is far from the truth. Priests, sisters, and brothers helped their fellow human beings in the inner city after Vatican II, but their actions took on the pale of social work, even though they happened to be ordained and/or professed. If Christ is not at the heart of the activity, then there is nothing spiritually nurturing about it. It will not be life-giving, and the people involved will become disillusioned by their lack of "results."

> In Christ, personal failure is not the whole truth about our lives. Rather whatever else it may be, failure is also a divine invitation to enter more deeply into communion with the Holy Trinity. And so, with the Apostle Paul, the disciple thanks God for his weaknesses.

Why? Because he (or she!) knows that grace is perfected in weakness (see 2 Corinthians 12:9). None of this is possible for the person who has never repented, never experienced divine mercy redeeming him (or her) from sin. Absent repentance, failure is just that, failure and a source of fear and shame.

In Christ however failure, like death itself, is overcome and transformed by grace into an experience of divine life. It is this life that is essential for us if we are to be Christians in anything other than name alone.[78]

When I talk about darkness within this study, I am recognizing the potential within all of us that embraces sinfulness over God's will in our lives. Seemingly "good" people seldom recognize their need for repentance in any deep-seated way apart from occasional confession, which is a far cry from the picture envisioned in the Gospel of Matthew. (See 5:38-48.) However, the impotence in dealing with chronic sin is a direct result of one's inability to take seriously the reality of the cross and the inability of one's own will to effect substantive change. A person's will is not sufficient to overcome sin on its own, since our propensity toward sin is covered in darkness. Only the Light of Christ can shine into it. It is no accident that Peter balked at Jesus' assertion that he would be rejected by the chief priests, suffer, and die—in two words: experience failure (Matt 16:22), and that Jesus called him, "Satan." God's way deals with the bleak circumstances of real life, whereas, human dealings look toward guaranteed success, an ego-based concern.

Fr. Thomas Keating, a Trappist monk, former abbot, and co-founder of the renewal of the practice of Centering Prayer, writes:

> Sometimes a sense of failure is a great means to true humility, which is what God most looks for in us. I realize this is not the language of success, but we have oversubscribed to that language.

---

[78] See, as of this writing (24 September 2014): http://palamas.info/repentance-and-discipleship/. See also John Chryssavgis (*Soul Mending: The Art of Spiritual Direction* [Brookline: Holy Cross Orthodox Press, 2000], 13), for a similarly worded explanation of repentance, underscoring Orthodox understandings.

We need to hear about the interior freedom that comes through participation in the sufferings of Christ, the symbol of God's love for everyone on earth.[79]

Weddell offers a workshop entitled, "the Called and Gifted," which can assist people in recognizing their charisms and God-given gifts, and help them to participate more effectively in a community. By recognizing one's charisms, a person can more easily align himself or herself with corresponding ministries. Such ministries will then be more fulfilling, since they come from God. However, manifesting charisms does not offset spiritual superficiality. It helps to ensure that people are fulfilled and engaging in ministries appropriate to them, but it does not address spiritual growth. I agree with Weddell's conclusion, however, about the necessity of spiritual support at the parish level.

> What we are discovering is that some are so distressed by the lack of support in their parish that they actually leave to find a community that understands what has happened to them....We need to recognize the presence of a *hidden hemorrhage fueled by spiritual growth* in our parishes....(Nine percent of all Protestants and 11% of all evangelicals were raised Catholic.) These people are motivated by a different kind of loss: a loss of spiritual hope that eventually turns into a loss of trust. Rebuilding or strengthening the trust of those who have left or are considering leaving because they long for more than they see around them requires that we be able to give them hope that their spiritual hungers will be met abundantly in and through the Catholic Church. For most, that will have to happen at the parish level.[80]

We as Catholics need to recognize sin in our lives. We need to accept it, own it, and invite Christ to shed light on it, and we need to take up the spiritual journey, not just say prayers and receive Sacraments. Though I do appreciate that Christ has taken away the impact of my sins through

---

[79] Fr. Thomas Keating, OCSO, *The Human Condition: Contemplation and Transformation* (The Harold M. Wit Lectures; New York: Paulist Press), 21.
[80] Weddell, *Forming Intentional Disciples*, 160-161.

Baptism and subsequently through faith, I can also appreciate that the residual effects of my sinful acts are a part of me and need to be appreciated as detrimental to my relationship with God, my self, and my neighbor. Holding a banner about the forgiveness of my sins does not absolve me of my responsibility to grow emotionally, which will impact how my spiritual life unfolds—the spiritual journey. The willingness to repair what we can and not just confess it goes a long way to mending the damage that we have done, as the Twelve Steps point out (esp. #8-9). As James Hillman, a Jungian psychologist and writer, whose work we will treat more extensively below, relates that a person can only forgive another person who acknowledges the need to be forgiven, just as the person betrayed (or sinned against) must recognize that this betrayal helps him or her to appreciate who he or she is without holding on to anything. This is the reality of faith. Those in recovery are light years ahead of most in our churches on the weekends, because they recognize the hard work of identifying the damage that they have done and the restitution that must be made.

Conclusion

Sherry Weddell has a great deal to say, and I admire her for her work. However, her emphasis on the example of Peter as a model disciple is problematic. Peter was invited by Christ to accompany him throughout his public ministry as one of his intimates. He was clearly the leader of the Twelve. But at crucial points on his journey of faith, Peter failed to demonstrate that he had depth of faith. From a realistic perspective, Peter then reflects most of us in our faith lives, but I believe that Weddell wants us to believe that we should take Peter's discipleship at face value as an ideal disciple without further examination. The picture that the Gospel of Matthew and the Letters of Paul depict point to a far more complex disciple who had trouble throughout his life living out his faith in Christ with all of its implications and cost. Peter ultimately paid with his life as testimony to his faith. I am not so sure that we can rest on our laurels that *his* faith, ultimately expressed, will be enough to offset *our lack* of faith, especially when our faith is untried or untested. Where is God? If he's not in one's heart, then one is looking for him in the wrong place. This searching into all the wrong places may make people feel good that "they're doing something fulfilling," but if it doesn't lead to a repentant heart, then I'm not sure we're on the right track.

11 MEANING AND INTERIORITY

Introduction

We can easily claim various roles and confessions for ourselves, such as I'm an American or I'm a Catholic. But when push comes to shove, and we are asked to recognize who we really are in given circumstances, how do we manifest our true selves? Can we do so? Viktor Fankl, a survivor of a concentration camp, offers his observations about the pre-requisites necessary for appreciating one's true self in light of bleak circumstances that may impose themselves upon a person. We offer his descriptions below, but also recognize that other social psychological experiments bear his conclusions out in many ways, thus inviting all of us to take a hard interior look to face our true selves, which is an essential part of the spiritual journey, as it involves facing our darkness and recognizing that all of us have it, not just Nazis.

Meaning

Frankl, already a medical doctor when imprisoned in a concentration camp, wrote his book, *Man's Search for Meaning*, over nine consecutive days in 1945 after his liberation. He intended to publish it anonymously; however, its publication did not occur in this way. In the book he notes that of all the many books that he subsequently wrote, *Man's Search for Meaning* was his most popular by far. His book does not deal with the atrocities of concentration camp life in vivid detail—he found that other works addressed this important topic. Instead, his work focused on what constituted meaning in people's lives, especially within the environment of a concentration camp, where there was so much suffering and brutality.

One of the most remarkable statements that he writes stems from his appreciation of those who had spiritual depth.

> In spite of all the enforced physical and mental preparedness of the life in the concentration camp, it was possible for spiritual life to deepen. Sensitive people who were used to a rich intellectual life may have suffered much pain (they were often of a delicate constitution), but the damage to their inner selves was less. They were able to retreat from their terrible surroundings to a life of inner riches and spiritual freedom. Only in this way can one explain the apparent paradox that some prisoners of a less hardy makeup often seemed to survive camp life better than did those of a robust nature.[81]

People who had "robust natures" were physically strong, yet, when their strength failed, which it would do under the extreme and chronic conditions of a concentration camp, others who had "delicate constitutions" survived better. The "life of inner riches" made all the difference in the world. They were coming from a deeper place. Depth mattered more than physical strength in light of the degradation one human being inflicted against another, especially over time, day in and day out.

In his description of a beating he received at the hands of an SS guard he notes something that affected him negatively at a deep level.

> I did not know what was going on in the line behind me, nor in the mind of the SS guard, but suddenly I received two sharp blows on my head. Only then did I spot the guard at my side who was using his stick. At such a moment it is not the physical pain which hurts

---

[81] Viktor Frankl, *Man's Search for Meaning* (Boston: Beacon Press, 2006), 36.

the most (and this applies to adults as much as to punish children);
it is the mental agony caused by the injustice, the
unreasonableness of it all.[82]

A child might receive punishment for disobeying his or her parents.
There is usually a cause and effect involved. Here Frankl saw no cause
and effect. He noted "unreasonableness." There was no reason for his
beating. The randomness of such things undoes an appreciation of cause
and effect, which, in effect, undermines any sense of justice. There can
be no hope where justice is undermined, but I believe that we will
continue to look for it—or notice it—if and when it appears. This is the
absence of the good manifested once again, but the good comes out even
more prominently within circumstances like those in a concentration
camp, as the following episode recalls.

> On returning from work, I was admitted to the cookhouse after a
> long wait and was assigned to the line filing up to prisoner–cook
> F-------. He stood behind one of the huge pans and ladled soup into
> the bowls which were held out to him by the prisoners, who
> hurriedly filed past. He was the only cook who did not look at the
> man whose bowls he was filling: the only cook who dealt out the
> soup equally, regardless of recipient, and who did not make
> favorites of his personal friends or countrymen, picking out the
> potatoes for them, while the others got watery soup skimmed from
> the top.[83]

Frankl saw blind justice, as our own imagery with a blindfolded Lady
Justice typifies. He noted it. It was not common and therefore stuck out.
But he goes on to say:

> But it is not for me to pass judgment on those prisoners who put
> their own people above everyone else. Who can throw a stone at a
> man who favors his friends under circumstances when, sooner or
> later, it is a question of life or death? No man should judge unless
> he asks himself in absolute honesty whether in a similar situation

---

[82] Frankl, *Man's Search for Meaning*, 23-24.
[83] Frankl, *Man's Search for Meaning*, 47.

he might have not done the same.[84]

Frankl was able to appreciate the actions of the people in the camp through the lens of compassion. However, the qualities of justice and unreasonableness stood out against what he and his fellow prisoners were experiencing.

> The majority of prisoners suffered from a kind of inferiority complex. We all had once been or had fancied ourselves to be "somebody." Now we were treated like complete nonentities. (The consciousness of one's inner value is anchored in higher, more spiritual things, and cannot be shaken by camp life. But how many freemen, let alone prisoners, possess it?) Without consciously thinking about it, the average prisoner felt himself utterly degraded. This became obvious when one observed the contrasts offered by the singular sociological structure of the camp. The more "prominent" prisoners, the Capos [Jews conscripted to work for the Nazis], the cooks, the store-keepers and the camp policemen, did not, as a rule, feel degraded at all, like the majority of prisoners, but on the contrary—promoted! Some even developed miniature delusions of grandeur. The mental reaction of the envious and grumbling majority toward this favored minority found expression in several ways, sometimes in jokes. For instance, I heard one prisoner talk to another about a Capo, saying, "Imagine! I knew that man when he was only the president of a large bank. Isn't it fortunate that he has risen so far in the world?"[85]

Once again Frankl notes the significance of "one's inner value" and its anchoring "in higher, more spiritual things." This is the underlying nature of this observation. At the same time we can appreciate that, when stripped of the identity that one has in terms of the world in which one lives, or, for that matter, given to a person—one's role—a person can be changed by it, rightly or wrongly. The anchor of the inner world or deeper place or true self makes all the difference in combating the driving force of one's environment toward devaluation or inflation, as

---

[84] Frankl, *Man's Search for Meaning*, 48.
[85] Frankl, *Man's Search for Meaning*, 62-63.

the following examples suggest.

The Milgram Experiment

Stanley Milgram, professor of Psychology at Yale University, wondered, in the aftermath of the Adolph Eichmann trial (1960), what impact "orders" had on people in certain circumstances, given that many of the guards who stood trial for the atrocities of the Holocaust at Nuremburg insisted that they were "just following orders." Milgram set about developing an experiment that would test this hypothesis. His experiment began in 1961.

> Milgram (1963) was interested in researching how far people would go in obeying an instruction if it involved harming another person. [He] was interested in how easily ordinary people could be influenced into committing atrocities for example, Germans in WWII.[86]

Milgram advertised for male participants in the newspaper. He paired those whom he chose from the applicants and designated one as the 'learner' and the other as the 'teacher,' where the 'learner' was always one of Milgram's confederates. The learner would enter a room and have electrodes attached to him. The teacher and the researcher would go to another room, where there was a gauge showing electric current from 15 volts (slight shock) to 450 volts (severe shock). It also read 'Danger' on the gauge at 300 volts.

The participants were between 20 and 50 years old and came from all walks of life in the New Haven area. They received money just for showing up. An actor played the researcher and wore a grey lab coat. The learner was given word pairs to learn and then was "tested" by the teacher. If the learner failed to remember the word pairs, then 'the teacher' was instructed to increase the level of shock each time 'the learner' was wrong—the gauge is marked in 15-volt increments.

The teacher was given four prods, asking him to increase the voltage

---

[86] http://www.simplypsychology.org/milgram.html (as of this writing, 9 November 2014).

with each wrong answer, which the learner deliberately provided.

Prod 1: Please continue.
Prod 2: The experiment requires you to continue.
Prod 3: It is absolutely essential that you continue.
Prod 4: You have no other choice but to continue.

Two-thirds of the participants (65%) continued to increase the voltage to the maximum of 450 volts. All participants went to 300 volts.

Milgram summarizes his findings in the following way:

> The legal and philosophic aspects of obedience are of enormous import, but they say very little about how most people behave in concrete situations. I set up a simple experiment at Yale University to test how much pain an ordinary citizen would inflict on another person simply because he was ordered to by an experimental scientist. Stark authority was pitted against the subjects' [participants'] strongest moral imperatives against hurting others, and, with the subjects' [participants'] ears ringing with the screams of the victims, authority won more often than not. The extreme willingness of adults to go to almost any lengths on the command of an authority constitutes the chief finding of the study and the fact most urgently demanding explanation.[87]

Does the statement: "We were just following orders," actually have merit? We turn to another experiment for additional data.

Zimbardo Experiment

In 1971, a group of researchers led by Philip G. Zimbardo of Stanford University brought together 18 college students over a period of two

---

[87] Stanley Milgram, "The Perils of Obedience: A social psychologist's experiments show that most people will hurt their fellows rather than disobey an authority," *Harper's Magazine* (December 1973): 62-66, 75-77. Milgram ("The Perils of Obedience, 75) writes: "The subjects do not derive satisfaction from inflicting pain, but they often like the feeling they get from pleasing the experimenter. They are proud of doing a good job."

weeks to complete an experiment of the psychological effects of prison life.[88] They sorted through the applications, selecting those who seemed "most normal." The researchers built cells in the basement of the Psychology Building, and solicited volunteers who would randomly take the positions of guards and prisoners, determined by a flip of a coin. They enlisted the help of the local police, who went to the volunteers' homes and arrested them. They were then brought in for booking, but were transferred to the makeshift cells in the basement of the Psychology Building at Stanford for holding.

The prisoners were stripped naked and deloused, then dressed in a smock with a number on it; each prisoner would be identified by number, not name, for the duration of the experiment. The guards began to abuse the prisoners within a short time of the beginning of the experiment. Some prisoners had emotional breaks and had to be released. The experiment, originally intended to last two weeks, was terminated after six days.

Zimbardo makes the following conclusion about the study:

> By the end of the study, the prisoners were disintegrated, both as a group and as individuals. There was no longer any group unity; just a bunch of isolated individuals hanging on, much like prisoners of war or hospitalized mental patients. The guards had won total control of the prison, and they commanded the blind obedience of each prisoner.[89]

---

[88] See, as of this writing (17 August 2014), http://www.prisonexp.org/, which offers a slideshow of the events by Philip Zimbardo, the chief researcher. Note that the number of those selected was 24, but the other six were "on-call" in case they were needed. See also Zimbardo's book, *The Lucifer Effect: Understanding How Good People Turn Evil* (New York: Random House Trade Paperback, 2007).

[89] A prisoner participant relates of his experience: "I began to feel that I was losing my identity, that the person that I called Clay, the person who put me in this place, the person who volunteered to go into this prison—because it was a prison to me; it still is a prison to me. I don't regard it as an experiment or a simulation because it was a prison run by psychologists instead of run by the state. I began to feel that that identity,

For college-age young adults, socialization, sexuality, and their peer group become dominant concerns. Competition is also a strong force within their interactions as their egos develop ego-strength, which means people win at the expense of others. The prisoners' group identity, which would feed into their individual identity, was completely undermined, because the guards were in competition with them to maintain their own cohesion, control, and identity. This "competition" resulted in psychological breaks for some of the prisoners.

But Zimbardo himself admits that he had too much identified with his role in the experiment, so he was "unable" to recognize how matters had gone so wrong that he did not stop the experiment sooner. He notes that Christina Maslach, his girlfriend, was the only person who had an effect on him.

> Christina Maslach, a recent Stanford Ph. D. brought in to conduct interviews with the guards and prisoners, strongly objected when she saw our prisoners being marched on a toilet run, bags over their heads, legs chained together, hands on each other's shoulders. Filled with outrage, she said, "It's terrible what you are doing to these boys!" Out of 50 or more outsiders who had seen our prison, she was the only one who ever questioned its morality. Once she countered the power of the situation, however, it became clear that the study should be ended.

Zimbardo had himself been co-opted by his own experiment. Only someone close to him who could break through his adherence to his "role" could bring him back to himself. He had been subsumed into the group-ego, which could do no wrong, as we related earlier in our study.

Though this experiment occurred in 1971, a more recent episode of young makeshift guards abusing and humiliating their prisoners occurred at a prison at Abu Ghraib, about 20 miles from Baghdad in Iraq.

---

the person that I was that had decided to go to prison was distant from me—was remote until finally I wasn't that, I was 416. I was really my number."

Wikipedia reports:

> From late 2003 to early 2004, during the Iraq War, Military Police personnel of the United States Army and the Central Intelligence Agency committed human rights violations against prisoners held in the Abu Ghraib prison. They physically and sexually abused, tortured, raped, sodomized, and killed prisoners.[90]

I would suggest that Abu Ghraib was the real-life manifestation of the cruelty innate to human beings, outside of the controls of experimentation, where human beings degraded other human beings in the name of control. The level of atrocities speaks for itself. We can appreciate that our own government—an institution—endorsed these tortures, so as to advance its "values." It is not surprising that young soldiers (college-age) are at the center of the perpetrated humiliations. The military provides them with identity, and the situation at Abu Ghraib put them in competition with the prisoners, over whom they had to assert their authority and control.

In December 2014, a Senate committee released a "Torture Report," detailing practices used by the Central Intelligence Agency (CIA) to obtain information from detainees allegedly involved in activities related to 9/11, including water-boarding. Two psychologists, Bruce Jessen and James Mitchell, received $80 Million for developing the methods used by the CIA, because the CIA "was unprepared to run an interrogation program," according to NBC News.[91]

President Obama is quoted in an interview used during the broadcast as calling the methods "enhanced interrogation techniques," not torture. The Senate Report stated that "the vast majority of intelligence came before the torture." Andrea Mitchell, reporting for NBC, stated that morale at the CIA was "shattered" and that colleagues had to "pick people up off the ground" after the Report came out. (Ret. Gen. [USAF]) Michael Hayden, former Director of the CIA (2006-2009), states in the

---

[90] See, as of this writing (17 August 2014), http://en.wikipedia.org/wiki/Abu_Ghraib_torture_and_prisoner_abuse
[91] *NBC News*, 10-11 December 2014.

piece: "The people feel like they had the rug pulled right out from under them....These people who thought that they were doing what we wanted them to do—that's unprecedented [that they would have support removed in this way.]"

We can blame Adolph Hitler for his "Final Solution" that made concentration camps a reality, but we cannot turn our backs on the fact that human beings, in experimental and real-life situations, become cruel when the circumstances are "right."

One More Experiment

In 1973, two researchers conducted an experiment using seminary students from Princeton Divinity School to discover what factors determined their willingness to help someone in need, taking their lead from the Parable of the Good Samaritan (Luke 10:29-37).[92]

Seminary students were told in one location that they would be giving a talk in another building. Some were told that they would be speaking on the Parable of the Good Samaritan, whereas others would be talking on another subject. Besides the difference in talks that the students were to give, the only other difference was whether a student was told that he or she should hurry to the other building to deliver the talk or that the person had some time before the talk was to be delivered. A person in need (an actor participating in the experiment) was located somewhere on the way to the talk location.

The experiment concluded that:

> Subjects in a hurry were likely to offer less help than were subjects not in a hurry. Whether the subject was going to give a speech on the parable of the Good Samaritan or not did not significantly

---

[92] For their findings, see John M. Darley and C. Daniel Batson, "'From Jerusalem to Jericho': A Study of Situational and Dispositional Variables in Helping Behavior," *Journal of Personality and Social Psychology* 27 (1973): 100-108.

affect his helping behavior on this analysis.[93]

The study reports that some participants actually stepped over the person in need in order to get to the other building. So the need to hurry made a difference in the response. But the study's authors also note another characteristic of those students who were willing to assist the person in distress.

> [Those who helped the victim], who conceived their religion as involving an ongoing search for meaning in their personal and social world, seemed more responsive to the victim's immediate needs and more open to the victim's definition of his own needs.[94]

In other words, where the person recognized a personal commitment to "an ongoing search for meaning," he or she was able to cut through the "institutional" requirement of hurrying to attend to the needs of the group, as the Samaritan had done in the Parable. The priest and the Levite avoided the man who had been abused by robbers in the Parable, as their "offices" are identified, whereas, the Samaritan is the one who shows him compassion. The study describes the Samaritan in the following way:

> A major intent of the parable would seem to be to present the Samaritan as a religious and ethical example, but at the same time to contrast his type of religiosity with the more common conception of religiosity that the priest and Levite represent.[95]

We should also note that a Samaritan would be at odds with Jews (John 4:9) and would have been looked down upon by Jews (Luke 17:17). In other words, Samaritans are as far from being religious insiders, as are the priest and Levite, as one can get within a Jewish environment. Samaritans can sympathize with outsiders.

---

[93] Darley and Batson, "'From Jerusalem to Jericho'," 104. See also 105-106.

[94] Darley and Batson, "'From Jerusalem to Jericho'," 107.

[95] Darley and Batson, "'From Jerusalem to Jericho'," 101.

Conclusion

Meaning matters. Interiority matters.

Viktor Frankl underscores the importance of one's inner spiritual life for combating the harshness of concentration camp life. Though we as modern observers will never be able to appreciate the nature of the pain that these prisoners experienced, we cannot simply absolve ourselves from the actions of the guards in concentration camps with statements like "I would never do that" or "How could the guards do such things?" The experiment at Stanford and the episodes at Abu Ghraib, and the revelations from the Congressional "Torture Report," should alert us to the depth of our own darkness as human beings, which we can easily gloss over as though it is not there. Such disregard can only be done to our own detriment and the peril to our true selves and those within our reach.

A recollection from Fr. Thomas Keating relates the comments of a Holocaust survivor with whom he sat on a panel:

> She had started a humanitarian organization to prevent such horrors [as the Holocaust] from being repeated and mentioned casually, "You know, I couldn't have started that organization unless I knew that, with the situation just a little bit different, I could have done the same things that the Nazis did to my parents and the others in the concentration camps."[96]

The experiment involving the Parable of the Good Samaritan helps us to appreciate that wishful thinking about altruism can be undermined by an inclination "to hurry." We are constantly in a hurry to do things, whatever they might be, but, even people who are looking to help others, like seminary students, can be diverted from helping others by a concern for "doing things" rather than "helping people"—who are not "things." The personal component is what makes the difference. And this is precisely what the study also demonstrated.

Where there was a personal commitment on the part of the individual to

---

[96] Keating, *The Human Condition*, 38-39.

grow in meaning about the circumstance or study or whatever it may be, this interior turn enriches the true self; this is true soul food. No one can take this away from someone, as the descriptions from Viktor Frankl underscore. A personal commitment to meaning, interiority, and spiritual enterprise has far-reaching implications, so that we are firmly grounded not in an institutional, oftentimes impersonal, awareness, but in a personal appreciation of and for our true selves. The cruelty described above points toward qualities of unreasonableness and a general lack of justice, as it serves to break down one's values from the outside in, but it comes from people who are pawns of an institution fulfilling a role. If, however, one has a strong foundation or anchors within one's identity, not developed through force of will or strength of physical prowess, but crafted in the crucible of suffering and human experience, then one can withstand the ebbs and flows of life, even the horrors of a concentration camp. This is the house built on solid rock. (Cf. Matt 7:24-25; Luke 6:48.) I would suggest that so much energy is expended maintaining the exterior world in the name of institutional ends and goals, as important as these are, that the task of moving interiorly is being neglected and even undermined. The summation by the lawyer Mr. Galvin, played by Paul Newman, in the movie *the Verdict* brings out the sense of the frustration that such a lack of justice can foster.[97]

> So much of the time we're just lost. And please, God, tell us what is right, tell us what is true. When there is no justice, the rich win; the poor are powerless. We become tired of hearing people lie. And after a time we become dead. A little death. We think of

---

[97] "*The Verdict* portrays a 1982 courtroom drama film which tells the story of a down-on-his-luck alcoholic lawyer who pushes a medical malpractice case in order to improve his own situation, but discovers along the way that he is doing the right thing. Since the lawsuit involves a woman in a persistent vegetative state, the movie is cast in the shadow of the Karen Ann Quinlan case. The movie stars Paul Newman, Charlotte Rampling, Jack Warden, James Mason, Milo O'Shea, and Lindsay Crouse," from http://en.wikipedia.org/wiki/The_Verdict, as of this writing (18 August 2014).

ourselves as victims. We become victims. We become, ... we become weak. We doubt ourselves; we doubt our beliefs. We doubt our institutions. And we doubt the law.

But today you are the law. You are the law. Not some book, not the lawyers. Not the marble statue or the trappings of the court. Those are just symbols of our desire to be just. But they are, they are, in fact, a prayer. A fervent and frightened prayer.

In my religion they say, "Act as if you have faith. Faith will be given to you." If, if we are to have faith in justice, we need only to believe in ourselves and act in justice. I believe that there is justice in our hearts.

Meaning matters. Interiority matters.

12 CORPORATE AMERICA

Introduction

It is my contention that remaining fixed in the Stage of the Ego will have detrimental effects on society at large, but this is hard to demonstrate. Or is it? If we turn to the business world, at least from the perspectives of a few individuals, I believe that there is evidence to suggest that we as a society need a way of seeing things from a vastly different perspective. Though formulated in different ways, I would suggest that the accounts below support my claim about the need for a movement to a deeper sense of self for carrying out business, but also for addressing other areas of life as well.

Ruthlessness Becomes the New "Way of Proceeding"

> The turmoil in corporate America is forcing the nation's business leaders to undertake the most radical reassessment of their practices and beliefs since the end of World War II. But out of this soul-searching, a new set of management precepts is emerging, with profound impact on individual companies and the country as a whole.[98]

These words begin an article by Steven Prokesch in *the New York Times*

---

[98] Steven Prokesch, "Remaking the American C.E.O.," *The New York Times*, 25 January 1987, p. 1.

from 1987, as he goes on to relate how various companies have had to adjust their ways of doing business in order to remain competitive in light of foreign markets and competitors. "What is making [CEO's] ... so willing to adapt their operations is a perception spreading through executive ranks—that corporate survival cannot be taken for granted."[99]

The game plan for companies immediately following World War II could assume that countries in Europe and Asia had to rebuild after the War. They had no infrastructure or research & development underway, because they had to dig out from the rubble and devastation of war, so their resources were directed here. America "called the shots." This has all changed, as has American expectations that market success is a given. This has given rise to a new order of doing business.

> The new order eschews loyalty to workers, products, corporate structure, businesses, factories, communities, even the nation. All such allegiances are viewed as expendable under the new rules. With survival at stake, only market leadership, strong profits and a high stock price can be allowed to matter.

In other words, nothing matters except for profits. "The new management ways are paying off for the moment." Companies are realizing profits for their stock-holders, but, with golden parachutes the rage, it seems that taking chances using these "new management ways" is something that affects only employees, communities, and dependent businesses. CEO's are insulated.[100] In other words, everyone is expendable, except CEO's, who can operate with reckless abandon.

> Many of the top officers of major companies are adopting the new practices. Most of these executives are in their 40's and 50's and have come into their jobs in the last five years. This is the landscape of the individuals who are now running America's largest companies.

---

[99] Prokesch, "Remaking the American C.E.O.," 1.
[100] For one article among others, see, as of this writing (14 August 2014): http://www.washingtonpost.com/blogs/on-leadership/wp/2014/03/26/dismantling-ceos-golden-parachutes/

It's important to note the ages of these people, since, if they are working solely for the bottom line, then they are egotistical people, who have little sense of anyone else's needs but their own. They are using markets up as quickly as they can to garner as much profit as they can. They have not worked to develop foundations or infrastructure. They would have no trouble not giving anything back to the community or to anyone else for that matter. Prokesch's original statement quoted above about doing some soul-searching reveals that these individuals have egos, but when we look at true selves, we would be hard pressed to find any evidence of this. If we equate success with possession of money, then these people are working toward success; however, they are spiritually bankrupt. Because of their golden parachutes, they are also insulated from the impact of poor, bad, or immoral decisions.

> "When you are the only store in town, and people had to take your service, you really did not have to work as hard," said Richard A. Clarke, CEO of Pacific Gas & Electric Company, who now visits customers himself.

The ruthless or cruel manner in which companies have dealt with their companies—employees and all—has sacrificed creativity and vision for the bottom line. Gone is the fostering of relationships with other companies and communities, because: "You can't be emotionally bound to any particular asset," says Mr. Davis of Gulf & Western. The term "asset" can also be a person; it does not have to be an inanimate object.

This is the description of corporate America as reflected by Prokesch. In light of increased competition from outside, companies have had to do more work in order to maintain market share and boost revenues or go out of business, or so they say. They sadly adopt cruel means, which may deliver profits, but people are left in the lurch.[101]

---

[101] See Dr. Milton Friedman of the University of Chicago, who writes: "What does it mean to say that 'business' has responsibilities? Only people can have responsibilities. A corporation is an artificial person and in this sense may have artificial responsibilities, but 'business' as a whole cannot be said to have responsibilities, even in this vague sense." The web-site where this quote is found is (as of this writing [27 January 2015]):

We saw above how bottom-line leaders, who view themselves from external references and are therefore co-dependent, will ultimately lead a company to failure. Such individuals are failures at being human. The lack of emotional connection, as Davis relates above, severs ties with humanity. Ruthlessness and cruelty in business begets more ruthlessness and cruelty. Suggesting that such morally bankrupt individuals will lead to a deeper appreciation of anything, especially success, would be idiotic. But there is still more to consider.

Paul Tudor Jones

Paul Tudor Jones, a billionaire with assets reported to be $3.6 Billion, was interviewed on CBS' *60 Minutes* in a segment entitled, "Robin Hood."[102] Jones had seen an episode of *60 Minutes* himself and had been inspired by the actions of another wealthy individual who was putting up the money for some students at a certain high school to attend college. Jones wanted to do something for others, because he recognized "a hole in [his] soul."

Jones reported that, when he was growing up, his mother wanted him to be a preacher, whereas, he wanted to be a millionaire. Scott Pelley, the interviewer from *60 Minutes*, was baffled about how "his ruthlessness" had paid off for him from a business perspective, but now he was so giving with regard to the homeless of New York City, which stands at 20% of the population of New York. In light of this staggering figure, Jones developed the Robin Hood Foundation, which provides money and expertise to various programs around the City. In his own words, the foundation is at the "forefront of kicking poverty's ass." He forces soup kitchens and other charitable organizations to develop business plans and strategic goals to foster the continued success of their programs, when they apply for help from his foundation.

The segment shows Jones making an impassioned plea to the 1% of the

---

http://www.colorado.edu/studentgroups/libertarians/issues/friedman-soc-resp-business.html, which quotes Milton Friedman, "The Social Responsibility of Business is to Increase its Profits," *The New York Times Magazine*, September 13, 1970. Copyright @ 1970 by The New York Times Company.

[102] Air date: 17 April 2014.

1% who attend a gala in New York City, a fund-raiser for his foundation. During the gala showcased in the segment, he raises more than $80 Million. Since its inception, the Robin Hood Foundation has given away $1.25 Billion. Before the segment concludes, however, Pelley notes that the figure of 20% that reflected the number of homeless before the Robin Hood Foundation was still the figure that reflects the amount of homelessness after the Robin Hood Foundation has done its work.

This should not be surprising, since the ruthlessness that Jones engaged in never changed.[103] To obtain a billion dollars, one has to be ruthless or cruel, just like the guards in the concentration camps, just like the guards at Abu Graib: this is the opposite of compassionate. Just because someone seems to be doing God's work to change something, doesn't make it real. Jones calls his fellow millionaires and billionaires "brothers and sisters." He can pretend that he's a preacher now, but I believe that his mother's point was to use his power of persuasion to advance the Kingdom. This is not happening. Nothing has changed. Can we call this success? Unless he moves to a deeper level, he's not doing God's work; he's paying guilt money for his ruthlessness. Making up for dishonesty and being a loving person are not the same thing; however, we do need to note that Jesus recognized that payment of alms can make up for sins committed.[104] (See Matt 19:16-22 and parr.; Luke 11:41.)

---

[103] The film *Fifty Shades of Grey* (2015 release) involves the budding relationship of Mr. Christian Grey, a young billionaire, who is in pursuit of a (sexual) submissive to his dominant. He describes his origins as the son of a drug addict who worked as a prostitute. He was abused and bears the physical scars. He is then adopted by a family when he is four years old. One of his adoptive mother's friends takes Mr. Grey as her submissive for six years beginning at the age of fifteen. Mr. Grey helps to fight hunger in Africa, because "it is good for business." The perpetuation of cruelty and its association with the accumulation of wealth underscores how this film dramatizes the dynamics that we have been examining.

[104] Patrick W. Skehan, and Alexander A. Di Lella, OFM, (*The Wisdom of Ben Sira* [AB 39; New York: Doubleday, 1987], 156) state: "At least since the time of the author of the Book of Tobit (the third or second

Another Author, but the Same Problem?

Chris Argyris, a professor of Education and Organizational Behavior at the Harvard Graduate School of Education, in his article, "Skilled Incompetence," suggests through his case studies that leaders within companies lack the ability to communicate with colleagues and so they skillfully maintain deadlock in making important decisions. Each "side" wants to hold its ground, so there are constant impasses that surface, never to be resolved.

> The ability to get along with others is always an asset, right? Wrong. By adeptly avoiding conflict with coworkers, some executives eventually wreak organizational havoc. And it's their adeptness that's the problem. The explanation for this lies in what I call skilled incompetence, whereby managers use practiced routine behavior (skill) to produce what they do not intend (incompetence). We can see this happen when managers talk to each other in ways that are seemingly candid and straightforward. What we don't see so clearly is how managers' skills can become institutionalized and create disastrous side effects in their organizations.[105]

Being "nice" and avoiding conflict all the time delivers nothing but impasse. Altercations point to unresolved issues, but addressing conflict takes a leader who is willing to deal with messy situations. Avoidance of conflict, which keeps everyone's ego from being "checked" as to whether it reflects reality, leads nowhere, whereas, the ability to recognize the ego-play going on from a more authentic place can help deliver the desired result: creative solutions to problems, so that company energies can be focused in more advantageous endeavors and directions, rather than protecting people's egos and never calling assumptions into question.

---

century BC), alms-giving was considered to be righteousness *par excellence*; cf. Tob 1:3; 2:10; 4:7-11; 14:9, 10, 11."

[105] Chris Argyris, "Skilled Incompetence," *Harvard Business Review* (1986): 1-7, here 2.

Because executives don't say what they really mean or test the assumptions they really hold, their skills inhibit a resolution of important intellectual issues embedded in developing the strategy. Thus meetings end with only lists and no decisions.[106]

Argyris points out that:

Built into decentralization is the age-old tug between autonomy and control: superiors want no surprises, subordinates want to be left alone. The subordinates push for autonomy; they assert that by leaving them alone, top management will show its trust from a distance. The superiors, on the other hand, try to keep control through information systems. The subordinates see the control devices as confirming their suspicions—their superiors don't trust them.[107]

This could also be a description of the way in which children and parents interact. Children, especially when they enter adolescent years, want to make their own decisions to demonstrate self-determination and ego-strength. They see parents as standing in the way of this, so they will engage in passive aggressive activities of not doing chores when asked or making up excuses or lying about having done them. Parents will become overbearing and "force" the children to comply through privations, groundings, or other punishments. Mature discussion virtually never takes place, because the authority of the parents, itself precariously understood and undergoing change because of the maturing children, cannot tolerate such questioning. I would suggest that this dynamic is also operative at the corporate level within this description. Two sets of egos: parents and children, are at odds, but the top-down authority structure is viewed as the only plan for addressing the problem. Only someone who comes from a deeper place, namely, beyond ego-based concerns and turf-wars, is able to accommodate some demands from "the other side" to ensure that both parties are respected and the work gets done. But if no one is willing to take the first step—which will be seen by egotistical people as weakness, rather than strength—then stalemate is

---

[106] Argyris, "Skilled Incompetence," 3.
[107] Argyris, "Skilled Incompetence," 3.

the result.

Argyris continues:

> My experience is that people cannot build on their appreciation of others without first overcoming their suspicions. But to overcome what they don't like, people must be able to discuss it. And this requirement violates the undiscussability rule embedded in the organizational defensive routines.[108]

Argyris recognizes that certain aspects of office culture are undisscussable, therefore, off limits. I do not disagree with this point; however, I do disagree with Argyris' statement from a different perspective.

People who have little ego-strength and who see themselves from the perspective of the group-ego are suspicious of others. People will avoid discussing difficult issues if at all possible, unless they are comfortable with themselves. Those who are bullies or in positions of authority, who are forced into discussions, are obviously "required" to discuss matters, but they are no more comfortable with themselves than anyone else involved. Such a discussion requires a person who has moved to the Stage of Authenticity to offer perspectives that only such a person can provide. A person who can observe matters at hand outside a primarily egotistical view has the type of perspective necessary for bringing people together. Argyris calls this "a skill." This is not something that can be picked up from a book. The skill stems from one's true self, which is an organic reality.

> Problems won't be solved by simply correcting one isolated instance of poor performance.... To overcome skilled incompetence, people have to learn new skills—to ask the questions behind the questions.... [But] [h]ere's the real problem. These executives and all the others I've studied to date can't prevent the counter-productive consequences until and unless they learn new skills. Nor will it work to bypass the skilled

---

[108] Argyris, "Skilled Incompetence," 5.

incompetence by focusing on the business problems, such as, in this case, developing a business strategy.[109]

In order to appreciate the impact of not moving to a more authentic sense of things, Argyris recognizes the implication:

> Why open this can of worms if we have already solved the problem? *Because defensive routines prevent executives from making honest decisions.* Managers who are skilled communicators may also be good at covering up real problems. If we don't work hard at reducing defensive routines, they will thrive—ready to undermine this solution and cover up other conflicts.[110]

We note that Argyris maintains that "honest decisions" are not happening. We must conclude that dishonest or inauthentic ones are occurring. Companies are operating on a basis of dishonesty. I'm not sure that this is where anyone wants to be, but if profits are at stake, then this will be the course that a company will follow.

Elsewhere in his article, Argyris quotes the CEO of the small company that he is using as a case study to demonstrate his point:

> The CEO explained, "This is a group of lovable guys with very strong egos. They are competitive, bright, candid, and dedicated. But when we meet, we seem to go in circles; we are not prepared to give in a bit and make the necessary compromises."[111]

Though the CEO is talking about business executives, we can still see that all of these individuals—at least as far as the description from the CEO goes—are locked into egotistical understandings. The word suspicion is used throughout the article—a quality of the ego and, even more, the group-ego—and nothing gets done because of it. I would suggest that the impasse stems from an inability to get beyond ego-based concerns for the good of the company, an institution. Only a leader

---

[109] Argyris, "Skilled Incompetence," 5-6.
[110] Argyris, "Skilled Incompetence," 7. Emphasis mine.
[111] Argyris, "Skilled Incompetence," 3.

willing to lead the team beyond its egostistical posturings can help the company make any progress. If there is no value elicited by the CEO for something more—and he clearly had no idea where to go, hence his need to consult with Argyris—then the stalemate would have continued, and the company would not have been able to move forward. I do not call authenticity a skill to be learned, but a movement of one's ego into a different frame of reference as it also recognizes a deeper sense of self, namely, the true self.

What Would Jesus Do?

In an episode that I believe demonstrates the problems that are described above, we can appreciate Jesus' actions in the following account.

> Luke 9:43 While they were all amazed at his every deed, Jesus said to his disciples, 44 "Pay attention to what I am telling you. The Son of Man is to be handed over to men." 45 But they did not understand this saying; its meaning was hidden from them so that they should not understand it, and they were afraid to ask him about this saying. 46 An argument arose among the disciples about which of them was the greatest. 47 Jesus realized the intention of their hearts and took a child and placed it by his side 48 and said to them, "Whoever receives this child in my name receives me, and whoever receives me receives the one who sent me. For the one who is least among all of you is the one who is the greatest."

After Jesus has made a statement that the disciples cannot understand, namely, that Jesus "will be handed over to men" (v. 44), due to their own concerns about "success"—they are at the Stage of the Ego—they are described as "afraid to ask him about this saying" (v. 45). I would suggest that their fear stems from dashing their egos' hope in a sense of success that has Jesus taking a prominent place as the new political leader of Israel, the Messiah. Rather than getting feedback from Jesus about their sense of what it means for Jesus to be the Messiah, they simply pass over Jesus' disturbing remark without comment. The statement stirred them, however, to consider their prominence, as the episode reveals, so they argued about who was the greatest (v. 46), because, when Jesus assumes his kingship, they will be ready to fall into place on his coat-tails. (See chapter 1.)

Jesus recognized their intention (v. 47), because he is coming from a deeper place, and offers them the example of a child, who has no concern about position or ego, and Jesus underscores how one offsets the pull of one's ego: "Whoever receives this child in my name receives me, and whoever receives me receives the one who sent me. For the one who is least among all of you is the one who is the greatest" (v. 48). This is how Jesus the leader responds. He identifies in a kind way the idiocy of the disciples' concerns and offers the model of the child that will address their focus on their egos, but will also take them to a deeper place. There is no impasse here. The truth is stated. The problem is addressed. An invitation to something deeper is provided. This is true leadership.

Show Me the Money

The Baltimore Sun on three different days printed comments from three different individuals expressing their outrage with the manner in which the Ray Rice case was handled. Ray Rice of the Baltimore Ravens punched his then-fiancée in the face in an elevator in Atlantic City, New Jersey, which was caught on tape. The National Football League (NFL) went along with business as usual. An editorial in *the Baltimore Sun* noted an inconsistency in the delivery of justice in its 9 September 2014 edition: "The Ravens supported Ray Rice after his domestic assault charge until a video of the incident made it bad business."[112] Another commentator, Thomas Schaller, a professor of political science at the University of Maryland (UMBC), compared Michael Brown, the youth killed by a policeman in Ferguson, Missouri, and Ray Rice, noting the differing treatment each received.

> The commodification of American justice is nothing new. Those with the means have always enjoyed the better legal representation in the courts, presuming their wealth failed to shield them from arrest in the first place. Beyond wealth, sociological distinctions

---

[112] "Reckless and callous," *the Baltimore Sun*. 9 September 2014, p. 12.

have also conferred judicial advantage.[113]

Schaller holds that the institution known as the NFL ensured that Rice would receive different treatment. Though he compares the treatment of Michael Brown and Ray Rice, his conclusion seems sound.

> The differences in treatment for Mssrs. Rice and Brown cannot be attributed to race or gender or wealth, even though one man is rich and the other man was poor. Beyond money or celebrity, Mr. Rice appears to have benefited from the status accorded to him because he is—or was, for now—associated with the NFL. New Jersey prosecutors have said they treated Mr. Rice as they would any first-time offender, but that strains credibility.[114]

Schaller recognizes the problematic nature of the statements made by the New Jersey prosecutors, as does another commentator who uses a different case to illustrate a similar point of differing treatment on the part of law enforcement.

Another commentator, this time former state delegate Connie DeJuliis, in her piece, "Tribal law in America," notes a similar disconnect between the treatment of Rice and Shaneen Allen, a woman who lives in another state. Allen was carrying a gun in her car, with a permit to do so, whereas, when she went into New Jersey and was stopped. She identified that she had a gun in her possession, in light of which she was taken into custody.

> Ms. Allen spent 40 days in jail before being released on bail. Rice has not and will not spend a minute behind bars. Ms. Allen petitioned [court officials] for release into New Jersey's Pretrial Intervention Program. So did Mr. Rice. Ms. Allen was denied, and Mr. Rice was accepted, despite a grand jury indictment on aggravated-assault charges. So what exactly made Mr. Rice a good candidate for this program? According to his attorney, Mr. Rice will not need rehabilitation. The profoundly violent incident was

---

[113] Thomas Schaller, "Another bias: institution-based privilege," *the Baltimore Sun*, 17 September 2014, p. 19.

[114] Schaller, "Another bias," 19.

"a momentary lapse of reason" and "out of his character." Ms. Allen, by contrast, appears to have acted very much in character. She was a law abiding citizen and had obtained a legal gun permit after twice being a victim of crime, so when she was pulled over by a New Jersey police officer she did what any law abiding person would do: she admitted that she was carrying a weapon. Perhaps that is why she was deemed ineligible for pretrial intervention—she truly was not in need of rehabilitation.[115]

DeJuliis notes that one's "tribal affiliation" matters when one is being "dealt" justice.

Mr. Rice belonged to the National Football League, a tribe so powerful that it was going to be allowed to mete out its own form of justice and, in doing so, send a message to its other members. That is, after all, how tribal societies work. The NFL sent a powerful message. Mr. Rice was suspended for a whole two weeks. Go ahead, beat up a woman, said the tribe. Women don't matter. It was only after the tribe itself felt under threat that they changed their tune. Once a gossip site released the second videotape of the brutal beating, the NFL finally suspended Mr. Rice indefinitely.[116]

DeJuliis notes that "pro-gun enthusiasts" have come to Allen's defense, but not without attempts to advance their own "tribal affiliations."

From whatever angle one argues the point, the situation with Ray Rice was handled badly. Money and business became more important than people or the issue of domestic violence. This is a real-world demonstration of how authenticity will be undermined by people and institutions with money, who will always be insecure and protective of their "holdings" (which means ego-extensions). Authenticity and justice are irrelevant. The NFL and the Ravens' owner Steve Biscotti will act in their own interests, until something or someone is willing to come

---

[115] Connie DeJuliis, "Tribal law in America," *the Baltimore Sun*, 22 September 2014, p. 15.
[116] DeJuliis, "Tribal law in America," 15.

forward—at great personal peril—to confront them in their lack of authenticity.[117]

But these episodes show us that money and power and the people who control them are morally bankrupt, no matter where they are found. We heard about Shaneen Allen and her circumstance, but only because of Ray Rice and only as a comparison. A gun group used her to advance its agenda. Her personal freedom was merely a slogan to advance a business or ideological decision.

The Church Does It, Too

In an article in *Due Process, Law and Love*, a newsletter from the organization called Justice for Priests and Deacons, we find statements about similar miscarriages of justice against priests. Rev. Michael Salvagna, a Passionist priest stationed in Pennsylvania, describes a case involving a priest, "Francis," who was falsely accused and later exonerated. However, the damage done to his reputation was such that it was insurmountable. Fr. Salvagna recognizes the institution of the Church in the following way:

> Ecclesiastical authorities always have the upper hand when it comes to accusing an individual priest or religious. The Vatican position acts on the principle that if the ordinary or the religious superior with jurisdiction is the source of the accusation against a priest, then the Congregation of the Doctrine of Faith considers its

---

[117] *The Baltimore Sun* (12 February 2015, p. 2) reported the following under the title: "Sex assaults at Naval Academy fall" in light of a report issued the day before by the Pentagon. "In 13 cases at the Naval Academy detailed in Wednesday's report, just one suspect was convicted at court-martial. Meanwhile, 44 percent of students across the academies who reported an attack said they suffered backlash—including disciplinary measures and 'social retaliation.' Susan L. Burke, a Baltimore attorney who has represented hundreds of service members who allege that they were sexually assaulted in civil actions against the military, said a low conviction rate and a high incidence of retaliation discourage victims from coming forward. 'Why would you open yourself to almost certain retaliation when your odds of getting justice are next to zero?' she asked."

responsibility to be reinforcement of local authority. The case against Fr. Francis was simply ratified up the chain of command almost by reflex. There is no justice when the accuser is powerful and his judgment is not questioned. Yet Vatican officials have a serious responsibility to dispense justice lest a priest or religious be victimized.[118]

I have met other priests who have been similarly treated. Institutions tend to protect the group-ego, rather than the individual. However, a voice that recognizes this lack of authenticity is quoted in the same issue of *Due Process*. Bishop Howard Hubbard, retired Bishop of Albany, New York, himself accused of sexual abuse, yet later exonerated, offered a critique of the current "no strikes" policy in June 2002, which overrides an earlier policy adopted by the United States Conference of Catholic Bishops (USCCB).

> I would argue that such a proposed policy, understandable as it may be from a public opinion perspective, is not consistent with the nature of who we are as a faith community which proclaims the central importance of conversion, repentance, forgiveness, compassion and reconciliation in responding to the Good News.[119]

Bishop Hubbard goes on to call to mind an earlier pastoral letter from the USCCB entitled, "Responsibility, Rehabilitation and Restoration: A Catholic Perspective on Crime and Criminal Justice." He wonders if, given the statements in this earlier policy, the United States Bishops are willing to recognize mercy [my term] for criminals, victims, and others, whereas, priests are left out of the bishops' concern. Hubbard wonders: "Do we accept this biblical concept as beneficial for the community at large but not for our own priests and other church personnel?"[120]

---

[118] Rev. Michael Salvagna, CP, "How Could This Happen? Tribute to a Friend," 8, in *Due Process, Law, and Love* 5 (2014).
[119] Bishop Howard J. Hubbard (ret.), "Episcopal Critique at Dallas Bishops' Meeting," June 2002, p. 5 in *Due Process*.
[120] Hubbard, "Episcopal Critique," 5.

The Limits of Institutions

Thomas Merton (1915-1968), a Trappist monk and prolific author, makes the following assertion in his tape series, "Prayer and Growth in Christian Life," about the function of a university to foster a student's growth as a person.[121]

> The function of a university is then first of all to help the student to discover himself, to recognize himself and to identify who it is that chooses. This description will be recognized at once as unconventional and in fact monastic. To put it in even more outrageous terms, the function of the university is to help men save their souls and in so doing to save their society. From what? From the hell of meaninglessness, of obsession, of complex artifice, of systematic lying, of criminal evasions and neglects. It will be evident from my context that the business of saving one's soul means more than taking an imaginary object, a soul, and entrusting it to some institutional bank for deposit until it is recovered with interest in heaven.

Merton recognizes the need to appreciate how institutions can be seen from two different perspectives:

> Society tends to make things easy for itself by enforcing certain roles on others, and demanding that the person be untrue to himself. Punishing for not accepting these roles. People are constantly being rewarded for betraying themselves and betraying those whom they love as an act of sacrifice of homage to the supremacy of the organization. *True dedication is the escape from this kind of trap. False dedication is the confirmation of this trap.* True dedication is not mere anarchy, without institution whatever, but the reason why people are called by the Holy Spirit to the dedicated Christian life is in order to free them from the tyranny of

---

[121] All quotes in this section come from this tape series, which Merton recorded for the Sisters of Loreto in light of a request from them related to their General Chapter presumably of 1967, when the series was recorded.

being defined by others, in order to affirm the supremacy of an institution which becomes further and further away from what they can identify with. (Emphasis mine.)

From one perspective, the institution takes the place of God: "The institution has all the rights of God Himself." One then dedicates one's life to this sense of institution.

The institution has the right to destroy us if it wants to.... This is like an Aztec human sacrifice. As long as this type of dedication remains alive in the religious life, then the religious life is through. A lot are finished in light of this. Meaningful life is correlative to its ability to overcome this wrong idea of dedication.... A community that demands this kind of immolation is no community at all.

Merton rightly sees the limitations that an institution, even the Church, has in light of its ability to ask people to sacrifice themselves for the "good" of the institution. No one should lose his soul or true self at any time. We noted from the episodes in chapters 11 and 12 how this can occur. We must fight against such promptings.

Conclusion

An authenticity-based institution or company or organization would take on a formational (parental?) role in the lives of its employees, with the understanding that relationships and roles must evolve over time. This is true in a family, but it should also be the case within institutions and organizations. The potential of each member of the organization must be respected, appreciated, and fostered. This is a different sense of community, but one that reflects Gospel values, instead of the myopic focus on the almighty dollar, which permits scape-goating and maintenance of archaic understandings to protect holdings as people are sacrificed. By fostering the growth of one's employees, which can only be done by someone coming from the Stage of Authenticity, a leader recognizes that the bottom-line now is not the only variable in the equation that leads to profit. By eliminating creativity, leaders are undermining their ability to grow their companies and organizations into the future by taking their profits and running. Ego-based leaders, as CEO's under the protection of the Golden Parachute demonstrate, have no stake in anything real; their assumptions are ethereal. Real people are hurt by their lack of humanity and moral bankruptcy—including their own families.

We conclude this chapter with the parable pronounced by Nathan the Prophet, describing the misdeed of David taking Bathsheba, the wife of Uriah the Hittite, as his own and covering it up with his murder. The story underscores what people in high places are willing to do to get what they want and try to cover it up. God, however, sees all.

2Sam. 12:1 The LORD sent Nathan to David, and when he came to him, he said: "Judge this case for me! In a certain town there were two men, one rich, the other poor. 2 The rich man had flocks and herds in great numbers. 3 But the poor man had nothing at all except one little ewe lamb that he had bought. He nourished her, and she grew up with him and his children. She shared the little food he had and drank from his cup and slept in his bosom. She was like a daughter to him. 4 Now, the rich man received a visitor, but he would not take from his own flocks and herds to prepare a meal for the wayfarer who had come to him. Instead he took the poor man's ewe lamb and made a meal of it for his visitor." 5 David grew very angry with that man and said to Nathan: "As the LORD lives, the man who has done this merits death! 6 He shall restore the ewe lamb fourfold because he has done this and has had no pity." 7 Then Nathan said to David: "You are the man! Thus says the LORD God of Israel: "I anointed you king of Israel. I rescued you from the hand of Saul. 8 I gave you your lord's house and your lord's wives for your own. I gave you the house of Israel and of Judah. And if this were not enough, I could count up for you still more. 9 Why have you spurned the LORD and done evil in his sight? You have cut down Uriah the Hittite with the sword; you took his wife as your own, and him you killed with the sword of the Ammonites. 10 Now, therefore, the sword shall never depart from your house, because you have despised me and have taken the wife of Uriah to be your wife.' 11

Thus says the LORD: "I will bring evil upon you out of your own house. I will take your wives while you live to see it, and will give them to your neighbor. He shall lie with your wives in broad daylight. 12 You have done this deed in secret, but I will bring it about in the presence of all Israel, and with the sun looking down.'" 13 Then David said to Nathan, "I have sinned against the LORD." Nathan answered David: "The LORD on his part has forgiven your sin: you shall not die. 14 But since you have utterly spurned the LORD by this deed, the child born to you must surely die."

Marc Lanoue

13 SPIRITUAL JOURNEY, PART I

Introduction

The resources that a person has: physical, intellectual, emotional, spiritual, and psychological—not that this list is exhaustive—can determine a person's direction in life, but one's spiritual life can flower without any external stimulation through the others, especially in light of pain, confusion, and distress, as we saw in the descriptions from Victor Frankl. But the need to endure extreme or greatly unusual circumstances does not do justice to understanding what goes into nurturing one's spiritual life from a day-to-day existence that may be devoid of great trauma. I believe that we need to look at some of the factors in play from the standpoint of the flow of life in general that impact one's perspectives and thus one's openness to growth on one's spiritual journey.

The Concerns of the "Adult"

In sum, I equated the concerns of the egotistical adult with wealth, long life, children, and reputation. Long life today might be the willingness to watch one's weight or otherwise follow a healthy lifestyle: to eat healthy foods and to exercise, for instance, but the goal is to live a long life, as long as one's quality of life is also maintained. The other values are clear. Whatever we can say about these four values, we can appreciate that they can be developed without consciousness of God. Non-believers and believers alike have these values. But concerns over these values represent only one stage of life. If, however, they are the only values you ever know, your growth and experience will be stymied.

> A financial planner, now semi-retired from his successful business worth tens of millions of dollars, returned to the office only to handle accounts that involved assets over $100 million. He took his entire extended family—three generations—on vacation for two weeks to a private resort, because of the importance that he placed on his family. His brother, a successful psychologist, made sure that he always called him doctor to emphasize his education. This bothered the financial planner.

A financial planner requires a respectable reputation to conduct business. Clients with assets in the amounts above avoid controversy and drama; they recognize the need for a good reputation in the ways of business. His family (children) is important to him. His wealth is substantial, as is his health and work toward longevity, not stated, but evident. The brother, also in his late sixties, regards his title as of paramount importance, because it points to a superior education over his brother (an egotistical concern). This is success to many people, but the question is whether there is any chance for further growth without spiritual values as well.

An 82-year-old priest from a religious community shared the following with a person who asked him how he was, since he had been hospitalized for major illnesses twice within a short span of time.

> I'm fine. If you need any money, don't ask me, because I don't have any. The secretary will have to help you. I get a pension of $50,000 a year from the military that goes to the Order. You know, I've visited 225 parishes. I am the confessor to 35 priests, 27 sisters, and 16 permanent deacons. I read three books a week and have a doctorate. Oh, I've got to go to prepare for Mass. I'll talk to you later.

The emphasis may be different, but this older priest is concerned with the same things that the financial planner is. His reputation is caught up in his ability to be a confessor to so many people. His "spiritual children" are the priests, sisters, and deacons whose confessions he hears. He may not have money in hand, but his pension demonstrates his worth. All of these accomplishments can be called ego-extensions, which is why this is the Stage of the Ego.

> Luke 6:31 Do to others as you would have them do to you. 32 For if you love those who love you, what credit is that to you? Even sinners love those who love them. 33 And if you do good to those who do good to you, what credit is that to you? Even sinners do the same. 34 If you lend money to those from whom you expect repayment, what credit [is] that to you? Even sinners lend to sinners, and get back the same amount. 35 But rather, love your enemies and do good to them, and lend expecting nothing back; then your reward will be great and you will be children of the Most High, for he himself is kind to the ungrateful and the wicked. 36 Be merciful, just as [also] your Father is merciful (Luke 6:31-36).

The people reflected in the account about the financial planner and older priest above want to be "successful." Their success is determined by their manifestation of the values mentioned earlier, though they might not use the same terminology. But if there is no one to lead them beyond these values as constitutive of "success," they will never turn interiorly to recognize something more, especially if any sort of suffering is viewed as the enemy. Decisions within one's life will be made from this perspective, always based on ego values, which are self-centered and insecure. Competition is always operative as are dualistic notions, since resources are finite, and if I do not have them, then you must have them. I will be competing to obtain them. This is what is known as the "zero-sum" game.[122]

---

[122] Jung ("The Stages of Life," 18) writes: "Whoever carries over into the afternoon the law of the morning, or the natural aim, must pay for it with damage to his soul, just as surely as a growing youth who tries to carry

A Movement to a New Stage

But if we are open to something more within ourselves and are able to appreciate inner movements that the values above do not satisfy, then a person will embark on a search that leads to a different sense of success and a different focus for one's life.

As children, we may or may not adopt moral principles from our parents or other sources depending upon a multitude of factors. However, once a person is no longer preoccupied with the voice of the ego alone or a group-ego, then options for moral living become more evident and important. This usually, though not exclusively, occurs at mid-life. This is the Stage of Authenticity or the Stage of the True Self, when one seeks a more authentic existence in light of everything around and one's interior movements. But we also have to recognize other changes.

If we again recall the 46 year-old woman from above (chapter 9), she no longer saw her children as ego-extensions. She was, of course, their birth mother and care-giver and she still loved them. However, as we all know from adult children taking in (aged) parents, whose health might be failing, our relationships with others change. This is a natural development. Life is constantly changing, so our relationships with parents also change. That our parents gave us birth will never change, but the content of "mother" and "father" takes on a new dimension as time goes on. As children go off to college or set up housekeeping for themselves, "empty-nest" syndrome is a sense of loss that, in light of no further care-giving responsibilities, a mother and father must view themselves and their children differently because of these changes in life. This is the type of opening that permits other interior movements to take place. If, however, one does not recognize these subtle changes going on

---

over his childish egoism into adult life must pay for this mistake with social failure. Money-making, social achievement, family and posterity are nothing but plain nature, not culture. Culture lies outside the purpose of nature. Could by any chance culture be meaning and purpose of the second half of life?" Jung uses morning metaphorically to describe one's youth, afternoon as one's mid-life, and night and evening to describe old age.

inside or does not even recognize their possibility, they might be ignored. Ignoring such movements will prove disastrous for the person—and those around him or her—as the movement is meant to bring people to a new level of understanding of God, which is founded in truth, justice, and mercy in our relationships with ourselves and others. If this does not occur, then the person will remain frozen in ego-based concerns and their associated insecurities. Such a person will not move to another stage of life, and everyone around that person will pay the price. Freedom and creativity are undermined to maintain this frozen state. Those who are looking to help others on their journeys will encourage them not to remain anchored in former ways of being, but will encourage them in their growth and development, as Chuckie Sullivan did for Will Hunting in *Good Will Hunting*.

Key to Happiness

If the critical mass of people who make up one's environment does not change its perspective or if there is no one to guide people to a growth beyond the Stage of the Ego, then some people will always avoid the pain of change and they will not move beyond the precarious value system based on the insecurities of the ego.[123] Trapped in the notion that happiness is found outside of oneself, where references point outward to: wealth, long life, children, and reputation, "the American Dream," we do not recognize that true happiness, that is, the happiness that comes from God, comes from interior values.

> The key [to happiness] ... was not lost outside ourselves. It was lost inside ourselves. That is where we need to look for it.... The chief characteristic of the human condition is that everybody is looking for this key [to happiness] and nobody knows where to

---

[123] The story of Abraham haggling with God over the fate of Sodom can have many interpretations. One of them involves appreciating why Abraham stopped at ten righteous inhabitants in Sodom. Without this number of righteous people, the others in Sodom could not have been converted. We recognize that the family of Lot was evacuated through heavenly intervention, which meant that there was not a sufficient number of people to rectify the conduct of the citizens of Sodom. (See Gen 19:16-17.)

find it. The human condition is thus poignant in the extreme. If you want help as you look for the key in the wrong place, you can get plenty of it, because everybody is looking for it in the wrong place, too: where there is more light, pleasure, security, power, acceptance by others. We have a sense of solidarity in the search without any possibility of finding what we are looking for.[124]

When we realize that these four natural values will not deliver happiness in any lasting way, this realization should push us to reconsider where we are coming from: being valued by external references to what we have or by internal references to our true selves. This movement can be difficult, since we only know a false self, embedded in worldly values. But as painful as the shift within may be, it is critical to true and lasting happiness, compassion, and turning from cruelty.

Resistance

One way of fending off interior movement is by not dealing with the suffering that comes from the normal course of life. But if we first examine the extreme end of avoidance of suffering, namely, by looking at someone who is an addict, we can appreciate that the purpose of addiction or one's "fix" is to avoid dealing with the suffering of a situation or trauma or life in general, which in turn arrests interior emotional and spiritual growth.

But as puberty signals a change in our bodies drawing us to a different physical stage of life, so too does mid-life signal another sort of change. It is not accidental that the woman above is 46 and facing mid-life. More often than not, people seek spiritual or other help at junctures in their lives, especially mid-life. But there are other events that compel us to see things in a different way from the Stage of the Ego, and these include: major trauma, to ourselves or to those whom we love; major health issues, such as cancer; terminal illnesses, both for ourselves and those around us; catastrophes, such hurricanes or other natural events; caring for disabled children and adults; loss of a child; divorce; disillusionment;

---

[124] Keating, *The Human Condition*, 10.

job loss; betrayal, and the list goes on. These are happenstances that can occur which are unexpected consequences of our worldview clashing with physical reality, which means outside of our control. However, they can lead us to interior growth if we face our limitations and recognize another dimension and depth to ourselves. The key term here is "outside of our control." The ego wants to be in control of everything—it's god-like yearning. However, when it recognizes that it is not god, a person must reassess what makes a person who he or she is. These are the types of events that can bring interior growth.

Not Growing Up

Because of resistance over movement to a new stage of life, issues will develop between those who choose to lead authentic lives (Stage of Authenticity) and those who choose to stop in the Stage of the Ego. (Remember John the Baptist and Herod and Jesus and the Chief Priests and Pharisees.) Fr. Keating's words from above ring true: "We have a sense of solidarity in the search without any possibility of finding what we are looking for." "Success" in this case means returning to the first stage of life over and over again, especially when we are on the cusp of another Stage.

> Here, then, is the beginning of what might be called the addictive process, the need to hide the pain that we suffered in early life and cannot face. We repress it into the unconscious to provide an apparent freedom from pain or develop compensatory processes to access forms of pleasure that offset the pain we are not yet prepared to face. We are thrust because of circumstances into the position of developing a homemade self that does not conform to reality. Everything entering into the world that makes survival and security, and affection and esteem, and power and control our chief pursuits of happiness has to be judged on the basis of one question: Is it good for me? Hence, good and evil are judged not by their objective reality, but by the way we perceive them as

fitting into our private universe or not.[125]

By the unwillingness to recognize the limitations inherent to a specific stage of life, growth is thwarted, and damage is done, especially to spouses, children, and other family members. A false sense of self remains entrenched, though not without enormous expenditures of energy. We are meant to get beyond the domination of the ego at mid-life (if not before) in order to go deeper within ourselves, which means dealing with darkness, our unconscious—the reason or reasons blocking our ability to move to the next stage of life. If we do not engage in the encounter with our darkness through a deeper sense of prayer and interior discernment, our lives will be impacted in major ways. We will inflict damage on others by our unwillingness to grow, especially in compassion. Those who are ego-based seldom recognize the damage that they are inflicting on others, because they do not come from a deeper place and their actions do not spring from its by-product—compassion.

Fr. Keating describes the process necessary for dealing with our darkness, which involves recognizing the fear inherent to dropping something that we have known for most of our lives—the false self.

> The contemplative journey, because it involves the purification of the unconscious, is not a magic carpet to bliss. It is an exercise of letting go of the false self, a humbling process, because it is the only self we know.[126]

Most people whom I have encountered attempt to address the darkness of their unconscious through rational/logical means. Such an attempt will never work. The search for meaning, and other non-linear and non-

---

[125] Keating, *The Human Condition*, 14. An opinion piece in *the Baltimore Sun* by psychiatrist Gordon Livingston, entitled, "Can we still claim to be the 'home of the brave'?" wonders how apt our national anthem is in light of people living in fear. He opens his column: "One of the most difficult tasks we face as human beings is to see ourselves as we truly are." He later writes: "Perhaps our sense of perspective has become distorted by the politicians and media who profit from our fears." *The Baltimore Sun*, 5 October 2014, p. 25.

[126] Keating, *The Human Condition*, 20.

rational methodologies are appropriate for dealing with the unconscious, personal and collective, such as ritual, parables, and other common stories. The ego seeks to control. If happiness is seen from a perspective embedded in the Stage of the Ego, then invitations to growth from God will be fear-instilling and resisted.

> God has not promised to take away our trials, but to help us to change our attitudes toward them. That is what holiness really is. In this life, happiness is rooted in our basic attitude toward reality.[127]

Can one be called "free" if he compels his brother to call him, "Doctor" or "Monsignor"? Does one need to list his "holdings" to impress others? Is there freedom in the need to divorce and establish a new family every time a new stage of life is in the offing? Freedom comes from a much deeper place, not a false sense of self that is ego-based. The project of dealing with one's darkness is not a pleasant experience for anyone, hence most people's wish to avoid it. However, not dealing with this vital component of our lives has serious implications.

> I don't know whether we can make progress in such a project without a contemplative practice that alerts us to our own biases, prejudices, and self-centered programs for happiness, especially when they trample on other people's rights and needs.... The false self is looking for fame, power, wealth, and prestige. The unconscious is very powerful until the divine light of the Holy Spirit penetrates to its depths and reveals its dynamics. Here is where the great teaching of the dark nights of St. John of the Cross corresponds to depth psychology, only the work of the Holy Spirit goes far deeper. Instead of trying to free us from what interferes with our ordinary human life, the Spirit calls us to transformation of our inmost being, and indeed of all our faculties, into the divine way of being and acting.[128]

Most people plod along and attempt to change objectionable habits and

---

[127] Keating, *The Human Condition*, 21.
[128] Keating, *The Human Condition*, 21-22.

perspectives piecemeal in their lives. The process of accepting one's darkness, owning it, and then giving it over to God changes a person at the root in the deepest way. Every fruit will, in turn, change as well. There's no need to "work on" something in one's life. Everything flows through God now as we accept our true selves and God as God, rather than as a projection of ourselves. This is done through resting in God, which we call Centering Prayer, a simple prayer of presence to God, which permits God to "unload" our unconscious and let God's Presence fill the gaps.[129] (We offer an outline for beginning this prayer form in Appendix I of this work.)

Conclusion

In the next chapter, we will explore how the value system changes from ego-based to authenticity-based concerns usually at mid-life. This is crucial for understanding ourselves, but it is also crucial for appreciating how we as human beings will address the problems of our time. Ego-based measures pass away. Authenticity-based concerns endure. The question is whether a sufficient number of people will adopt the spiritual journey as a way of life, which means turning inwardly in order to let transformation occur according to God's plan.

---

[129] We will discuss below the founders' reliance on Merton for their understanding of Centering Prayer. Thomas Merton (*New Seeds of Contemplation* [New York: New Directions, orig. 1961; 1972], 227) writes about the experience of contemplation, the purpose of Centering Prayer: "God touches us with a touch that is emptiness and empties us. He moves with a simplicity that simplifies us. All variety, all complexity, all paradox, all multiplicity cease. Our mind swims in the air of an understanding, a reality that is dark and serene and includes in itself everything. Nothing more is desired. Nothing more is wanting. Our only sorrow, if sorrow be possible at all, is the awareness that we ourselves still live outside God."

14 SPIRITUAL JOURNEY, PART II

Introduction

I suggested in the last chapter that we can stop growth in our lives, either through direct means or through the lack of awareness that anything more is possible on the "stages of life." If we are "successful" in the only value system that we acknowledge, then why would anyone go further? This is a legitimate question. Only when one can appreciate interior values over external references will one be willing to undertake the spiritual journey with all one's resources. We all look for the pay-off in any endeavor. If interior movement does not deliver, then we will abandon it for what is clear and obvious in the material world. But we need to see what a change in value entails.

Change in Value System

As our physical lives press us toward different stages of life, so too our spiritual understandings need also to mature, impacted as they are by our emotional lives. The spiritual journey requires emotional maturity, which means acceptance of growth as an organic requirement, not to be avoided, but embraced. Those on the spiritual journey will experience a change in their values corresponding with changes in other arenas, such as the physical and intellectual. For instance, from the ethical perspective, when doling out cookies to children, people may appreciate justice as one cookie per child. But as we mature, we must recognize that other factors determine our moral stances.

Retributive justice, as described in Deuteronomy 28, comes down to a sense that if one is good to God, that is, that one follows the Lord's commandments, God will be good to you, and vice versa, which will occur in this life, since there is no sense of an afterlife under the Torah-based value system. If we consider possession of wealth, long life, children, and reputation as blessings from God, we need to ask ourselves the question: Is someone cursed who dies young, childless, lacking a reputation or in poverty? This was Jesus' situation when he died unmarried (and therefore childless) and was executed as a Messianic pretender at the relatively young age of 33. From the value system based on Retributive Justice, we would have to affirm that Jesus was cursed in God's eyes, which calls for a reassessment of these values, especially from the sayings of Jesus himself.

> John 9:1 As [Jesus] passed by he saw a man blind from birth. 2 His disciples asked him, "Rabbi, who sinned, this man or his parents, that he was born blind?" 3 Jesus answered, "Neither he nor his parents sinned; it is so that the works of God might be made visible through him."

The understanding on the part of the disciples, which was reflective of Jewish society at large, was that a disability was punishment for sin on the part of someone, the parents or the person with the disability. Instead, Jesus appreciates the blindness of the man as an opportunity for God to manifest his glory or power over all things. There is a change in the value system going on here. Another episode illustrates yet another change taking place.

> Luke 13:1 At that time some people who were present there told [Jesus] about the Galileans whose blood Pilate had mingled with the blood of their sacrifices. 2 He said to them in reply, "Do you think that because these Galileans suffered in this way they were greater sinners than all other Galileans? 3 By no means! But I tell you, if you do not repent, you will all perish as they did! 4 Or those eighteen people who were killed when the tower at Siloam fell on them — do you think they were more guilty than everyone

else who lived in Jerusalem? <u>5</u> By no means! But I tell you, if you do not repent, you will all perish as they did!"

Jesus is questioning whether someone can interpret negative occurrences in someone's life in a negative light, that is, as a curse (from God) on them. The account above seems to suggest that things happen to people, which should not be interpreted positively or negatively with regard to punishing someone's lack of righteousness, but one ought always to be ready to answer for one's life at any given moment. Appreciating sufferings or difficulties as growth opportunities sent by God is found throughout the Old Testament, as is also the sense of Retributive Justice. But I would suggest that the Book of Wisdom, written around the first century BC, dramatically illustrates the collision among several value systems, and the implications that such collisions bring about.

The Book of Wisdom and Two Value Systems at Odds

The biblical sense of God's intervention in the life of the people of Israel is too lengthy to examine here. I believe, however, that a broader belief in the afterlife impacts one's appreciation of how to interpret the blessings or values of this life, especially in light of the suffering that human beings perpetrate against one another. At least two value systems are at odds in the Book of Wisdom. Representatives of a value system that reflects neither Retributive Justice nor the "laissez-faire" understanding of Jesus speak first.[130]

> <u>Wis. 2:4</u> Even our name will be forgotten in time, and no one will recall our deeds. So our life will pass away like the traces of a cloud, and will be dispersed like a mist. Pursued by the sun's rays and overpowered by its heat. <u>5</u> For our lifetime is the passing of a shadow; and our dying cannot be deferred because it is fixed with a seal; and no one returns. <u>6</u> Come, therefore, let us enjoy the good things that are real, and use the freshness of creation avidly. <u>7</u> Let us have our fill of costly wine and perfumes, and let no

---

[130] We must recognize that the author is presenting both views, so they will be skewed to express a specific perspective. We admit this from the outset.

springtime blossom pass us by; 8 let us crown ourselves with rosebuds ere they wither. 9 Let no meadow be free from our wantonness; everywhere let us leave tokens of our rejoicing, for this our portion is, and this our lot. 10 Let us oppress the needy just man; let us neither spare the widow nor revere the old man for his hair grown white with time. 11 But let our strength be our norm of justice; for weakness proves itself useless. 12 Let us beset the just one, because he is obnoxious to us; he sets himself against our doings, Reproaches us for transgressions of the law and charges us with violations of our training.

From this reading, we can see that life is fleeting and pointless (v. 4). There is no enduring legacy, either through perpetuation of one's name (v. 4) nor is there an afterlife understood (v. 5). Life lends itself to use of creation for pursuing pleasure (vv. 7-9). Strength is the dominant value (v. 11a). Those who do not have strength: the widow, old, and weak, should be oppressed by the strong (vv. 10, 11b). This is the way of the world. The just man is oppressed by the strong (v.12). This is the world of the strong, which is at odds with that of "the just one," subsequently presented.

Wis. 3:1 But the souls of the just are in the hand of God, and no torment shall touch them. 2 They seemed, in the view of the foolish, to be dead; and their passing away was thought an affliction 3 and their going forth from us, utter destruction. But they are in peace. 4 For if before men, indeed, they be punished, yet is their hope full of immortality; 5 Chastised a little, they shall be greatly blessed, because God tried them and found them worthy of himself. 6 As gold in the furnace, he proved them, and as sacrificial offerings he took them to himself. 7 In the time of their visitation they shall shine, and shall dart about as sparks through stubble; 8 They shall judge nations and rule over peoples, and the LORD shall be their King forever 10 But the wicked shall receive a punishment to match their thoughts, since they neglected justice and forsook the LORD. 11 For he who despises wisdom and instruction is doomed. Vain is their hope, fruitless are their labors, and worthless are their works. 12 Their wives are foolish and their children wicked; accursed is their brood. 13 Yes, blessed is she who, childless and undefiled, knew not transgression of the marriage bed; she shall bear fruit at the visitation of souls. 15 For the fruit of noble struggles is a glorious one; and unfailing is the root of understanding. 16 But the children of adulterers will remain without issue, and the progeny of an unlawful bed will disappear. 17 For should they attain long life, they will be held in no esteem, and dishonored will their old age be at last; 18 While should they die abruptly, they have no hope nor comfort in the day of scrutiny; 19 for dire is the end of the wicked generation.

Wis. 4:1 Better is childlessness with virtue; for immortal is its memory: because both by God is it acknowledged, and by men.

Death is viewed on the part of those in the first passage as punishment in their eyes (vv. 2-3). We see that the traditional values are still in play here, but they are re-evaluated. Verses 13 and 15 laud a childless woman with virtue, whereas, the children of sinners are doomed (vv. 16; 4:1), not having a good reputation (v. 17), even if their lives be long. There is a sense of an afterlife, which casts the former values in a new light. One's conduct in this life matters and impacts one's eternal reward (vv. 18-19). It is no longer a simple task to discern if wealth, long life, children, and reputation are coming from God or simply from the natural course of human interactions. Together with this, there is an appreciation of deeper values, which are brought out from a person through suffering: "As gold in the furnace, he proved them, and as sacrificial offerings he took them to himself" (3:6). Gold is heated to high temperatures in order to burn off impurities. Suffering is viewed through this metaphor. Justice, virtue, and faithfulness are some of the values that are celebrated in this passage, as we can recognize a change in perspective. But we can also appreciate that those with no sense of these values are described as inflicting suffering on those who are just in the eyes of God. *Those inflicting harm are necessary for the just to manifest their virtues. Suffering takes on a role of being able to purify a person's intent and virtues.* In other words, things are not how they appear to the undiscerning eye, but a movement from one stage of life to another brings a different perspective.

Betrayal

We as Catholics tend to downplay it, but part of the Eucharistic ritual is the sense of betrayal found in the "Words of Institution," those words used by Christ when he celebrated the Last Supper with his Apostles. They begin, "On the night he was betrayed...." Judas is, of course, the betrayer, but his part to play in the drama is kept in the margins, as he remains unnamed.[131] However, we should appreciate the role of betrayal, since it is found frequently in the Old Testament.

James Hillman, a Jungian psychologist, in his essay entitled "Betrayal," comes at the subject of betrayal from an archetypical perspective, citing episodes from Greek mythology as he also notes stories from the Old Testament that have betrayal at their heart.[132]

> Since the expulsion [from the Garden], the Bible records a history of betrayals of many sorts: Cain and Abel, Jacob and Esau, Laban, Joseph sold by his brothers and their father deceived, Pharaoh's broken promises, calf-worship behind Moses' back, Saul, Samson, Job, God's rages and the creation almost annulled—and on and on, culminating in the central myth of our culture: the betrayal of Jesus.[133]

But I believe that we can look at betrayal from a simpler perspective and still gain insight. Betrayal is the recognition that whatever "structure" bound a person to another, that is, an institution, family, union, group, or other relationship, is never one hundred percent sure or secure. The implication is that betrayal is an opportunity for individuation against the backdrop of friendship, partnership, etc., as we saw above in the Book of Wisdom. "Relationships" are abstract concepts, which have no real existence apart from human to human interactions. As we've seen earlier, the more one adopts the identity of the group-ego, the more one loses oneself. Betrayal helps a person to recognize that institutions have gaps and are insecure, which is the nature of anything having to do with the

---

[131] See Matt 24:10; 26:21, 23; Mark 14:18; Luke 22:21; John 6:64, 71; 12:4; 13:11, 21; 21:20.

[132] James Hillman, "Betrayal," 69.

[133] Hillman, "Betrayal," 64. See also Ps 55: "If an enemy had reviled me, that I could bear; If my foe had viewed me with contempt, from that I could hide. But it was you, my other self, my comrade and friend, You, whose company I enjoyed, at whose side I walked in procession in the house of God" (vv. 13-15).

ego or, in this case, the group-ego.

In light of this type of understanding, Hillman appreciates an interior conviction that the sting of betrayal, seen played out exteriorly, points to an inner questioning of one's own willingness to betray oneself.

> What one longs for is a situation where one is protected from one's OWN treachery and ambivalence.... In other words, primal trust in the paternal world means being in that Garden with God and all things but Eve. The primeval world is pre-Eve, as it is also pre-evil. To be one with God in primal trust offers protection from one's own ambivalence.... We want a Logos security where the word is Truth and it cannot be shaken. We are led to an essential truth about both trust and betrayal: they contain each other.... We can be truly betrayed only where we truly trust—by brothers, lovers, wives, husbands, not by enemies, not by strangers. The greater the love and loyalty, the involvement and commitment, the greater the betrayal. [134]

Commitment to another determines the level of betrayal possible. An enemy is expected to betray, whereas, a friend is not. It is this sense that Hillman is exposing, at the same time that he recognizes the level of trust that must be present in order to appreciate being betrayed. It is appropriate that Jesus was betrayed by Judas' kiss. We saw earlier in the chapter on "the Absence of the Good" that betrayal comes from the sources where we would least expect it. Trust opens up the opportunity for betrayal. This is the nature of any opening to the heart: it can also be an opening to a negative situation.

Hillman continues:

> [Primal] trust will be broken if relationships are to advance; and, moreover, that the primal trust will not just be outgrown. There will be a crisis, a break characterized by betrayal, which according to the tale is the sine qua non for the expulsion from Eden into the 'real' world of human consciousness and responsibility.

---

[134] Hillman, "Betrayal," 65-66.

For we must be clear that to live or love only where one can trust, where there is security and containment, where one cannot be hurt or let down, where what is pledged in words is forever binding, means really to be out of harm's way and so to be out of real life.

The broken promise or broken trust is at the same time a breakthrough onto another level of consciousness.[135]

In effect, we can see that, when trust is betrayed, we can either walk away or we can embrace a different level of trust that no longer involves what we perceived to be important. But we cannot leave this topic without recognizing that broken trust can also lead to blockages for someone who is not willing or ready to move from one level to another level of consciousness.

A woman confessed to seeking out child pornography, which she found strange. She seemed to be drawn to it, though she had experienced incest as a child. She wondered where God was during her ordeal. She was fed up with psychology and wanted everything to be over.

This woman needed a professional to assist her in dealing with the "absence of the good" that she had experienced. No one can expect a child to be able to process such an incident emotionally without such assistance. This circumstance, however, would block this woman from leading a "normal" life, unless a professional assisted her.

The alienation from one's self after betrayal is largely protective.... For it was just through this trust in these fundamentals of one's own nature that one was betrayed.... We are rather like Judas or Peter in *letting down the essential thing,*

---

[135]Hillman, "Betrayal," 66-67. Hillman ("Betrayal," 79-80) writes further on the topic: "Psychologically, carrying a sin means simply recognizing it, remembering it. All the emotions connected with the betrayal experience in both parties—remorse and repentance in the betrayer, resentment and revenge in the betrayed—press towards the same psychological point: remembering."

the essential important demand to take on and carry one's own suffering and be what one is no matter how it hurts.[136]

Hillman is here talking about "carrying" or "holding" one's own suffering. The breach of relationship leads one to experience pain—something that is inevitable in everyone's life, but, as we have discussed earlier, can be arrested by trauma. By avoiding pain, we avoid growth. By holding our sufferings, however, we are able to expand our horizons and grow emotionally. The point of this expansion of our hearts is, of course, to grow in compassion, which means being compassionate with oneself first. Suffering with others (loving them as they are) can only occur when someone is ready to appreciate the commonness of suffering. Individual sufferings widen our abilities and capacity, whereas, fleeing from such occurrences closes us in on ourselves. Forgiveness is the outcome for holding our sufferings.

> It may well be that betrayal has no other positive outcome but forgiveness, and that the experience of forgiveness is possible only if one has been betrayed. Such forgiveness is a forgiving which is not a forgetting, but *the remembrance of wrong transformed within a wider context*, or as Jung has put it, that salt of bitterness transformed to the salt of wisdom.... Wisdom would here take to be that union of love with necessity where feeling finally flows freely into one's fate, reconciling us with an event.
>
> Just as trust had within it the seed of betrayal, so betrayal has within it the seed of forgiveness.... *Neither trust nor forgiveness could be fully realized without betrayal.*[137]

We must, of course, call to mind the Our Father prayer: "Our Father, ..., forgive us our trespasses, as we forgive those who trespass against us...." God measures our capacity for forgiveness by the capacity and openness that we are willing to extend to others. Jesus also says: "Give and gifts will be given to you; a good measure, packed together, shaken down, and overflowing, will be poured into your lap. For the measure with which

---

[136] Hillman, "Betrayal," 73-74. Emphasis his.
[137] Hillman, "Betrayal," 78-79. Emphasis his.

you measure will in return be measured out to you" (Luke 6:38).

> It is a strange experience to find oneself betraying oneself, turning against one's own experience by giving them the negative values of the shadow and by acting against one's own intentions and value system. In the break-up of a friendship, partnership, marriage, love-affair, or analysis, suddenly the nastiest and dirtiest appears and one finds oneself acting in the same blind and sordid way that one attributes to the other, and justifying one's own actions with an alien value system. One is truly betrayed, handed over to an enemy within. And the swine turn and rend you.[138]

We need to come from a deeper place in order to offset the impact of betrayal as Hillman presents above. The Spirit of God and Its penetration of our depths are the only way to address this darkness or shadow living within each of us.

> If we don't allow the Spirit of God to address the deep levels of our attachments to ourselves and to our programs for happiness, we will pour into the world the negative elements of our self-centeredness, adding to the conflicts and social disasters that come from over-identifying with the biases and prejudices of our particular culture and upbringing. This is becoming more important as we move into a global culture and into the increasing pluralism of religious beliefs.[139]

Betrayal also lets us see who we really are as our individuated selves. This is where the group-ego can no longer sustain us. The pain of betrayal (and others, too) pushes us to re-examine who we are in light of external encounters. God moves front and center, as we relate to the one who invites us to a deeper level of self and experience.

> Instead of finding support that will back up our own belief system, we might look more profitably for the self differentiation that enables us to be fully ourselves, with the acceptance of our

---

[138] Hillman, "Betrayal," 73.
[139] Keating, *The Human Condition*, 36.

limitations.... The latter, under normal conditions, is responsible for his or her choices.[140]

Responsiveness and responsibility are not owed to institutions anymore in the Stage of Authenticity; they are recognized as our life's blood. The prophecy from Ezekiel that God's Law would be written on our hearts becomes a reality (Ezek 35:25-27). We are not individuals with no connection to anyone, where our motto is "whoever dies with the most toys wins." We are individuated persons who recognize an underlying connection with everyone, with God at the center. The ego needs to be put in its place in order to help us to recognize what our true purpose is. Our true self must emerge as the director of our lives as we move in concert with the other "players" in this symphony called life.

We look again to Fr. Keating for a description of the movement from the Stage of the Ego to the Stage of Authenticity.

> We spend the first part of our lives finding a role—becoming a father or mother, a professor, a doctor, a minister, a soldier, a businessperson, and artisan, or whatever. The paradox is that we can never fully fulfill our role until we are ready to let it go. Whoever we think we are, we are not. We have to find that out, and the best way to do so, or at least the most painless way, is through the process that we call the spiritual journey. This requires facing the dark side of our personality and the emotional investment we have made in false programs for happiness and in our particular cultural conditioning....

> Rest in Centering Prayer provides us with profound healing. To be really healed requires that we allow our dark side to come to full consciousness and then to let it go and give it to God. The divine therapy is an agreement that we make with God. We recognize that our own ideas of happiness are not going to work, and we turn our lives over completely to God.[141]

---

[140] Keating, *The Human Condition*, 36-37.
[141] Keating, *The Human Condition*, 35. This last statement about

I have noted in the lives of several people who have approached me for spiritual direction that they come at these cusps in their lives: the break with the ego, their desire to live life in authenticity, and the Stage of Surrender. However, I also see that people come to a break-through point and attempt to ignore it. They try to regain what they need to leave behind, so people become new mothers and fathers at mid-life, when typically a more authentic existence is dawning. I have also noted that in every case that I have seen, some person or environment or condition (addiction/co-dependence) is holding them back. I can also note from my personal and professional life many people who hold on to the egoic life and do not convert or go deeper, because they do not want to give up what their present religious tradition offers them in terms of reputation or networking or the four traditional blessings. Conversion is appreciated by these people as a way to realize a more authentic life, but, as the call comes, they think that they will lose too much to go forward. God takes all of us where we are, but a lack of integrity or faith must also be acknowledged. The organic need for a deeper experience of life and God can be avoided, and often is, for many different reasons, some unknown due to pathology, and some quite clear due to the hold that the ego has on the person's life. The question that everyone must ask himself or herself is: Is it worth it? Without faith at a deeper level than the surface, this movement is impossible. If the egoic values as stated above have been one's only way of life, then it is well nigh impossible, especially for those who have benefited from the four values and God's connection with them has been remote, if not questionable. They have relied upon their own devices and equated such success falsely with God's blessings. It is a fearful thing to place oneself in God's hands, when one has never done this before. Courage is an

---

"[turning] our lives over completely to God" refers to the third stage of life, namely, surrender. This stage occurs around the time of retirement or when one's health fails. One turns everything over to God and recognizes a new level of freedom.

exceptional virtue.

Centering: A Deeper Prayer

Fr. Basil Pennington, the late Trappist monk of St. Joseph's Abbey in Spencer, MA, was one of the founders of the revival of Centering Prayer.[142] He gave a lecture on "the Contemplative Attitude" in 1981.[143] During that talk, and subsequent ones on the topic, he recognized that, if we did not do something to get to a deeper level of prayer, then he believed nuclear holocaust was inevitable. Though his fear has not been realized, we can certainly not view the current state of affairs as anything but wrought with crisis. Solutions to problems will only manifest themselves from the experience of a deeper state of being. Two business practices of this year (2014) reflect the need for such a change in how we conduct ourselves. 1. General Motors' revelation that a record number of cars needed recalls, but, due to cover-ups, such recalls were put off for years as people died. 2. The discovery that Veterans Administration officials were falsifying service delivery wait times, as some veterans died while waiting. These business models are dishonest and corrupt. They come from the mind-set of people seeking egotistical ends. We cannot look to such spiritually and morally bankrupt people as these for solutions facing our communities, nation, and world. Spiritual and emotional childishness has sadly become normative. Even the Church has sometimes been complicit with such values.

Fr. Keating understands the purpose of Centering Prayer as a way of dealing with the unconscious. He holds that, spending sessions in the

---

[142] Fr. Thomas Keating, Fr. Joseph Meninger, and Fr. Basil Pennington, all of St. Joseph's Abbey, Spencer, MA, have presented or written on Centering Prayer within various venues.

[143] Fr. Basil Pennington, "The Contemplative Attitude" (Kansas City, MO: National Catholic Reporter, 1981). Fr. Pennington cites Thomas Merton and his writings as the actual source for his understanding of Centering Prayer during this lecture. Merton (*New Seeds of Contemplation*, 227) writes: "A door opens in the center of our being and we seem to fall through it into immense depths which, although they are infinite, are all accessible to us; all eternity seems to have become ours in this one placid and breathless contact."

Presence of God, simply "wasting time on God," will bring up the irrational unconscious. He states that this must be offered to God.

As someone who has practiced Centering Prayer for years, I can attest to its "efficacy," though we should appreciate this as a positive by-product. I have also noticed that my unexpressed "needs" often tend to take care of themselves, and family members tend to benefit as well without vocal intercessory prayer. I describe that it is as though the Lord reads my heart, as one's beloved would do, when people are very close. Other people who practice Centering Prayer, including Fr. Pennington, note similar experiences. However, keeping goals out of the equation can be a difficult task for those with ego-based understandings.

> A permanent deacon in his early sixties, who had had many spiritual directors, but who was left without any support after they all died, sought out someone to direct his spiritual life. He recognized that something was missing, given that he was busy with ministry for much of the day and week. He needed something to get him focused, so that, should the need arise, he would be able to do even more if the situation warranted. He faithfully said many devotional prayers, the Divine Office, and followed a Carmelite method of meditation, though he admitted that he was just saying prayers, not praying.

This deacon needs to commune with God. He admitted that he was ego-based in his focus, which means, even at his age, he had not yet moved to the Stage of Authenticity. I encouraged him to practice Centering Prayer, which he had reservations about, which he admitted later on was intense fear of God. I suggested that Centering Prayer would help him "to waste time on God," so that God could transform him. He asked about the goal of the prayer—an ego-based concern. I asked him why he had married his wife, and he said that it was to start a family, a typical response. I asked him if he saw his wife as a baby-making machine? He laughed, "Of course not." I invited him to recognize that his time spent with God would be as fruitful for his interior life as his married life had been with his wife. It's about getting to know a person. If this is a goal, so be it, but it seems to defy such a pat definition.

Using this prayer to achieve a goal is counter to its purpose. Seeking God for himself is its purpose; everything else is a by-product. Such an encounter will transform in a way unique to the individual, since God knows what's best for the person. But I also believe that Fr. Keating is overly optimistic in one's ability to deal with one's unconscious. I was guided into using the prayer decades ago, but I never recognized what it was about until I read Fr. Keating's book, *The Human Condition*, where he summarizes what is going on. The suggestion that someone will *obviously* understand the troublesome thoughts that come up in Centering Prayer and recognize what to do with them seems a stretch. Nonetheless, having encountered them, I am now in a position to offer them to God. This takes me beyond my darkness into the deeper darkness of God, which is the source of all Light.

Conclusion

We are attempting to deal with problems in our selves, our families, workplaces, nations, and even the world, without recognizing our own darkness and our need for God, for healing, and for compassion on ourselves, which we can then share with others. If we are living egotistical lives, we may never see a way beyond this reality and we may constantly be attempting to formulate plans of attack to "win" against our darkness, projected on the latest scapegoat: Isis, terrorists, or child immigrants from Central America, who "threaten" to take what is ours. Our unconscious is non-rational. Why would anyone believe that a rational approach could combat something that is not rational? God and religious and archetypal meaning are beyond the realm of the rational. Their help takes us beyond the realm of the ego, which stands in the way of depth of meaning and the ability to respond to problems from a deeper level of being and consciousness. Revolution is inevitable in this country should we not move to a deeper level. Schism is in the air as we deny Christ's statement: "You cannot serve God and mammon." This truth comes from the Way, the Truth, and the Life. We are called to more. It's about time our leaders invited us to partake of it, but that would require that they venture there first. A true leader is willing to recognize the hard work required by the present that will bear fruit in the future. If a child prodigy can do it on the piano, why can our politicians and religious leaders not do the same?

We close with an invitation from St. Anselm (ca. 1033-1109), Bishop of Canterbury.

> Insignificant man, escape from your everyday business for a short while, hide for a moment from your restless thoughts. Break off from your cares and troubles and be less concerned about your tasks and labors. Make a little time for God and rest a while in him.[144]

---

[144] From Saint Anselm, *Proslogion*, Cap. 97-100, *Opera Omnia*, Edit. Scmitt, Secovii, 1938, in *Liturgy of the Hours* (4 vols.; New York: Catholic Book, 1975), 1. 184.

15 JOHN THE BAPTIST AS LEADER

Introduction

John the Baptist is celebrated in the Church through several feasts commemorating his significance in salvation history. He was a forerunner of Christ and pointed the way to him. He did not perform any miracles himself (John 10:41), but led his life in accordance with God's will as a quest to prepare the way of the Lord. His life serves as a model for qualities that we should exhibit in carrying out God's will ourselves.

Luke 3:7-19

The statements found about John the Baptist in chapter three of the Gospel of Luke are unique in the New Testament in that they offer the lengthiest statements attributed to him, which most scholars believe reflect his actual words, or at least a close rendering of them.

> Luke 3:7 [John the Baptist] said to the multitudes that came out to be baptized by him, "You brood of vipers! Who warned you to flee from the wrath to come? 8 Bear fruits that befit repentance, and do not begin to say to yourselves, 'We have Abraham as our father'; for I tell you, God is able from these stones to raise up children to Abraham. 9 Even now the axe is laid to the root of the trees; every tree therefore that does not bear good fruit is cut down and thrown into the fire."

Luke 3:10 And the multitudes asked him, "What then shall we do?" 11 And he answered them, "He who has two coats, let him share with him who has none; and he who has food, let him do likewise." 12 Tax collectors also came to be baptized, and said to him, "Teacher, what shall *we* do?" 13 And he said to them, "Collect no more than is appointed you." 14 Soldiers also asked him, "And we, what shall *we* do?" And he said to them, "Rob no one by violence or by false accusation, and be content with your wages."

Luke 3:15 As the people were in expectation, and everyone questioned in their hearts concerning John, whether perhaps he were the Christ, 16 John answered them all, "I baptize you with water; but he who is mightier than I is coming, the thong of whose sandals I am not worthy to untie; he will baptize you with the Holy Spirit and with fire. 17 His winnowing fork is in his hand, to clear his threshing floor, and to gather the wheat into his granary, but the chaff he will burn with unquenchable fire."

Luke 3:18 So, with many other exhortations, he preached good news to the people. 19 But Herod the tetrarch, who had been reproved by him for Herodias, his brother's wife, and for all the evil things that Herod had done, 20 added this to them all, that he shut up John in prison.

The first block (vv. 7-9) describes people coming to John the Baptist to be baptized. Purification by water was not a novelty to Jews. Pools for performing a *miqbah* or ritual purifications have been found throughout Israel at least from the period of the first century. One would enter a pool of water via steps in an unclean state and emerge from the pool ritually clean on the other side of it. The ritual act of submersion in water is symbolic of dying to an old self (through symbolic drowning), as the water washes the outside of the body clean. The people are coming to John the Baptist in light of his preaching about upcoming eschatological events, so that they may be ritually clean for the event, achieved by repentance of their sins and the ritual act of baptism that John is performing. The difference is that they are permitting John to effect the rite upon them; those who performed *miqbah* ablutions did so to themselves.

In v. 7, John mentions "the wrath to come." This is a cataclysmic event that would inaugurate the "end times," when there would be great upheaval brought about by the hand of God. John denounces those who believe that their hereditary connection through their bloodline with Abraham is sufficient to save them from the negative consequences of immoral conduct in light of the wrath (v. 8). Instead, he insists that deeds demonstrating an interior change are necessary to show true repentance and thus salvation from the wrath to come. God's power to "raise up children to Abraham" from stones (an act achievable solely by God) is contrasted with the human generative process of procreation.[145] Additionally, those who do not produce "good fruit" are contrasted with those who do, in that those who engage in wrong-doing will be thrown into the fire. John sees that repentance must produce fruit, that is, have deeds that issue from it, for it to be considered of real or lasting worth.

The second block of verses, vv. 10-14, coheres around the theme of ethical conduct, as it presents three groups of people asking John what they should do in their lives to reflect a repentant life. First, the multitudes ask what they should do (v. 10). John tells them that they should share what they have with those in need (v. 11). Second, tax collectors approach him with the same question (v. 12). Tax collectors offered the Romans a sum of money to collect taxes for them, and the area collection would go to the highest bidder. The tax collector would need to recoup his costs with a profit. John invites them to keep their tax collection business, but understood is that they should not defraud people paying their taxes in order to obtain a profit (v. 13). Third, soldiers ask

---

[145] Weddell (*Forming Intentional Disciples*, 27-28) writes: "In contrast, Catholic pastoral practice still assumes that religious identity is largely inherited and stable throughout one's life span. So firm is our sense of Catholicism as a 'faith into which one is born' that many Catholics are surprised to discover that millions of their brothers and sisters are converts. What we have taken as normative is, in fact, the far end of the 'religious bell curve.' Catholicism has the second highest percentage of 'native' members of any major faith in the United States. All other US faiths, with the exception of Hinduism, have a higher percentage of converts, including Judaism, Orthodoxy, Islam, mainline Protestantism, and Buddhism."

him the same question (v. 14a), and he tells them not to use their position to intimidate and extort people so as to supplement their income. Soldiers serve in a specific capacity, which he does not denounce. Instead, John encourages the soldiers not to use their position to bully people or to obtain "security money," given that they have weapons for use, and Palestine at this time is a police state under Roman occupation. They are also not to use their positions to bear false witness to influence imprisonment or other punishments on the people under occupation.

The third block of verses, vv. 15-17, centers around whether John the Baptist is the expected anointed one, the Christ (Greek) or Messiah (Hebrew), who would come to inaugurate God's rule on earth. (We will take this up further below.) John denies that he is this expected figure. By his own admission, he is, instead, insignificant in comparison with that figure, not worthy even to untie the thong of that person's sandal (v. 16). He further notes that he has been baptizing with water, whereas the new figure will baptize "with the Holy Spirit and with fire." This statement is followed with the image of separating wheat from chaff, where the wheat (the fruit) is kept, whereas the chaff (the husk) will be burned. The Holy Spirit or divine power that this figure will use will be superior to what John effects, as purification by fire is superior to purification by washing. For example, gold is heated to high temperatures to burn off impurities. The level and depth of purification occurring seems to be the point of the difference between John's baptism and the purification effected by the coming figure.

John preached this "good news" to the people (v. 18), meaning that the people were encouraged that they no longer had to be mired in their sins, but could repent of them and be made right with God through John's baptism. John the Baptist preached the good news to people in all walks of life: the multitude, tax collectors, and soldiers, and he also confronted Herod about taking Herodias, his brother Philip's wife, as his own (v. 19). Herod, in turn, put John into prison because of this (v. 20).

Summary of Luke 3:7-20

We see that John the Baptist spoke with conviction and authenticity to such an extent that people from all walks of life came to hear him and to be baptized by him. The people thought that he was the one whom they expected, namely, the Messiah or Christ, but he made it clear that he was not this figure. In humility, he accepted his place as someone in a lesser category from the figure whom the multitudes were expecting. John noted that the figure coming after him would purify in a way that was superior to his baptism. He, therefore, accepted his place and spoke his truth, which was "good news" for the people, but it did not sound like good news to those who were in power, namely, Herod the tetrarch nor those who did not produce the fruit of repentance in their lives.

John the Baptist was imprisoned for making known that Herod had married his brother Philip's wife, Herodias. The truth may set a person free at an interior level (John 8:32; 14:6), but it can also have political consequences for those who are in power and want to appear ethical. Nonetheless, John the Baptist spoke the truth: Everyone knew it, though their actions and reactions betray how welcome it was in their lives.

Thomas Merton offers this thought about the place of purification.

> Therefore if you spend your life trying to escape from the heat of the fire that is meant to soften and prepare you to become your true self, and if you try to keep your substance from melting in the fire—as if your true identity were to be hard wax—the seal will fall upon you at last and crush you. You will not be able to take your own true name and countenance, and you will be destroyed by the event that was meant to be your fulfillment.[146]

Purification, then, is meant over time to help us become more pliant to God's will rather than our own. It takes recognizing sinful actions and their implications. It also takes a change of heart, so that we deliver fruit from the reality of its experience. If there is no fruit, then true repentance remains elusive. Purification is a process, not a one-shot occurrence.

Mark 6:14-29

Mark's Gospel has the most detailed version of the events leading up to John's death at the hands of Herod. We examine this passage for what it

---

[146] Merton, *New Seeds of Contemplation*, 161.

reveals about King Herod and what affects his decisions and actions.

> Mark 6:14   King Herod heard of [Jesus's fame and inquired about him]. Some said, "John the baptizer has been raised from the dead; that is why these powers are at work in him." 15 But others said, "It is Elijah." And others said, "It is a prophet, like one of the prophets of old." 16 But when Herod heard of [all of this] he said, "John, whom I beheaded, has been raised." 17 For Herod had sent and seized John, and bound him in prison for the sake of Herodias, his brother Philip's wife; because he had married her. 18 For John said to Herod, "It is not lawful for you to have your brother's wife." 19 And Herodias had a grudge against him, and wanted to kill him. But she could not, 20 for Herod feared John, knowing that he was a righteous and holy man, and kept him safe. When he heard him, he was much perplexed; and yet he heard him gladly. 21 But an opportunity came when Herod on his birthday gave a banquet for his courtiers and officers and the leading men of Galilee. 22 For when Herodias' daughter came in and danced, she pleased Herod and his guests; and the king said to the girl, "Ask me for whatever you wish, and I will grant it." 23 And he vowed to her, "Whatever you ask me, I will give you, even half of my kingdom." 24 And she went out, and said to her mother, "What shall I ask?" And she said, "The head of John the baptizer." 25 And she came in immediately with haste to the king, and asked, saying, "I want you to give me at once the head of John the Baptist on a platter." 26 And the king was exceedingly sorry; but because of his oaths and his guests he did not want to break his word to her. 27 And immediately the king sent a soldier of the guard and gave orders to bring his head. He went and beheaded him in the prison, 28 and brought his head on a platter, and gave it to the girl; and the girl gave it to her mother. 29 When his disciples heard of it, they came and took his body, and laid it in a tomb.

Several figures are expected in the minds of the people during the period when John the Baptist and Jesus walked the earth—all of them prophets. Because of the miraculous deeds that Jesus performs, some people believe that, in light of John's death, he is John the Baptist come back from the dead. Since, during his lifetime, John did not perform any miracles, it was thought that the power of resurrection effected miraculous deeds. Another expectation is the return of Elijah before the wrath of God comes (see Mal 3:23).[147] All of these prophetic figures are attempts to explain where Jesus gets his ability to perform miracles and his connection with John the Baptist.

When John told Herod that it was unlawful for him to take Herodias as his own wife, Herodias wanted to kill John (v. 19). But we see that "Herod feared John, knowing that he was a righteous and holy man, and kept him safe" (v. 20a). The ability to recognize the truth comes from a deeper insight than just comparisons with others about how they view things. John had touched that deeper sense for Herod, and Herod recognized it. Herodias, however, could not bear the truth, so she sought to eliminate the one who had dared to bring it to light.

"When [Herod] heard [John], he was much perplexed; and yet he heard him gladly" (v. 20). Herod appreciated the truth that John spoke, as well as his holiness and righteousness. John was the voice of truth, which oftentimes calls us to account. Our ability to accept the truth is dependent on many factors, but that Herod could appreciate what John said and who he was seems clear.

Herodias gets her chance to do John in through her daughter's dance at Herod's birthday banquet. Delighted by her performance, Herod vows to grant her whatever she desires, "even half of my kingdom." Herodias seizes the opportunity and tells her daughter to ask for John's head (v. 24b). Verse 26 describes the conundrum that Herod wrestles with: "[The] king was exceedingly sorry [that she made this request]; but because of his oaths and his guests he did not want to break his word to her." Herod keeps his word, believing that honesty means keeping it. However, the source of the request comes from a grudge against the truth. Honesty and

---

[147] In John's Gospel (1:19b ff.), priests and Levites from Jerusalem come to John inquiring whether he is "the prophet," which most likely denotes "the prophet like Moses" described in Deut 18:15ff. See also 4:25-26. The Gospel of Matthew mentions Jeremiah the Prophet by name (16:14) as an expected figure to return.

truth are thus used to placate hurt feelings; the consequences are fatal for the bearer of good news.

Additionally, the manner in which Herod portrays himself to his invited guests is of paramount importance, not the truth that has been his experience of John the Baptist. He has made an oath, not taking into account its full ramifications. Herod has been played like a fiddle, and John the Baptist loses his life because of it. King Herod's sense of truth, which came before John entered his life, is determined by his wish to placate his step-daughter and not lose face among the courtiers attending his birthday celebration. His capacity for truth was diminished as its deeper sense was replaced by immediate circumstances and his desire to please others.

Herod led as tetrarch; John led through an innate authenticity. Both exercised leadership. Ronald Heifetz and Marty Linsky of the Harvard Business School offer the following reflection on the implications of exercising leadership:

> To lead is to live dangerously because when leadership counts, when you lead people through difficult change, you challenge what people hold dear—their daily habits, tools, loyalties, and ways of thinking—with nothing more to offer than perhaps a possibility. Moreover, leadership often means exceeding the authority you are given to tackle the challenge at hand. People push back when you disturb the personal and institutional equilibrium they know. And people resist in all kinds of creative and unexpected ways that can get you taken out of the game: pushed aside, undermined, or eliminated.[148]

Though Heifetz and Linsky are talking about business, their words are poignant for Herod and John as well. Herod knew the truth, and it caused him pause. But the concerns drawing him away from an inner truth "compelled" him to act in an inauthentic way, which undermined the truth and ultimately cost John the Baptist his head. John the Baptist was collateral damage in Herod's attempt to placate those around him and

---

[148] Heifetz and Linsky, *Leadership on the Line*, 2.

maintain his image. Authentic leadership has serious implications. Anything else is play-acting. But both were drawing from a truth. The problem was that one was drawing from authenticity, the other from fraudulence.

Luke 7:18-30

In a third episode involving John the Baptist, we see that John seeks further clarification about Jesus and his deeds. Jesus, in turn, describes John's place in salvation history.

> Luke 7:18 The disciples of John told him of all these things [about Jesus]. 19 And John, calling to him two of his disciples, sent them to the Lord, saying, "Are you he who is to come, or shall we look for another?" 20 And when the men had come to him, they said, "John the Baptist has sent us to you, saying, 'Are you he who is to come, or shall we look for another?" 21 In that hour he cured many with diseases and plagues and evil spirits, and on many that were blind he bestowed sight. 22 And he answered them, "Go and tell John what you have seen and heard: the blind receive their sight, the lame walk, lepers are cleansed, and the deaf hear, the dead are raised up, the poor have good news preached to them. 23 And blessed is he who takes no offense at me."
>
> Luke 7:24 When the messengers of John had gone, he began to speak to the crowds concerning John: "What did you go out into the wilderness to behold? A reed shaken by the wind? 25 What then did you go out to see? A man clothed in soft clothing? Behold, those who are gorgeously appareled and live in luxury are in kings' courts. 26 What then did you go out to see? A prophet? Yes, I tell you, and more than a prophet. 27 This is he of whom it is written, 'Behold, I send my messenger before thy face, who shall prepare thy way before thee.' 28 I tell you, among those born of women none is greater than John; yet he who is least in the kingdom of God is greater than he." 29 (When they heard this all the people and the tax collectors justified God, having been baptized with the baptism of John; 30 but the Pharisees and the lawyers rejected the purpose of God for themselves, not having

been baptized by him.)

John the Baptist is awaiting "the one who is to come," which is an expression denoting the expected figure we discussed earlier.[149] He sends his disciples to Jesus to discover if he is, in fact, the one whom he is awaiting. Jesus does not tell John's disciples plainly, but instead invites them to share what they have seen with John, so that he can make his own decision about him. Jesus' identity is not caught up with titles or others' expectations. Many expectations seem to be floating around among various groups, but Jesus does not claim any of them, nor does he exactly fit any of them. All of them are pointers to a more profound truth. Jesus, using a beatitude or macarism, pronounces "blessed" the one who takes no offense at what he is doing. This is a far cry from making an assertion about his identity.

Jesus then describes John and his place as he speaks with the crowds about him. He questions them as to what their expectations were as they went out to the desert to see him. Were they looking for "a reed shaken by the wind," that is, a person who would bend at the slightest resistance? Or were they instead looking for someone in soft clothing, that is, someone who was familiar with luxury and the "courting" of opinions—someone found where positions are sought, and power is brokered? Jesus tells the people plainly that if they were looking for such a person, they were going to the wilderness with the wrong intention. John was a prophet by Jesus' own admission, yet he was more. Jesus asserts that it was about John that the statement from the Prophet Isaiah was intended: "Behold, I send my messenger before thy face, who shall prepare thy way before thee." John the Baptist is the one who prepares the way before the Lord when he comes. Jesus even describes John as the greatest human being, as he also recognizes that the "least in the kingdom of God is greater than he." The parenthetical remark in vv. 29-30 highlights that the tax collectors and people "justified God," because they had received baptism by John, recognizing that his message was authentic, whereas, the Pharisees and lawyers did not.[150] They doubted

---

[149] See Rev. Joseph A. Fitzmyer, SJ, *The One Who Is To Come* (Grand Rapids: Eerdmans, 2007), vii, 1-2.
[150] See Mark 11:30ff. and parr.

John's legitimacy, which is counter to what Jesus does.

Two different sources of power are reflected here: John the Baptist's and that of the Pharisees and lawyers. "The people" and those tax collectors here referenced recognized their need for repentance, as they also accepted the authenticity of what John had to say. He came from a place, the wilderness, where there was no other witness apart from God, and he appeared as one who did not come from the standard trappings of royalty or society. From every angle, at least as Jesus describes it, John reflected someone who was authentic in his living out his life according to God's plan. This was difficult for others to accept, and the Gospels demonstrate that he was not accepted.

In sum, then, we can see that John the Baptist lived out his truth in the following way:

> John the Baptist spoke the truth to everyone, regardless of position or station in life.
> He didn't sugarcoat the message that came from God.
> He pointed out that some people were not living repentance authentically, both those who had been baptized and those who had not been.
> He was practical in his assertions about what people needed to do to demonstrate repentance.
> He recognized his place and did not attempt to usurp the place of "the one who was to come."
> He appreciated what he offered, as he also appreciated the superiority of what "the one who was to come" would offer.
> John wondered if Jesus was "the one who was to come."
> As tough as the words were from John, they are still described as "good news."
> Both rank and file people, as well as royalty (Herod) recognized John's holiness and righteousness.
> Speaking the truth proved fatal for John; he was collateral damage as Herod catered to inauthentic desires, both from his wife and himself.
> Jesus recognizes that various types of people went to John. John's sense of integrity was clear, despite mistaken and misguided reasons for going to him.
> John was a prophet and also the greatest of human beings; however, those born into the kingdom of God are greater.

"In what does man's wretchedness actually consist?" asked Pope Benedict XVI. He answers that the root of human wretchedness is loneliness, the absence of love—the fact that our personal existence is not embraced by a love that makes our existence necessary. Our misery arises when we live without love strong enough to justify our existence no matter how much pain and limitation go along with it. What our heart is crying out for is a true companion in whose love we experience how truly necessary and valid and invaluable our existence is. John the Baptist preached a message that brought people to God, because they had lost the sense that God believed them to be "good enough" to return to him. The Christ-event will further elaborate about this message, but John's message is sufficient to recognize God's action to bring those who were far off back to him.

One of my favorite parables comes from Fr. Anthony De Mello's *The Heart of the Enlightened*, where he describes a prisoner in a concentration camp.[151]

> Once upon a time in a concentration camp there lived a prisoner who, even though he was under sentence of execution, was fearless and free. One day he was seen in the middle of the prison square playing his guitar. A large crowd gathered to listen, for under the spell of the music, they became as fearless as he. When the prison authorities saw this, they forbade the man to play.
>
> But the next day there he was again, singing and playing on his guitar with a larger crowd around him. The guards angrily dragged him away and had his fingers chopped off.
>
> Next day he was back, singing and making what music he could with his bleeding fingers. This time the crowds were cheering. The guards dragged him away again and smashed his guitar.
>
> The following day he was singing with all his heart. What a song! So pure and uplifting! The crowd joined in, and while the singing

---

[151] De Mello, The Heart of the Enlightened: A Book of Story-Meditations (New York: Image/Doubleday, 1991), 19.

lasted, their hearts became as pure as his and their spirits as invincible. So angry were the guards that this time they had his tongue torn out. A hush descended on the camp, a something that was deathless.

To the astonishment of everyone, he was back at his place the next day swaying and dancing to a silent music that no one but he could hear. And soon everyone was holding hands and dancing around this bleeding, broken figure in the center while the guards stood rooted to the ground in wonder.

We can appreciate that the prisoner knows his inner voice or true self and is not willing to let anyone or anything stand in the way of his ability to express it. It often means torture and, sadly, execution, because those who espouse the "truth" of the group-ego are innately insecure and wish to suppress or even eradicate anyone who calls them to accountability. They maintain their control of people and circumstances through disinformation, intimidation and violence. However, like Gandhi, Martin Luther King, Jr., Jesus, and John the Baptist, and countless others, some people have the innate sense of their own truth and value. They are a threat to those seeking to maintain the status quo, not because of what they do, but because of who they are. This is what makes them dangerous, revolutionaries, and a host of other derogatory and demonizing labels.

However, I wish to appreciate the exceptional quality of this type of witness to one's inner truth. The group-ego usually wins out. There are flashes of truth possible, which cause others to begin the process of working out their own truth. They fight the group-ego, but without directly doing so. Their innate sense of self or truth calls the group-ego and its values into question at the same time that such people work to build an infrastructure to foster the new growth and acceptance of truth. Max Weber (1864-1920), the German sociologist, noted in his monumental works that bureaucracy is the logical outcome as time progresses beyond the era of the founder of any group and the incorporation of the spirit of his or her charism takes place. Truth is sterilized into laws and practices which can never capture the essence of the person's truth, which can never be encapsulated, anymore than God can be. Those willing to be who they are will experience push-back from those who do not. Freedom comes with a price, but non-freedom's price is greater. People can tell you this, but one can only know it for oneself. This is the Passion. This is the Life of Christ. "It is no longer I who live, but Christ who lives in me," and Christ was crucified. He also rose from the dead.

One final question: Do you have the courage to be you?

CONCLUSION

If we were to examine the qualities of an ideal leader, we would probably observe qualities from all of the leadership types that we have examined. Narcissists have great vision and forward-thinking. As-if leaders recognize the need to ensure that whatever group we are speaking about, be it a family, an organization, a business, or a church, that it conducts itself according to external regulations, so that the norms of the group or organization are the rule, not the exception. The Talking Head understands that the "bottom line" matters or systems will cease to exist in the long run, so every system must be financially aware and be ready to use methods to trim what tends toward excess or is not working to preserve its future. Recovery means that honesty governs one's conduct and interactions, so an ideal leader is honest and has integrity both toward him or herself and one's charges. Ideal leaders respect those whom they lead and value their input and recognize that they are human beings themselves. Additionally, the ideal leader is ready to make the hard decisions and implement them, which may not be popular, but he or she knows that it is the ethically appropriate thing to do when assessing all variables under consideration. Ideal leaders do not take short-cuts, but grow their systems gradually, so as to achieve results in a human way, since human beings have limits and grow incrementally. Leaders sometimes limit expansion or growth for the good of the system.

The co-dependent leadership types that we initially explored have one thing in common: an inability to understand the place of emotion in the human equation. Emotions limit us, which is what makes us human. Only God is limitless, so ignoring or denying emotions ignores or denies our humanity. The leadership types that we examined are also unhealthy ways of dealing with situations and people. In worldly terms, the style may be successful in financial terms, but in human terms these types of people are disasters and they will wreak havoc, more or less, depending on the severity of their inability to deal with emotion, both on themselves and those whom they "touch" through their leadership. Compassion, love, mercy, or forgiveness, or a host of other correlative terms, will not be found in great quantities in these people. One's spiritual life rides piggyback on one's emotional awareness and depth, as Thomas Aquinas says, "grace perfects nature." To deny emotion is to be spiritually and morally bankrupt, since there is no basis in humanity for grace to alight. Spiritual "success" beyond the Stage of the Ego is unlikely without humiliations of marked variety, such as catastrophic illness, serious loss, gross impairment, a recovery program—or a miracle. These sick ways of dealing with others we may summarize under the heading of Bernard's Law, where the means to an end do not matter, so long as one is "successful" in achieving the result and regardless of collateral damage.

The arenas where we saw leadership styles operate were many, but so were the lessons learned. From Corporate America, we saw that when companies had not prepared for the competition of companies in Europe and Asia after World War II, they became cruel, attempting to address their lack of preparation by becoming ruthless. However, when we look inside some companies, we see that when competition is operative without restraint inside its walls it fares no better. Ego-based personnel making decisions operate in particular groupings, reminiscent of peer groups from earlier young-adult development. The adage, "birds of a feather flock together," conveys the sense that people with similar views will consort with one another. Such actions at the corporate level place people at odds with one another in competitive situations with counter-productive results. A leader coming from a deeper place, which is not a skill per se, but a state of being, is necessary to bridge the gap between factions. Someone who is able to confront conflict, appreciating its purpose, but who is also able to step out of the way of seeming opposites, is necessary to negotiate terms that stem from a deeper perspective. Such a person will not collude with the drama, so as to make the best decision for the system and its people possible. This scenario from the business world helped us to appreciate the debilitating nature of not having access to a deeper level for realizing long-term results instead of "get-rich" schemes. People coming from a deeper place change systems, but getting to a deeper place is wrought with problems.

Many experiences in our lives can have debilitating effects on us, so as to stymie our emotional growth, which, in turn, stands in the way of spiritual growth. There are certain aspects of our lives that, when so affected, lead to roadblocks. We have expectations from outside ourselves: society, culture, family, that reflect value systems that provide us with meaning. These value systems—group-egos—have trained us to question ourselves before we question them, especially in early development, because we lack interiority to handle life as it is. If this value system fails us, as, for example, when we experience "the absence of the good," then there will be additional trauma to overcome, but this must be done at the individual level. If we have experienced physical or emotional abuse, especially as children, then a child's emotional sense of an incident needs to be recognized and appreciated if any progress is to occur in getting beyond this blockage. This was the purpose of the story surrounding "black-dog syndrome." Additionally, we must recognize that group-egos will not accept correction until there is a critical mass of individuals to object to the trauma that the group-ego is inflicting on people, because too many take their identities from the group-ego.[152] The group-ego does not operate from a deeper level, hence one's only remedy is to stick it out and grow into oneself. This is the most effective weapon against any system unwilling to acknowledge the pain it has caused, but it is also a difficult, lonely, and isolated path to trod.

---

[152] The film *Selma* (2015 release) dramatizes the Civil Rights Movement as it pits the strategy of Martin Luther King, Jr., and his compatriots against the concerns of President Lyndon Johnson and those of Governor George Wallace of Mississippi. The media's ability to show live, unedited video footage from the march from Selma to Montgomery, MS, and the carnage that ensued, pit one opinion—one national group-ego—against another local group-ego in Mississippi. History shows the group-ego that became normative, though resistance will always exist.

Our belief systems can stand in the way of our growth as individuals as they offer limited approaches to recognize God as God, instead of relying on one's personal experience of God. I often tell people that Saints build ladders to heaven through spiritual practices and the living out of their lives. These can offer us helps to create our own ladders, but once a Saint arrives in Heaven, his or her ladder is destroyed. Everyone's ladder is unique. So too are our experiences. The Church can point the way to boundaries for appreciating God and right conduct, but people need to do the work of plodding their own paths within these guidelines, since no one can walk the way for another. Doing the hard work associated with advancing toward the Kingdom helps us to deepen our sense of self, which is what coming from a deeper place means.

When we talk about coming from a deeper place, we owe a debt to Carl Jung and his understanding of the Stages of Life. We noted that when one does not seek to come from a deeper place, through ignorance or deliberate acts, then superficiality and instinct remain our operative modes of interaction. We can make claims about Peter's faith, that he was coming from a deeper place, but this point did not ring true as we followed his reactions to the stimuli that came his way, until he came to the end of his life, when there was no alternative for him. This helped us to view Peter and ourselves in a new, yet more realistic, way. When the hype about his discipleship was stripped away, we could see him as an example of discipleship that more clearly reflected the path most of us also take toward discipleship—halting. We have spurts of fervor, but more often we become complacent in our lives and seek security, not constant change.

When the veneer of civilization is removed, and an atmosphere of cruelty or stress obtains, as, for instance, in a concentration camp or an experiment mirroring prison life, we demonstrate in raw truth what we are made of. Our "selves" as they emerge from behind any pretense, be they selves from the realm of the ego or the realm of authenticity, reflect how we have "handled" the lessons offered to us in our lives to date. Our willingness to permit them to affect us makes all the difference for growth. Accepting these lessons means acknowledging and dealing with our darkness and accepting ourselves with compassion. This is the seedbed for offering compassion to others and also to receiving it. This depth is necessary for anyone making the spiritual journey, but also living a life worth living. Many are the ways to avoid pain, suffering, and growth or seeking distractions. In order to foster a deepening within ourselves, we explored a deeper prayer form to deal with our darkness and unconscious through the practice of Centering Prayer. Centering Prayer or the Prayer of Quiet is a deeper communion with God not concerned with self-aggrandizement, but with the appreciation of God as God. The ego is not in charge; God is. "Wasting time on God" is the type of experience that brings about deep-seated change at one's root, which prepares a soul for movement to a deeper and more authentic level of being and living.

As we take the spiritual journey, we can have helps along the way, but if one does not hold one's sufferings oneself, then progress is impossible. Depth is replaced with superficiality. The unwillingness to deal with one's sufferings emotionally does not lead to a deeper place, nor to the Kingdom, and such avoidance will lead to damage in one's life and in the lives of others. We can accept others' actions as detrimental to our growth, or we can recognize in them opportunities for us to see ourselves as we truly are so as to gaze ever more lovingly and deeply on ourselves and others. When we experience someone's cruelty, it can offer us a learning opportunity and a way of purging ourselves of ego-based designs. The Book of Wisdom and its change in value system helped us to appreciate meaning in the sufferings that we may experience at the hands of others. Also consider: "But I say to you, offer no resistance to one who is evil. When someone strikes you on [your] right cheek, turn the other one to him as well" (Matt 5:39).

How we deal with betrayal and forgiveness, so much a part of our tradition, especially as we recount the Lord's betrayal at the Last Supper, leads us in a direction that begs for compassion for all parties concerned as we consider our own ability to betray and be betrayed. There are surely consequences to our actions, but we can recognize a deeper sense if we are able to get beyond our false selves and make our way to more authentic being.

John the Baptist closed out our work as we saw him carry out his mission in the desert to call people to repentance. They heeded his summons and came to him to have him baptize them in the Jordan River. They wanted to leave their former lives behind and lead God-centered lives, as they willingly confessed their sins and accepted John's baptism. John admitted that his was a baptism with water, but it was meaningful for so many, except for the professional clergy, who wondered the rationale behind why he was doing it (John 1:24) and who he thought he was in doing it (John 1:19). King Herod had a divided heart in listening to John, since he recognized John's authenticity in what he said, but the people around him and the trappings of the court hemmed in his ability to live from a deeper place. He chose to execute John rather than abandon the system that brought him great rewards and great inner turmoil. This would require courage. Co-dependents like King Herod and Herodias have no courage, because courage comes from a deeper place, where deeper values are at stake. Not even life itself can inhibit those living from a deeper level. As we saw in the Book of Wisdom: "The souls of the just are in the hand of God and no torment shall touch them." All of us cling to the ways of the false self, because we know no other way. Only the interiorly free are able to foster the growth of the true self and trod paths unique to them, though paradoxically all of these varied ways lead to the same Kingdom.

I was recently struck by the efforts of war veterans, whose connection in coming together was that each of them had had a limb or multiple limbs amputated because of injuries suffered due to their military deployments in the Middle East. Tim Medvetz, founder of the Heroes Project, was someone who had to confront his own physical problems after an accident left him with multiple metal plates in his body. Traditional rehabilitation would simply not work for him, so he set his sights on Mt. Everest. As the effort in climbing and reaching the summit changed him, so he set about bringing some veterans to the tallest peaks on the seven continents. The *60 Minutes* story, entitled simply, "Up," detailed the veterans' efforts to make their way to the tops of the mountains.[153] Their grueling efforts pay off in the experience of reaching the summits they

---

[153] "Up," *60 Minutes*, air date: 11 January 2015.

climb with Medvetz and others' help, though the physical climb is done by their own blood, sweat, and tears. It's a life-changing experience for all of them. They are overcoming more than just a mountain. All of them experienced depression, even suicide, attempting to see where life would take them. One veteran says, "Going through my injury, I lost myself; I was suicidal." Another responds: "[The achievement] answered it for me. Injury does not define my life."

These men were making the trek of the hero, which is the journey to selfhood, which recognizes limits, even possible death, but also recognizes the indomitable nature of the human spirit. The veterans cannot look at themselves again in the same way. Someone even says of them, "They forget that they have lost their legs." But I see the spiritual journey in their efforts, because their limitations may be physical, but there is always a way around the limitation. The physical aspect can seem insurmountable, until we face our fears, most especially appreciating who we are in some physical ability. These wounded warriors paid the price in suffering to get to the tops of those mountains—the physical was necessary, since it impacted their souls, they had to pull from so deep. Medvetz states during the piece, "At some point, [the climb] becomes more mental than physical." When a clear articulation of the problem is removed, as, for instance, through an inability to name one's suffering (the absence of the good) or when there is an oppression being (deliberately?) ignored, it makes this journey that much more difficult. It takes faith to make the leap to recognize that we are more than the hurts that have been done to us or that we have done to ourselves. Our true self cannot identify with these pains, hurts, difficulties, or limitations. We need to leave the false self behind, which does identify with such things. The True Self longs to sound forth its melody, unencumbered by the scars of the past, though acknowledging the past's reality, even if it is only I who does so.

The spiritual journey is one wrought with dangers at so many turns, from institutions, those leading sick lives, and those who are well meaning, but limited in their perspectives. All of these aspects feed on each other, because the most dangerous person in the world is not a terrorist or an enemy, it's the person who is truly unique, truly different, truly who God wishes that person to be. Such individuals call into question the systems that bring great prizes to those who benefit most from the systems' fruits. All of these prizes are external to oneself and can be taken away; this is how the system controls. The "pearl of great price" is something that cannot be taken away. This is what makes it most feared, not because of what one does with it, but because of who one is because of it. It's not a "something," it's a sense of one's being. When Jesus asked two disciples of John the Baptist what they were seeking, they answered, "Rabbi, ... where are you staying?" (John 1:38). They sought a person, the Messiah, who was going to lead them where they needed to go. Others tried to use crucifixion and other forms of murder and torture to eradicate Jesus and his message. Holy Week and Easter Sunday tell how well that plan worked. People will continue to develop plans to resist what is unknown. "The devil that you know is better than the devil that you don't," or so the saying goes for those who cling to the false self. The problem is: This spiritual journey leads to God. Will you let fear keep you back from your meeting?

APPENDIX I

Centering Prayer

Fr. Basil Pennington, Fr. Thomas Meninger, and Fr. Thomas Keating, all Trappist monks of St. Joseph's Abbey in Spencer, MA at the same time, worked collaboratively to foster the resurgence of a specifically monastic method of prayer known as Centering Prayer or the Prayer of Quiet.[154] Fr. Pennington, as noted above, cites Fr. Thomas Merton, the late monk of Our Lady of Gethsemani in Kentucky, as the impetus behind this prayer form.[155] It is based on the twelfth century book, *The Cloud of Unknowing*[156], by an unknown author. There the author suggests a simple way to pray.

---

[154] Fr. Thomas Meninger, OCSO, has an undated four-part cassette tape series entitled, "Contemplative Prayer: For God Is Love," produced at St. Joseph's Abbey, Spencer, MA. Fr. Thomas Keating, OCSO, has numerous works relating to Centering Prayer, among them: *Intimacy with God: An Introduction to Centering Prayer* (New York: Crossroad, 1994); *Awakenings* (New York: Crossroad, 1990) and *Reawakenings* (New York: Crossroad, 1992).

[155] Fr. M. Basil Pennington, OCSO, *Daily We Touch Him: Practical Religious Experiences* (Garden City: Image Books, 1979), 54.

[156] One edition of this work is William Johnston, ed., *The Cloud of Unknowing* (New York: Image, 1973), which includes *The Book of Privy Counseling*.

The purpose of this prayer is to be present to God, the source of all Presence. God will transform you by that encounter, as subtle as it may be. If you've ever heard the statement: "Dance with the Devil and the Devil doesn't change. The Devil changes you." The implication of the statement is that a person is permanently altered by one's encounter with the Devil. How transformative, then, should one's encounter be with God?

We generally have goals associated with spiritual exercises, expressed in statements like: "I made a good meditation today" or "I got a lot out of the sermon today." The practice of Centering Prayer is vastly different, since there are no goals per se, apart from being with God, and the benefits or by-products are elusive. The assumption is that God is worth "wasting time on," using a phrase from Fr. Pennington. The world can go on without us. By spending time with God, we permit Him to change us from the inside out, as a beginning to praying always, as the Lord encourages (Luke 18:1).

This is not the time for reading or other "thinking" about anything. As with a person whom you love, your time with God should be a period where silence between you and God is not awkward, but welcomed. Your withdrawing to God should be like going to meet an intimate friend, someone who knows you better than you know yourself. You are going to "rest" in God.

If you're looking for some method to help you to focus better or be at peace or something else, then you are looking at the wrong prayer type for you. If you are looking for a prayer form that uses your imagination, such as that of St. Ignatius of Loyola, then you will not find that here. Centering Prayer is about a direct encounter with God, whether you recognize that this is happening or not. If you are looking for some sign or goal, then this prayer may not be for you. If, however, you are faithful to Centering Prayer, then your by-products will be as personalized as your encounter with God will be.

Practical Concerns[157]

Place. Anywhere will do as a location for this prayer as long as there are no jarring sounds or overt disturbances, such as a garbage truck backing up or the neighbor's dog barking continuously. Sit upright in a chair of your choice, where your back can be supported. Place your hands on your thighs. Sit up straight as a way of freeing yourself, not at attention, as though you were in the military. Your posture should be upright without being oppressive to your body. Close your eyes.

Now place yourself in God's Presence through a short prayer, such as, "Lord, have mercy on me. I now enter into your Presence." That's it. Rest in the Lord for 15-20 minutes each session, attempting to have two sessions of Centering Prayer per day. When you do this is dependent upon you.

Distractions. As a river flows along, you can see the detritus on the top, but there is an under-current operating beneath the surface of the water that is unseen. When thoughts develop (the detritus), do not give your attention to them. Instead, upon recognizing that you are paying them attention, pray a sacred word interiorly to bring you back to the Presence of God (the under-current). The word "God" usually has little meaning for people, since it is so generic a term. Instead, try "Abba" or "Father" or "Jesus" or develop your own sacred word over time. It is holy and intimate for you to bring back your attention at an interior level to remain in your prayer. The type of thoughts that you have are not important. Let them go and return to your sacred word.

When you wish to end your prayer, acknowledge this slowly with a prayer: "Lord, I bring this prayer to a conclusion. Our Father, ..." This brings you back slowly to "reality."

If you fall asleep during this prayer, then accept that you needed the physical rest and try again later. If you consistently fall asleep, then you may want to try another time for this prayer. I generally perform my first

---

[157] For more detailed considerations, see Pennington, *Daily We Touch Him*, 56-72.

session for thirty minutes shortly after I rise, get ready for the day, and offer my first hour of the Liturgy of the Hours. My second session usually occurs mid- to late afternoon. Your times will depend on you, your temperament, and your circumstances.

Please note that the two sessions work in tandem. If you are only able to have one session during the day, celebrate that. But I have found, and others have confirmed, that having two sessions greatly magnifies the effects of the sessions. It is as though you get 30% with one session and 100% with two. No one has offered an explanation of why this is, but it is my experience and others'.

By-Products

You will not be able to recognize what is happening to you in light of this prayer. Be open to others' observations about you: "There's something different about you. I can't quite put my finger on it," or "You seem more peaceful." These are the types of comments you may hear. Your encounter with God is sufficient in itself. Have faith that He is transforming you from within. Your thoughts during this prayer, if they trouble you, need to be turned over to the Lord. At the start, getting the nuts and bolts together seems more important than remembering any of your thoughts. See chapter 13 above for Fr. Keating's understanding of the unloading of the unconscious.

APPENDIX II

Spiritual Exercises

If you'd like to use these exercises to help with spiritual growth, recognize that your full presence joined with God's Presence is the essential component that brings healing, since this is the essence of prayer, namely, communion with God. You can determine the length of time that you spend with each exercise.

The directions for getting the most out of the prayer are mostly the same: Go to a secluded place and ensure that the television is off; you're not playing with your cell phone or texting anyone; and you're not using the Internet. Just share some time (three minutes at a time?) with God and pray. What you pray will change with each exercise. This is what is meant by the words at the close of each of these exercises: "Go to a secluded place..." The prayer will change for each exercise, but your seclusion will not.

1. Recognizing your fears.
Invite God to come to you. In God's Presence, name and write down your fears the best that you can after some consideration. Your fears can hold you back from growth and real life. It may take more than one day. Ask the Lord to grant you insight into any pattern that emerges. Ask the Lord to help you to befriend them and own them. The biggest fear we can have is not to be who we are. Your fears hold you back especially

from being this. Pray to the Lord to help you to be you. As a prayer or penance, go to a secluded place.... and share some time with God, praying: "Lord, help me to recognize and accept my fears, so that they don't limit me form being who I am."

2. Appreciating your scars.

Someone once said: "Our scars help us to recognize that our past was real." All of us have scars: physical, emotional, psychological. Physical scars are usually the easiest to accept, whereas, emotional wounds often run deep, and they can be hard to name. But you are more than anything that has been done to you or anything that you have suffered. As a prayer or penance, go to a secluded place.... and share some time with God, praying: "Lord, help me to recognize that I am more than the things that were done to me or the sufferings that I have endured." God wastes nothing. Even your scars have made you the person who you are. This is something to celebrate.

3. Put down your anchors.

What do you stand for? Most people don't know what they stand for from an interior perspective, so their lives tend to drift when something or someone catches their attention or excites them. Saying, "I'm an Italian American" or "I'm a Republican" are superficial external references. Having a sense of our interior qualities, which I call anchors, makes us less susceptible to external stimuli, so that we can live without having ourselves (or our "ships") tossed about by any little thing. Perform the following exercise to identify just one interior quality that reflects you. As a prayerful exercise, go to a secluded place....

> A. Take a piece of paper and write the numbers one through twelve down the left-hand side.[158]
> B. Write the names of eleven people whom you admire. These could be anyone: rock stars, saints, actors. It doesn't matter whom you choose; they are people whom you value. That's enough of a reason to list them.
> C. Now write your name in slot #12.

---

[158] Taken from John Martin, *Become Who You Are!*, chapter one. Kindle book. Publication data unknown.

D. On the right-hand side, write the quality that you admired in each person.

E. Examine these qualities and identify the one that best reflects you.

Put this paper in a place where you do your most work. This is your first identified anchor. Remember this when you are tempted or manipulated or wonder what you stand for or what you hold dear. Thank God for sending people into your life to help you to model who you are.

4. Mourning the absence of the good (unnameable).

Many people have hurt us in varied ways in our lives, and those whom we appreciate as the most influential—consciously recognized or not—are those who can hurt us the most: a parent, a teacher, a mentor, a best friend, a spouse, a partner. However, no matter what the hurt that this person caused, *you* cannot move on until you acknowledge the energy within you that sought the good, which was right to seek. But now this energy has to be rechanneled through mourning or else it will continue to seek affirmation which may never come. There is a hole in your heart from the absence of the good. As a prayerful exercise, go to a secluded place....and do the following:

A. Acknowledge that good energy that was never fulfilled—love, affirmation, acceptance, respect.

B. Now mourn that good you sought that never materialized.

C. Pray to the Lord to help you to accept that this good never came.

These steps may take several days to pray over each one. You need to accept the loss that went with this experience and move on with the rest of life. Sometimes such things will not be resolved until heaven. Your emotional and spiritual growth depends upon mourning it!

5. Mourning the absence of the good (nameable).

Those who have lost a child or have hopes for their children which never materialize need to go through a similar process of mourning as in #4. Parents want to see their children fair well in the world. It's hard to hold suffering or loss with regard to one's child, especially based on dashed hopes or dreams, if that child has profound autism or a debilitating disease, leading even to death. As a prayerful exercise, go to a secluded place....and do the following:

A. Acknowledge the good that you wanted for your child, but recognize that, through no fault of your own, that good will never be realized.

B. Mourn the good you were seeking for your child.

C. Pray to the Lord to help you to recognize and then accept this loss of the good that you sought.

D. Now pray to accept your child and his or her circumstance as it is.

E. Pray further that you will accept your child as he or she is and seek what's in your child's best interests, which is different from the "good" you sought.

You need to accept this loss and move on with the rest of life. Your emotional and spiritual growth depends upon it!

Note: This exercise may also be appropriate for accepting divorce, debilitating illness, such as, cancer or other chronic condition in yourself or someone else.

6. Accepting Jesus' yoke.

Some people think that by positive thinking they can pretend that their burdens aren't real or that they will go away. They are not being honest with themselves, since even Jesus recognized burdens.

> Matt 11:28 Jesus said: "Come to me, all you who labor and are burdened, and I will give you rest. 29 Take my yoke upon you and learn from me, for I am meek and humble of heart; and you will find rest for your selves. 30 For my yoke is easy, and my burden light."

Jesus wants to share our burdens. The image of the yoke is one where two oxen bear a burden together. Applying this image, you are bearing one part of the burden with Jesus bearing the other. As a prayer or penance, go to a secluded place.... and share some time with God. During your prayer, invite Jesus into whatever burden you are facing and ask him to help you to bear it. The point is not to take the burden away, but instead to recognize Jesus' willingness to help with it—in whatever way he deems fit. The courage comes in the willingness to permit Jesus to help you.

7. God's plan.

Many people live their lives as though *they* have a plan to their lives that *God* fits into, rather than recognizing that *God* has the plan into which *we* fit. Note well the difference! Who's at the center? God's gift of His Son Jesus pays the price for our sins, which makes things right between the heavenly and earthly realms. As a prayer or penance, go to a secluded place.... and share some time with God. Pray to God to recognize the great gift that has been given through the gift of His Son, and pray that you may recognize God's Plan in your life, rather than forcing yours on God.

8. Forgiveness.

Many people tell me that they have trouble forgiving another person, persons, and even God for something that happened in their lives. Exercise #7 might be a place to start in order to recognize where we fall in God's Reality. But all of us also need to come to terms with our darker selves, that we believe that we are owed something for a past hurt. This runs deep. James Hillman, a Jungian psychologist, writes:

> Resentment especially is an emotional affliction of memory which forgetting can never fully repress.... These emotions would seem to have as their aim keeping an experience from dissolving into the unconscious. They are the salt preserving the event from decomposing.[159]

Hillman is saying that human beings do not forget emotionally, even if they do intellectually. Many people believe that "forgive and forget" is a biblical statement. It isn't. This is the power of the emotions, and it is also why naming hurts is so important, otherwise, resentment can surface within us, and we don't know where it comes from. It's time to go to the Cross! Go to a secluded place.... and recognize Jesus on the Cross. Appreciate his suffering, but also acknowledge your own. See the person who has hurt you in your mind. Join Jesus in his prayer to the Father for some period of time, praying: "Father, forgive them [the people who have hurt you] for they know not what they do."

9. Hopelessness—in two stages.

Spiritual health piggy-backs on emotional health, so unless your emotional house is in order, your spiritual house will not be. This does

---

[159] Hillman, "Betrayal," 79-80.

not mean perfection, so called; it means that you have accepted yourself as you are, warts and all, weaknesses and strengths. Now recognize that this is true of everyone. No one can change another person; one can hardly make changes to oneself.

Stage 1. But unless people see themselves through emotionally healthy eyes, appreciating others as they are cannot take place. Such a situation can cause us to experience hopelessness or despair, because we see no way out of our situation, which is really our emotional sickness. It's time to go to the Cross! Go to a secluded place.... and recognize Jesus on the Cross. Appreciate his suffering, but also acknowledge your own. Join him in his prayer to the Father for some time, praying: "My God, my God, why have you abandoned me."

Stage 2. In recognizing your own emotional/spiritual sickness, you may appreciate someone else's, especially if you live with a sick person. You cannot change this person or these people. However, you must recognize that emotionally sick people can drag you into the sick and tumultuous tornadoes of their lives—that was the point of the chapters on sick leadership types. It may be difficult to extricate yourself from the downward spiral of such people, but you have every right by God to protect yourself from them, as Christ himself did, every time he said, "My hour has not yet come" (John 2:4; see also 7:30; 8:20). This meant that Christ avoided circumstances, situations, and events that would lead to the Passion before the Father's Plan could be fulfilled on Good Friday.

There are at least two kinds of suffering: redemptive suffering and senseless suffering. Redemptive suffering has a meaning and a purpose for helping a person to grow. Senseless suffering is suffering for suffering's sake or something that happens to you because of another's unwillingness to get help. Being mugged and injured and having to deal with your injury is senseless suffering, though you can turn it around. Avoidance of redemptive suffering can be problematic for our emotional growth, but it is the sign of healthy people, when they avoid senseless suffering and drama, which will lead nowhere. For this exercise, go to a secluded place.... and pray to Jesus for a time, praying: "Jesus, give me the insight to protect myself from those who want to bring me down."

Note: Such insights may take the form of going for a walk; not responding to an e-mail; saying, "No"; holding your own against others; establishing boundaries; seeking professional help; or any number of other things. Discern them and implement them. Live your own life. Don't live vicariously through the life of another.

10. "He used their love against them."

The Green Mile (1999) is a movie based on a book of the same name by Stephen King.[160] It recounts the story of Paul Edgecombe—played by Tom Hanks—a death row supervisor, who meets John Coffey—played by the late Michael Clarke Duncan—an unusual inmate who displays inexplicable healing and empathetic abilities. Coffey has been convicted of raping and murdering two small white girls, but Edgecombe later discovers that he is innocent of the crime. Coffey, using his healing abilities, attempts to revive the girls when he chances upon their corpses, but could not; they were too far gone. As Coffey weeps over them, he says, "He used their love against them." Another man had coerced the sisters to be silent by threatening to kill one if the other made a noise as he perpetrated his crime. Coffey accepts death by electrocution rather than live in the world that knows such cruelty. Coffey is a figure of Christ.

It's time to go to the Cross! Go to a secluded place.... and recognize Jesus on the Cross. Appreciate his suffering, but also acknowledge your own. Celebrate the fact that you loved or else you could not have been manipulated in this way. Healthy people love and are hurt many times. But your love is the important thing. Now pray for the people who "used your love against you"—that those persons will be healed of their sickness by recognizing who they are. Love them. You may be the first person who has done so in a long time, if only for a moment. Celebrate your capacity to love. Now you can better understand the Cross! Amen.

---

[160] See, as of this writing (24 February 2015):
http://en.wikipedia.org/wiki/The_Green_Mile_(novel)

Marc Lanoue

APPENDIX III

A Lenten Program

Lenten practices, like the Stations of the Cross and fasting, put us in the mood for Lent and help us to realize that this is a different time, one where we need to take stock of our lives at the same time that we recognize the prime events of the Christ-event: Jesus' Passion, Death, Resurrection, and Ascension, that paid the price for our sins. Ash Wednesday begins the holy season of Lent with fasting (no meat or more than one full meal) and the signing with ashes. The use of ashes is an ancient symbol, connecting us with the fact of our mortality. "Remember, man, you are dust and unto dust you shall return," where ash and dust are correlative terms. God made humanity from dust, which means that we are not God; we are creatures. Good Friday and its requirement of fasting help us to connect the physical loss in the pit of our stomachs with the death of Christ on the cross. Ash Wednesday and Good Friday form the bookends for the Lenten season. Refraining from meat on Fridays sustains the sense of time different from the usual.

You may follow various Lenten practices, such as giving up dessert, candy, soda, chips, or a host of other non-essentials. You may make charitable donations to the poor. Whatever your practices may be, I believe that they help us to recognize that Lent is a different time, a sacred time, when we are invited to become more introspective, but I also believe that these practices, as good and helpful as they are for maintaining the atmosphere of Lent, will not change a person at his or her core. After all, people can become nasty if they are attached to something that they give up, then everyone is on the receiving end of their wrath, because they resent giving it up! That's not helpful. I invite you to do something different for Lent—and much harder!

I invite you to observe your reactions in your interactions with others and while you are alone. Observe these behaviors in your life (if you practice them). *Don't judge yourself.* The observation is meant to help you to go more deeply into yourself and understand why you would adopt these behaviors into your life. It usually has to do with protecting some misguided sense of happiness. So I offer the following questions for you to ponder, when you get a chance to reflect on your interactions.

1. Do you manipulate or attempt to control people's responses? For example: "What are you doing tonight?" puts someone on the spot, so that, if they have no plans, you will swoop in and insist that they accompany you. Or you ask over and over again until you get your way, thus wearing the person's resolve down. Instead, how about: "I'm going to the movies tonight. Would you like to join me?" There is nothing manipulative about this statement. But the point is not simply to change your questions (superficial and temporary); it's to recognize the reason why you were manipulative to begin with (permanent sense of self understanding). This is the deep-seated discernment the Gospel demands. It's a hard thing! But it will have lasting effect. This is true repentance.

2. Can you be genuinely happy for someone else, or do you offer disparaging remarks about them to undermine their success or do you even demean them: you make them look bad against the backdrop of your (supposed) goodness. For example, "He's always been kissing up to the boss, that's why he received that promotion." Instead, "Congratulations on a job well done," as long as it comes from the heart. Again, faking the words has failed the purpose of the examination.

3. Apologize immediately for errors/mistakes. Cut down on excuses. "I'm sorry I was late. I apologize. It was my fault and no one else's." It's time to move on to try again.

4. Preferences are no issue for anyone. Attachments, on the other hand, replace the internal happiness with which everyone is endowed with an external sense of happiness that doesn't come from God. Preferences are choices, like vanilla vs. chocolate ice cream. You don't have a tantrum if you get one or the other, though you would prefer one over the other; there's no problem with this. An attachment is something inside of you saying, "I can't be happy without ....," where you fill in the blank. In the great symphony of life, you cannot be bogged down focusing on any one note, whether you hear it or you don't. You need to experience all the music. Attachments hinder you from doing so. If you get angry because you don't have something or someone (to own), then it's probably an attachment. All attachments, no matter their size, stand in the way of your God-given happiness.

5. Jesus said: "Let your 'Yes' mean 'Yes,' and your 'No' mean 'No.' Anything more is from the evil one" (Matt 5:37). Deal with people in person (when possible) and always on personal terms, not in ways that are passive aggressive, meaning that you do not convey your anger or other emotion, but instead use a passive way to convey your anger. Do not write something in an e-mail (nasty-gram) to avoid confronting someone and/or to avoid discussion. Confrontation is not sinful. Ask yourself why you cannot confront people or otherwise tell them what you think. There may be a legitimate reason why you refrain from doing so: mental illness, dementia, Alzheimer's. Your situation will vary. But for "normal" people, look deep within yourself to see why you cannot or will not speak with this person.

Values that reflect the Kingdom of God respect boundaries as they also reflect truth, the Will of God, genuine love, and respect for the value of every person. Healthy interactions reflect a healthy emotional life, which is necessary for a healthy and fruitful spiritual life. Leave judgment behind. Instead, observe, observe, observe. Watch yourself as a scientist would watch the behavior of ants in an ant farm.

ABOUT THE AUTHOR

Fr. Marc Lanoue is Associate Pastor at St. John the Evangelist Catholic Church in Severna Park, Maryland. He enjoys teaching on various topics, particularly those related to the Bible and human development as they impact the spiritual life. He is also interested in music from the Classical and Romantic periods.

Made in the USA
Lexington, KY
11 March 2015